SCREENWRITING

HISTORY, THEORY AND PRACTICE

By Steven Maras

WALLFLOWER PRESS
LONDON & NEW YORK

First published in Great Britain in 2009 by
Wallflower Press
6 Market Place, London W1W 8AF
www.wallflowerpress.co.uk

A catalogue record for this book is available from the British Library.

ISBN 978-1-905674-81-7 (pbk)
ISBN 978-1-905674-82-4 (hbk)

Book design by Elsa Mathern

Printed in India by Imprint Digital

CONTENTS

A NOTE ON TERMINOLOGY

Sometimes in this book 'screenwriting' will appear as one word, and at other times two, as in 'screen writing'. In most cases the compound version will apply to 'screenwriting' as the writing of screenplays, or the craft of screenwriting conceived as the writing of page-based scripts. In other cases, however, 'screen writing' relates to either a historical period when the meaning of screenwriting was still unstable or uncertain, and the two words 'screen' and 'writing' had yet to be fully coupled, or a practice of writing that is not solely page-based (as in writing with a camera). There are times when a third hyphenated form, 'screen-writing', is used, and this is generally linked to an author using this hyphenate form in their own work. I also use the term 'scripting' as a framework for expanding our understanding of screenwriting to include other approaches to screen writing which go beyond the manuscript (writing with bodies, or light) but which still occupy the space of 'writing' in an extended sense. Finally, the term 'film writer' or 'film writing' appears, which I borrow from Dziga Vertov and Dudley Nichols, as a term to describe the general area of writing for film, writing in film and film as writing.

ACKNOWLEDGEMENTS

A project such as this, which has taken shape over more than a decade, gathers some debts. Perhaps the most significant of these is to scholars I have never personally met, but whose work provided an entry point into the field: namely Tom Stempel, Edward Azlant and Janet Staiger. I doubt that this book could have existed without the commitment with which they approached their own work.

The earliest iteration of this book dates to 1989, at Murdoch University, Perth, Western Australia, when during a break from post-graduate study I was introduced to video production and questions surrounding the script by Josko Petkovic. For the patient supervision of my subsequent doctoral dissertation I thank Alec McHoul.

Since that time, the idea of writing a book about scripting went through various phases. In 1996, with the support of an F. G. Swain New Researcher Award, and the University of Western Sydney, Hawkesbury Foundation, I began to work seriously on the topic. My thanks to Chris Fleming, research assistant at the time, for his passion for photocopying and insightful observations. This initial research provided the impetus for my teaching a subject titled 'Constructions of the Script', and my sincere thanks to all of the students who undertook that subject between 1998 and 2004.

The project benefited from research leave in the second half of 1998, during which I spent some time on attachment with the Writing Department of the Australian Film Television and Radio School. My thanks to Ron Blair, Helen Carmichael, John Loney and Yvonne Madon in the department for their generosity in answering my questions and queries. My thanks also to Rod Bishop, Sara Bennett, Robin de Crespigny and Jane Mills for helping me to think harder about my research at that time. I am grateful to the staff of the Jerzy Toeplitz library at the School for their generous assistance during this period.

In March and April 2002 I benefited from a period of attachment with the School of Cinema-Television at the University of Southern California, Los Angeles. I am grateful to Dana Polan and Marsha Kinder for facilitating that arrangement. My thanks to

Karen Pedersen at The Writers' Guild Foundation James R. Webb Memorial Library for providing access to early Guild newsletters and encouraging me in my endeavours. Thanks also to Ned Comstock, Reference Librarian at the Cinema-Television Library at USC who pointed me in the right direction many times; Pat Hansen at the American Film Institute; and Brian Taves and Paul Spehr at the Library of Congress, for fielding some of my questions. Barbara Hall, Elizabeth Wertin and other helpful staff at the Margaret Herrick Library were similarly generous in their assistance. The research could not have been carried out without the support of a travel grant from the College of Arts, Education and Social Sciences at the University of Western Sydney, and the generous support of Bill Loges, Faculty Master of the Annenberg House at USC.

Attempting to research early screenwriting in the US from Australia has been challenging. Several libraries and librarians have proved indispensable to this research. I would like to thank staff of the Australian Film Institute Research & Information Centre for their assistance in October 1997 and again in October 2007. Deserving of special mention are Di Robertson of Document Delivery at the University of Western Sydney, Hawkesbury library, for sustaining me with hard to get books and articles, and Ute Foster in her role of Library Liaison Officer for the Humanities. At the University of Sydney I would also like to thank Bruce Isaacs at the Fisher Library, for his efforts in securing difficult to get items. For resolving some key final issues to do with copyright in the US my special thanks go to Rosemary C. Hanes, Librarian, Moving Image Section, Library of Congress, for generously providing a description of the applications and ledgers, and research assistance in the inspection of deposit material.

This project has benefited from the encouragement and support of some wonderful people and colleagues. Yoram Allon at Wallflower Press took on the idea of a scholarly book on screenwriting and allowed it to find its form – the latter enhanced by the expert editorial efforts and encouragement of Jacqueline Downs and Ian Cooper. John Belton and Janet Staiger as proposal reviewers, and the anonymous manuscript reviewers from Wallflower Press provided invaluable assessments of the project. Lesley Stern and Dana Polan have been a source of inspiration and advice, and likewise Jodi Brooks who provided perceptive comments on drafts of the introduction. Many thanks to my colleagues in the Humanities at the University of Western Sydney, Hawkesbury from 1995–2005 – their support for a cross-disciplinary research culture and the highest scholarly standards was (and continues to be) inspiring. From 2005 my insightful colleagues in the Media and Communications Department at the University of Sydney have provided material and moral support, including periods free for writing and special study leave to complete the book. My thanks go in particular to Catharine Lumby for looking at the proposal again with fresh eyes, Kate Crawford for her advice on chapter structure, Megan le Masurier for her insights on history writing, Gerard Goggin on the ins and outs of publishing etiquette, Anne Dunn for her discussions around video production, Richard Stanton for his encouragement close to the end and Marc Brennan and Robin Moffat for just listening. As this is my first book, I wish to acknowledge my parents Tomislav and Dragica for providing me with a formal education that they were never able to obtain in the mountains of post-World War Two Croatia. This book is dedicated to Teresa Rizzo, who has lived with this project over many years, and whose intelligence, intellectual generosity and companionship have

INTRODUCTION

This book aims to challenge your understanding of screenwriting. Because screenwriting is a complex entity this book also has to do with ways of thinking about film in general, the production process, the functions performed by the film script, and the nature of expression in cinema. This is not a screenwriting handbook in the sense that may be familiar to many readers. It is not a manual to writing 'screenplays that sell', or a guide to writing technique, but rather a handbook for opening up questions about screenwriting practice beyond solely 'business' or 'storytelling' issues. In the following I seek to create a bridge between scholarly work in film, media and screenwriting studies and practitioner-orientated discussions of craft and industry issues. This involves addressing different bodies of work, approaches to analysis and, indeed, ways of talking. Inviting readers with such varied backgrounds and interests to the table presents a challenge for any project, but the invitation is made in the conviction that our understanding of screenwriting can be advanced by such communication. While the book draws on scholarly work in film history especially, it is written for students or teachers of screenwriting craft, and readers with an interest in media studies (after all, screenwriting is a fascinating form of media practice). Readers with a broader interest in film issues and the film industry will find a different perspective on some familiar industry debates.

Given my interest in bridging different approaches to film and screenwriting, and practical concerns, an important question arises, namely, 'What do I mean by "screenwriting"?' In its (currently) commonsense definition 'screenwriting' is the practice of writing a screenplay, a manuscript understood through notions such as story spine, turning points, character arc and three-act structure. In subsequent chapters I explore the unique aspects of this approach to writing for the screen. In a different sense of the term, 'screen writing' (and I intentionally use two words here) can refer to writing not *for* the screen, but *with* or *on* the screen. It can refer to a kind of 'filmic' or 'cinematic' or audiovisual writing – and it is worth remembering here that both cinemato*graphy* and photo*graphy* are etymologically speaking forms of writing (see Derrida 1976: 9).

'Writing' can thus be linked to other media, not just the page. When cinematographer Vittorio Storaro refers to 'writing with light' (in Schaefer & Salvato 1984: 220), or F. W. Murnau refers to the camera as 'the director's sketching pencil' (1928: 72), or Alexandre Astruc to the 'camera-pen' or *caméra-stylo* (1968), they are activating literal (if not entirely literary) concepts of writing. Similarly, when Dziga Vertov speaks of being a 'film writer' (1967: 107), and 'writing' with recorded shots, or when Philip Dunne describes Gary Cooper's acting as writing 'in invisible ink directly on the film' (1980: 287), they are relying on a notion of screen writing in which the cinematographer, editor or actor may have equivalent standing to the 'writer'. This definition of writing is more distant from the idea of writing a page-based object, but still occupies the space of 'writing' in an extended sense, or what might also be termed 'scripting'. This space of scripting is broader than that of mainstream screenwriting, and potentially extends to audiovisual practices such as 'writing with sound' (as sound can be inscribed or transcribed on the optical sound track (see Potamkin 1977: 86–7)), as well as aspects of choreography, performance or 'writing with bodies'.

An extended theory of scripting can help counterbalance the focus on manuscript-based definitions of screenwriting, and help establish a framework for understanding diverse forms of screen writing. The concept of scripting opens up writing beyond the container of the page, focusing on 'writerly' input or collaborations across different areas of production (see Macdonald 2004a). But it also helps us look at how the space of scripting has been narrowed down and gradually shaped by the demands of film production into a normative idea of screenwriting, which in turn has been reinvented around the screenplay. This book forms a study of how screenwriting has emerged as a particular kind of scripting, as well as how certain ideas of screenwriting came to assume a dominant position.

The interplay between these two senses of screenwriting will be important throughout this book; there are two key reasons why. Firstly, it helps broaden our understanding of screenwriting; secondly, it helps draw attention to the tensions between different ideas of writing.

Turning to the first reason, the idea of scripting allows a broader understanding of screenwriting because it assists in thinking about screenwriting in non-normative ways. Through the concept of scripting I build a bridge between narrative or dramatic (in the sense of 'plot-based') approaches to screenwriting and alternative approaches to scripting of the kind that can be found in experimental or documentary-style filmmaking. This idea allows us to think about screenwriting in new ways, to look at variations in scripting approaches, and to put contemporary mainstream discourses on screenwriting into a different historical context and theoretical perspective.[1]

The concept of scripting provides an idea through which to examine and recon-sider the place of writing and screenwriting in the production process. It is not about setting up a prescriptive approach to story and storytelling or enforcing a ban on three-act structure in favour of 'non-narrative' film styles. It is not about limiting screen writing to a particular approach to working with material (direct inscription of celluloid, for instance, or self-reflexive experimentation with the apparatus of film), but about connecting mainstream scriptwriting to a broader field of possibilities.

This approach involves reconsidering the relationship between terms that are often kept separate in film studies and screenwriting discourse, namely structure, style and performance. It means rethinking the demarcation between creation and interpretation, writing and performance, and the boundaries between what is a matter of style in cinema and what is a matter of screenwriting. In his writing on film story, Australian film critic and theorist Adrian Martin reflects on the models avail-able for thinking about structure in film, and suggests that there is more to narrative than plot and character. In a discussion of *Elephant* (Dir. & Writ. Gus Van Sant, 2003), Martin details a different understanding of how suspense and tension can be written: 'from the movement of the camera, the rising arc of a sound, a gradual change of the colour palette of the screen, the choreography of a body' (2004: 85). These features can be treated as formal style elements, separate to screenwriting issues, but through the concept of scripting they can be treated as screen writing elements.

Not all forms of scripting are the same – an extended notion of scripting is not the same as a homogenised one – so it is important to remain mindful of different condi-tions, practices and materials involved. It is important to note that there are many traditions of screenwriting, varying from nation to nation,[2] and while there is wide-spread recognition of the centrality of 'American' screenwriting this diversity should not be overlooked. The main focus of this book is on North American feature film-making and the discourse surrounding the screenplay in the US. This does not mean that its focus is limited solely to the US, or to narrative cinema, as this book draws on thinkers and filmmakers from other cultures (primarily European) who develop their ideas through a dialogue or argument with American film. These non-US approaches form a vital perspective on screenwriting discourse, and are an important aspect of any archaeology of 'screenwriting'.

To highlight the point that screenwriting is a historically contingent form I shall refer to examples of other ways of working from different times and places. This is part of a broader commitment to a pluralistic approach to scripting which could be extended into a more detailed discussion of different forms of scripting. A more complete 'mapping' of these scripting practices might focus on the local screen cultures in which they emerge, and the collaborative creative context supporting them, the genres and forms drawn on (including video art, documentary, animation, games and new media), and the different understandings of scripting at play (from scribbling, to storyboard, to executable computer scripts, databases, flowcharts and navigation structures). Although it is beyond the scope of this book, this work would help not only to internationalise the arguments put forward here, but contribute to pluralism by changing the dynamics of what is considered 'proper' screenwriting and what is considered to be 'alternative'.

Turning now to the second reason why it is useful to distinguish the two senses of screenwriting discussed above, the gap between screenwriting as the writing of screenplays, and screen writing as scripting, is helpful for understanding some of the politics surrounding screenwriting which can often be traced to tensions between different ideas about writing. An example is the tension between the idea that 'movies are written in the camera' as opposed to on paper (Dunne 1980: 46). Screenwriting discourse has since at least 1909 been replete with normative ideas of standard practice: what a good structure is and how it should work (see Bordwell, Staiger & Thompson 1985: 106–7). Part of this has to do with ensuring narrative clarity so that audiences are satisfied. The practice continues today, in part due to the risky nature of film development and costs involved, leading to a great deal of attention being paid to the script before the film gets made (see Sainsbury 2003). But with these norms come particular, prescriptive conceptions of writing, privileging some approaches over others. This sets the scene for a range of political struggles in screenwriting, including those around auteur theory and authorship, acknowledgement of creative effort and control, tensions between 'literary' and cinematic approaches, and issues to do with the development of film ideas. I include here arguments about the way a dominant form of screenwriting, or model such as 'central conflict theory', can marginalise other understandings of working with film and produce a narrow conception of the possibilities of the medium (see Ruiz 1995).

When looking at the politics surrounding screenwriting it is easy to make generalisations about practice that inflame sensibilities. For this reason I take a prompt from Christian Metz, and try to avoid a too easy polarisation of terms such as 'film-maker's cinema' and 'script-writer's cinema', or 'plot' and 'writing', or 'old cinema' and a new 'cinema cinema'. As Metz reminds us, the very terms of these debates are exclusionary, and limit the dimension of the scenario to a belittling caricature (1974: 203).

One area of politics worth elaborating has to do with the way screenwriting has emerged as an autonomous area. Martin voices concern about this trend when he suggests that 'there has been a historical drift towards scriptwriting as an autonomous activity, breaking apart the ideal unity of script conception and screen realisation – an alienation that the current manuals help to reinforce' (1999). Leaving to one side the point that not all filmmakers share this notion of ideal unity (Sergei Eisenstein, for example), Martin here picks up a common concern regarding the treatment of the script as a distinct work, and the writing of scripts as a separate practice. For Martin, the extent to which scriptwriting has emerged as an autonomous activity can be gauged by the focus placed on scripts today, their publication as books in their own right.

Why should a drift towards an autonomous activity of screenwriting be of concern? Because it changes what it means to make film or cinema. In a point I shall take up more fully below, the movement towards autonomy takes the script out of its production context and potentially reinforces a fracture between conception and execution that impacts on the way we might imagine creativity and expression, and think about the medium. Martin is foregrounding the way a notion of scriptwriting as an autonomous activity reconfigures the act of conception and execution. Related to this concern is a broader issue, one examined in detail in what follows, to do with how to think about screenwriting in relation to the historical separation of conception and execution in the Hollywood system.

Distinct from the concern over the unity of conception and realisation, but related to it, is another issue embedded in Martin's use of the term 'alienation', namely that the area or field of screenwriting is developing in an isolated way, separate from other film practices. Indeed, there is a risk that the field of screenwriting as it is emerging in the UK, Australia and the US, embedded in a particular engagement with story, character and dramatic structure, is developing at a distance from not only other production disciplines, but areas such as screen studies, film history, media studies and literary analysis, which are regarded (narrowly and instrumentally) as failing to deliver (see Russell 2003). The introduction to a special issue on screenwriting of the *Journal of Film and Video* observes that 'screenwriting has grown hermetic' (Dancyger & Rush 1990: 3). While this comment arises out of a concern that many screenplays read the same and that a conformity of narrative style has developed, the idea can be extended to the field itself. The fact that in many academic institutions screenwriting is separated from film studies, or even other production disciplines, is perhaps confirmation of this autonomy. This book responds to this state of affairs by trying to understand how screenwriting came to be defined as an autonomous activity, and to encourage further dialogue between screenwriting and other areas of film/screen culture.

A key aspect of the development of screenwriting as an autonomous craft area has been the development of the screenplay as the primary script form. Screenwriting has not always been defined as the writing of screenplays, however, and tracing this idea means examining what different authors and institutions have said about screenplays and also other scripting forms. It also involves going further and looking at the screenplay as but one kind of script, and developing an understanding of the place of the screenplay in the production process. To achieve this task some groundwork is required as the script itself tends to be an underanalysed textual form. It is not self-revealing and has been subject to institutionalisation and codification over time. In response to this situation this book draws on a mix of history and theory to tease out the diversity and complexity of the script, in line with Tom Gunning's insistence that 'history and theory must proceed in tandem in film study' (1991: 4). Looking at the script also presents some methodological difficulties because the script is what has been termed an 'intermediate' entity, a structure that wants to be another structure, destined to 'vanish' into the film. Its 'place' in the process is by definition transitional and transformational, and is closely associated with particular modes of film practice and production. In short, it is a very unusual textual form.

The uniqueness of the screenplay itself is a complex issue. In terms of scripting practices there is little that is exclusive to the screenplay that is not present in the scene-based organisation of the scenario, the shot-by-shot format of the continuity script, 'the read' of the extended synopsis or dialogue of the playscript. Viewed in this light, the distinctiveness of the screenplay is elusive. What is most distinctive about the screenplay, I contend, is the work it does underpinning a form of discourse; one that articulates a perspective on writing for the screen, a script-centred way of speaking about production, and relations between different crafts. Contrary to expectations, I suggest that while screen writing is discussed in earnest from the 1910s, a discourse focused on the screenplay appears later in the 1930s and 1940s. This screenplay discourse has powerful effects, and enables screenwriters to rethink established scripting techniques within the studio context. It allows a new language-game and understanding of screenwriting in which the screenplay is a key 'integrated' creative form. While some aspects of this discourse have, as Martin puts it, alienating effects, it is nevertheless important to keep a broader perspective on screenwriting discourse and appreciate its different features and aspects. This book attempts to do this through discussion and analysis of different debates and issues in this discourse, including the way the idea of the script as screenplay, combined with notions of writing for the screen, and the idea of the script as a blueprint, define the parameters of our contemporary understanding of screenwriting.

In order to explore what I call the 'invention of the screenplay' I look mainly at the state of screenwriting in the period from the 1910s through to the 1940s, as it is expressed in handbooks and other writings. This study is not rigid in its historical periodisation, however, and as it is interested in contemporary understandings of screenwriting I shall also look at developments from the 1950s to the 1970s, and more recent academic writing on the history and theory of screenwriting as well. It is not my intention to provide a complete history of screenwriting to the present day. Rather, I attempt to provide the reader with a historical perspective on a contemporary understanding (or discourse) of screenwriting, which is closely tied to the screenplay.

Since the inception of cinema the activity of film writing has been under constant revision and redefinition. One of the surprising things about the study of screenwriting is the amount of relevant scholarship that exists but is rarely gathered together in one place. Here I am thinking of work by Sergei Eisenstein, Pier Paolo Pasolini, Dudley Nichols, Janet Staiger, Béla Balázs, Osip Brik and more recently Ken Dancyger, Jeff Rush, Claudia Sternberg, Ian Macdonald, Adrian Martin and a host of other authors to whom I refer in the discussion that follows – these figures have made significant interventions, trying either to define the function of the script or redefine the practice and theory of scriptwriting.[3] This book tries to bring a range of work by different authors and theorists of the script and screenwriting together in a way that has not been attempted before, and construct a conversation between different approaches.

Recent years have seen more attention paid to the script and screenwriting as an area of film history and film scholarship.[4] In what follows I engage with this work and seek to give it a broader readership. At the same time, I wish to highlight a significant issue for study in this area which has to do with the relationship between understandings of 'film practice' or 'screen practice' and screenwriting practice. This book operates on the assumption that the relationship between these diverse fields of practice has yet to be fully worked out, and although moves are being made in the right direction there is still a sense that screenwriting practice is only partly 'integrated' into ideas about film or screen practice.

In researching this book, what has become apparent is that film studies does not always know what to do with screenwriting, and screenwriting studies can have an ambivalent relationship to mainstream approaches within film studies. There seems to be a lack of recognition of interests between the two areas.[5] This state of affairs can be traced back to a range of factors. With Janet Staiger's work a notable exception, the careful analyses of the rise of narrative or continuity that exist in film studies often fail to provide a screenwriting perspective, only referring in passing to the work involved in providing a scenario or story. The place of the script and writing in the production process, the format of what is being written, is not always extensively considered – for some commentators there were no screenwriters in Hollywood prior to the 1930s. There exist methodological issues around thinking about screenwriting practice that have to do with working through the division of labour in early cinema and different ideas of screenwriting and scripting (with a figure such as Edwin S. Porter working as cameraperson and scriptor, as well as technician, drawing on a range of sources, such as comics and paintings; see Musser 1991: 340). There is a danger of retroactively projecting our current ideas of screenwriting back onto past screen practices of early cinema. Also, the 'textual' aspects of screenwriting practice – with the script serving as part text and part administrative or industrial tool – have yet to be fully integrated into current notions of film practice which focus heavily either on literary/narrative form or economic/industrial processes. All of these factors contribute to a situation where screenwriting is underanalysed in film studies,[6] and film theory underutilised in screenwriting. The two areas are beginning to invoke distinctly different readerships.[7] This is not to downplay the importance of works of scholarship in these fields that this book draws upon. Our understanding of film and screenwriting practice is converging to some extent in some areas, especially in relation to US cinema history; but the process of coming together still involves readjustment between different genres, 'fields' and screen cultural contexts.

On one level, the expectation that screenwriting be fully integrated into a notion of film practice might seem wrong-headed. Screenwriting can be studied effectively in terms of theatre or literature for instance, for it is fairly clear that early filmmakers borrowed many scripting and production methods from the theatre (see Loughney 1990: 211). But while this might be the case, such an approach risks overlooking the fascinating way screenwriting stands between literature and the factory, and the unique relationship between script and film. On another level, the notion of 'integration' might be seen as problematic, implying the absorption of screenwriting into a pre-determined idea of film, when in fact a highly developed account of scripting may change our ideas about film. Acknowledging these arguments, what seems reasonably clear is that our account of film practice will suffer if our understanding of scripting remains trapped in a particular model. An account of the diversity of film practices should ideally leave room for an account of the diversity of scripting beyond mainstream feature filmmaking.

Summing up, this book seeks to contribute to the 'integration' of screenwriting and ideas about film or screen practice by exploring screenwriting discourse in greater depth, examining key issues and debates such as the role of the script in production, treating the screenplay as literature, reading the screenplay and screenwriter perspectives on auteur theory. It traces the emergence of what it sees as a dominant, contemporary conception of screenwriting in the US, linked to key ideas such as the script as blueprint, writing for the screen, and the screenplay. At the same time, it tries to open the conventional idea or discourse of screenwriting out onto different notions about scripting, beyond normalised ideas of writing for the screen, the blueprint and the separation of conception and execution. The terms 'history', 'theory' and 'practice' all become key sites and terms for reflecting on screenwriting (I examine each of these and their relationship in more depth in the first chapter). It is conventional to offer at this point a chapter-by-chapter breakdown of what follows. Departing from this convention, I refer the reader to brief introductory passages at the start of each chapter, which explain the scope of that chapter and how it fits into the broader argument of the book.

1.

PUTTING HISTORY, THEORY AND PRACTICE TOGETHER

This chapter explains the methodological approach of this book, and stresses the importance of a historically and theoretically informed account of practice. It identifies an interest in speaking about screenwriting in novel ways, beyond issues of 'story and structure', and suggests that a theoretical interest in particular 'problems' in screenwriting can be useful. The chapter explores an 'object problem' in screenwriting, which refers to the difficulty of pinning down an object of discussion and debate, but also flags the separation of conception and execution, and particularism, as key issues for discussion. There is arguably a dearth of analytical frames for looking at these kinds of problems and in this chapter I suggest a new frame linked to the idea of screenwriting as both practice and discourse. In the area of history, I attempt to build a bridge between revisionist film history and the post-1970s historiography of screenwriting by focusing attention on the historical identity of screenwriting, as well as the discursive boundaries of our contemporary understanding of screenwriting.

This book is written at an interesting time for those concerned with screenwriting issues. We have been bombarded with manuals outlining formulas and structures for screenwriting for so long that there is now general understanding that there is no magic formula for good scriptwriting. There is recognition that every project is challenging in its own way, involving a rethinking of the rules. There is also healthy scepticism – evident in films such as *Adaptation* (Dir. Spike Jonze, Writ. Charlie Kaufman, 2002) – surrounding notions such as the three-act structure, the commercialisation of the craft of screenwriting and the packaging of advice about screenwriting by so-called 'script gurus' such as Syd Field (see Castrique 1997). These trends are evidence of an interest in new ways of talking about screenwriting beyond well-worn concepts of story and structure (see Millard 2006a) and plot and character (Martin 2004). But there is a lack of tools to aid in this task, and the discussion can get easily bogged down in old arguments and conflicts. Faced with the recognition that 'manuals are not enough' (Macdonald 2004b), there is a desire to speak about screenwriting in different ways.

One of the tools that can be useful for talking about screenwriting in new ways is theory. While theory is often linked to 'high theory' work in literary studies (see Culler 2000), many screenwriters are already consumers of theory. Theory is embedded in many screenwriting manuals: from the mythic 'archetypal' analysis of Christopher Vogler, to the structuralist tendencies of Syd Field, to the new critical or formal analyses of Robert McKee. There is a general sense that Aristotelianism is alive and well in Hollywood (see Hiltunen 2002). Were it not for an almost total absence of references to literary studies, screenwriting could almost be described as an applied sub-branch of the academic area of narrative studies.

Thinking about the uses of theory in relation to screenwriting can lead down at least two paths. The first path has to do with more diverse kinds of theory and philosophy, works of politics, history, culture and society, for instance, leading to a more informed screenwriting. Many screenwriters are open to this form of research-led practice, and keen to explore deeper aspects of the social and political issues and events they write about.

The second path has to do with teasing out in more detail theoretical issues and 'problems' (in the mathematical sense of the term) that are already present in screenwriting – and I have already alluded to some of these, including the separation of conception and execution, the intermediality of the script and the two senses of screenwriting discussed earlier. There are other 'problems' that exist, such as the difficulty of identifying an object in screenwriting (which is closely related to the issue of the separation of conception and execution, and to which I shall turn in a moment) and what I term below 'particularism', a tendency to align screenwriting with particular groups.

One obstacle to thinking about screenwriting in novel ways is a dearth of analytical frames through which to engage with screenwriting.[8] The term 'frame' here is borrowed from an approach in media and communication studies called frame analysis, where it refers to ideas of selection and salience: 'To frame is to *select some aspects of a perceived reality and make them more salient in a communicating text*' (Entman 1993: 52; emphasis in original). The term is often used to discuss media coverage of a particular event or issue. There are some very familiar frames through which to engage with screenwriting: among them are the practitioner frame, the story and structure frame, the business frame and the anti-screenwriting frame. Each of these frames highlights particular aspects of screenwriting. The practitioner frame tends to be about advice, experience and the so-called 'creative process'. The story and structure frame is primarily concerned with dramatic principles and storytelling problems. The business frame focuses on deals and pitching a project. The anti-screenwriting frame is suspicious of the literary dimension of filmmaking and tends to 'beat down' the writer.

Each of these frames produces a different perspective on screenwriting, at times even competing with one another. A business frame might focus on the script as package or property, while a story and structure frame might provide a different aesthetic focus that may be in conflict with particular marketing ideas. Different frames can change over time. The business frame of 1920s Hollywood (which itself could vary across companies specialising in gangster pictures, melodrama or musicals) looks different to that of today. While today the practitioner frame is dominated by discussion of screenplays and feature films, in the past it related to plots of action and photoplays.

Clarifying the 'Object Problem': Screenwriting as Practice and Discourse

A key issue arises at this point, which is that screenwriting, while intensely discussed and debated, is rarely fully defined. The 'object' of the above frames is underspecified. It could be argued that there is in fact a good reason for this, that screenwriting is not an 'object' in any straightforward sense: it is a practice, and as such it draws on a set of processes, techniques and devices that get arranged differently at different times. While this arrangement relates to what can be seen as an 'object' – say a script or a film – it is not clear that either the script or film is best treated as an 'object' in this context: scripts are in transition all through film production, they vary in form and function across different modes of filmmaking; and films are more than final products or outputs that only exist at the end of the process. The line between where the script stops and where the film starts can, furthermore, be mysterious and blurry.

What I term the 'object problem' in screenwriting refers to the difficulty of both defining screenwriting as an object, and identifying an object for screenwriting. Is the 'object' of screenwriting on the page or the screen? Does the script or its realisation exist independently from the film? Is the 'script' the final product of the screenwriting process, or just one aspect of the filmmaking process? Are we dealing with two objects (the script as read and film as distributed) or one? And what should be made of discrepancies between the script and film and then published script? If the screenplay is the object, how did it emerge and develop? These questions are not easily answered, and the 'object problem' not easily resolvable because of the unique relationship between script and film. The frames mentioned above do not always illuminate the problem well – although the practitioner and anti-screenwriting frame can produce some important insights (see Carrière 1995). The more one grapples with the complicated object-status of screenwriting, the more it becomes apparent that no one frame can fully account for it.

What would be helpful in this context is an approach that focuses on the changing nature of screenwriting practice, the status of the film and script in that process and the nuances of the object problem. Ideally, it would accommodate a historical perspective open to different received understandings of screenwriting, and not be prescriptive about how writing or scripting should be defined, or the place of writing in production. Also, it should be flexible enough to allow us to look at different frames together, and how they interact to construct a sense of an object (or different senses of an object) that maps onto the space of screenwriting. The perspective or frame I want to put forward is to think about screenwriting as a discourse. A discourse frame focuses on the way screenwriting has been shaped and talked about in particular ways. The concept of discourse does not solve the object problem entirely, but it allows us to clarify it, to focus on it more carefully, as well as to look at particular frames and what they say about screenwriting. Through the concept of discourse it is possible to grapple with the fluidity of screenwriting, the way it has changed over time and gets seen in different ways.

Elaborating on this approach further: screenwriting is a practice of writing, but it is also a discourse that constructs or imagines the process of writing in particular ways. Indeed, strictly speaking, discourses and practices are inseparable; the two meld together in skills and bodies, understandings and ways of speaking about the craft. Practice, here, is not something 'out there' beyond language or discourse. Instead of describing and analysing practice as a 'doing', separate from 'theory', I see practice as constituted in action, ideas and language. Screenwriting is thus a layered activity, drawing together skills, performance, concepts, experiences and histories – individuals and groups encounter and 'know' screenwriting through these constructs.

Thinking about discourse and practice together involves considering the very identity or make-up of a form of practice. In *On the History of Film Style*, David Bordwell comes close to a discourse approach to media practice when he focuses on stylistic norms, techniques and group style (see 1997: 118, 121). He comes closer still when he outlines a 'problem/solution model [that] recognises that individual action takes place within a social situation' (1997: 150). 'The filmmaker pursues goals; stylistic choices help achieve them. But no filmmaker comes innocent to the job. Task and functions are, more often than not, supplied by tradition' (1997: 151). However, filmmakers themselves are not blank slates, and often come primed with particular speaking positions in respect to 'the industry'. Bordwell's focus on tradition as 'supply' lacks a broader account of discourse and communication, and how that discourse (in)forms media practice.

A useful question to consider at this point is: 'What does analysing discourse involve?' Paying attention to discourse means being attentive to what people say about screenwriting, how they make sense of it and the way this shapes practice and what is possible in the world of scripting. As such, manuals and handbooks are especially rich sources for statements that shape the discourse. An awareness of historical changes in writing is important: screenwriting is not singular or static through time. Because screenwriting does not exist in a vacuum, also important are the 'border disputes' that can occur between different craft areas (thus, directors and producers can be seen as contributors to screenwriting discourse). More specifically, analysing screenwriting discourse involves thinking about speaking position (who is saying what at which time), working with the terminology or jargon used in screenwriting (how things are said), appreciating the different objects of scripting (what is spoken about, including formats of script and the nature of the work), as well as the way different individuals imagine the craft (giving us a sense of the broader field and its rules and norms).

Thinking about the discourse of screenwriting is not a process of focusing on discourse over here (what people say) and practice over there (what people do). What people say is shaped by doing, and vice versa; practice is shaped by discourse. Looking at screenwriting through a discourse frame involves exploring how the practice of screenwriting is constructed or constituted through statements that circulate through institutions, handbooks, trade magazines, academic studies, promotional materials and other writings. Using statements from writers and theorists to illustrate particular ideas or assumptions, I shall examine different 'ways of speaking' about the script and screenwriting in this 'archive'. This book can in a sense be thought of as a primer in how to tune into and listen to screenwriting discourse as it has emerged in the US and taken hold internationally, picking up on tropes and ideas that reoccur over time. I focus on what I consider to be many of the main tropes, but this is by no means a final analysis.[9]

Thinking about screenwriting in this way, it becomes apparent that screenwriting discourse in fact has a long history and that discourses about screenwriting already exist and circulate. In this sense, one challenge of a critical reflection on screenwriting is to think about the area differently (in terms of different time frames and conceptions or norms of writing). One particular discourse will be familiar to some readers, in the form of an account of the experience of writers from the East Coast of the US as they encounter the Hollywood studio system from 1930–1940. In *West of Eden: Writers in Hollywood, 1928–1940*, Richard Fine identifies some common themes in this account, including discrimination against writers and the philistinism of producers (1993: 107–115), as well as a gesture whereby one conception of writing and literary work is pitted against the efforts of scenario writers as the 'lowliest and most ignoble' kinds of labourers (1993: 72). Literary workers with established reputations in New York 'would quickly learn that in Hollywood the "writer" was defined not only differently, but diametrically so' (1993: 104). As a result, a powerful discourse *about* Hollywood emerges, intermingled with ideas about screenwriting.

Distinguishing between different levels or layers of discourse can be difficult, especially in an area such as filmmaking that involves the collaboration of many craft workers from different areas. Ultimately I am not interested in policing a rigid formal distinction between discourses *about* and *of* screenwriting. But I am interested in key differentiators such as practice, the object and also speaking position, in that they help us identify different discursive formations. For example, the discussion of screenwriting in *West of Eden* is often about the studios, producers or Los Angeles. It also emerges from writers who do not in the first instance derive their standing as writers from screenwriting but rather from other kinds of literary production. It is crucial to pay attention to speaking position. As Fine notes: 'this "writer's view" of the studio system cannot be taken as an accurate or objective description of the system; it is not how the studios *really* worked. Rather, it is evidence of the funda-mental beliefs, attitudes, and values *shared by these writers* which determined the way they, as *writers*, viewed their world' (1993: 104; emphasis in original). Not all New York writers are subject to this perspective, however. Writers such as Dudley Nichols and Sidney Howard, whom I shall look at more carefully in what follows, can be seen as contributors to this dominant discourse of screenwriting, but a closer reading of aspects of their work shows they are part of a different perspective on screenwriting as well.

Significantly, the term 'discourse' provides a link between thinking about screen-writing and recent developments in film studies. While it has become commonplace to see film history as involving three major forces – technology, social and economic conditions, and aesthetics and style – language and discourse forms a fourth crucial but less developed area. It has become common in the literature to hear about larger cultural and institutional discourses framing particular developments (see Decherney 2005: 42), 'public discourse' (Hansen 1985: 322), even 'critical' or 'industrial' discourse (Higashi 1994: 191, 195). Tom Gunning draws extensively on the concept of discourse in his study of D. W. Griffith and the origins of American narrative film. There, 'narrative discourse is precisely the text itself – the actual arrangement of signifiers that communicate the story – words in literature, moving images and written titles in silent films' (1991: 15). But the concept has a much broader function in his work, which is to get away from a closed notion of the text and connect it to social and industrial concepts; indeed a whole 'sea of discourse'. For Gunning, the notion interacts with others such as 'signifying system' and 'filmic system' to produce a highly nuanced approach to signification and its links to social forces. This enables an approach to works 'which acknowledges their aesthetic identity but is also attuned to their function as social discourse' (1991: 11).

The concept of discourse allows Gunning to range across aesthetic forms as well as modes of production, distribution and exhibition. Whereas for Gunning the focus is on individual films, in this book the focus is screenwriting discourse itself, on under-standings of the craft and statements about writing. In this respect, discourse will not be linked to the idea of a filmic system or a particular idea of context or reception, so much as a concept of media practice.

A discourse frame focuses on the way screenwriting has been structured in particular ways. Because the practice and discourse of screenwriting is interwoven, the history of screenwriting is inseparable from a history of discourses that surround and constitute screenwriting. Approaching screenwriting as a way of speaking about texts, writing and production allows us to question received understandings of what screenwriting should or could be. This focus goes against a dominant tendency in screenwriting circles to speak about 'the Script' (singular), and screenwriting, in very authoritative ways. It allows us to look at how screenwriting is 'discursively constructed', as cultural critics say. It also allows us to focus on an essential and neglected aspect of the history of screenwriting practice: which is how critics and writers invented a practice in discourse. The invention of screenwriting occurs through particular terms and constructs such as 'writing for the screen', the idea of the script as a 'blueprint' and the notion of the screenplay. As I hope to show, many handbooks and writings by screenwriters, film theorists and critics have sought to redefine and renovate film writing.

Taking History Seriously

This book could not have been written without the efforts, carried out by a range of authors since the 1970s, to pay more attention to screenwriting and redress a perceived neglect of the area (one exacerbated by auteur theory). Of course, the corporate history of screenwriting dates from before the 1970s (see Ross 1941; Sands 1973; Wheaton 1973; Ceplair & Englund 1980; Schwartz 1982; Bordwell, Staiger & Thompson 1985; Bielby & Bielby 1996; Buckland 2003), and an understanding of this history is useful to the study of screenwriting practice and issues related to screenwriters (such as the emergence of the Guild, and the Blacklist). Since the time that story became a priority in motion pictures the writer has been embroiled in a conflict of authority with the director and later the producer, a struggle for recognition of their expertise and craft and in some cases direct creative control. For William Goldman, 'writers have always been secondary in Hollywood' (1983: 52). But rather than get bogged down in grievance and even resentment, our understanding of this area can be extended in a critical fashion.

History is important in this book because it helps us understand that the story film did not arise in a vacuum, and the invention of screenwriting took place within a complex set of cultural and institutional practices and conditions. Part of the challenge of approaching screenwriting in a more analytical fashion is to get serious about the history and historiography of screenwriting. There are many forms of historical writing. For some readers, the term history will evoke a 'life and times' chronology of screenwriting from its earliest days to the present, identifying specific, different, periods of screenwriting and mapping the contributions of key figures onto its progress. Such an approach, however, can overlook important issues to do with how screenwriting works and functions. As Edward Azlant notes: 'Even the richest history of screenwriting may not tell us everything about the nature and structure of the screenplay' (1980: 6).

Since the 1970s, the area of film history has become highly sophisticated, imagining the technological, representational and socio-cultural aspects of screen practice in a relationship of 'constant, interrelated change' (Musser 1990: 16). A distinction between an early and 'primitive' cinema and a more mature narrative cinema, for example, has been problematised. Scholars looking at the cinema of the late 1890s and early 1900s highlight the presentational approaches surrounding the screen, often borrowed from lectures, travel shows and vaudeville. Film critics and historians attempt to explore an interaction between what Charles Musser calls cinema's mode of production (how it is made) and the mode of representation (how a story is told or subject represented) (see 1990: 7). One can imagine that screenwriting is of central importance to this interaction, as it is part of the process of making and central to representation. However, an emphasis on scenes, shots, editing and the visual aspects of film, has meant that screenwriting is rarely treated with the kind of specific attention to detail that is given to film form. A group of dedicated historians (among them Tom Stempel and Edward Azlant) have begun to address this situation by focusing on the history of screenwriting and screenwriters, but their work does not always pick up on the techniques of contemporary film history, is sometimes focused around a 'life and times' approach looking at who did what and when, and does not always build on or go beyond established historical sources (see McGilligan 1989).

In this book I present a purposive history that seeks to foreground some of the conceptual frameworks within which screenwriting is understood. Although this study draws on archive and historical material – especially early handbooks – it is not a detailed empirical investigation of actual examples of screenwriting practice and its variations through different production companies. Nor does it undertake a comparison of different writing styles or genres of screenwriting. Taking precedence over these approaches is an interest in the historical identity of screenwriting. As I have suggested above, rather than give a complete history of screenwriting to the present day, the historical scope of this book is defined by three key anchoring points: the emergence and institutionalisation of a notion of 'writing for the screen' as the hallmark of screenwriting, the 'invention' of the screenplay and, finally, the idea that the script is a kind of blueprint for production. In other words, I want to explore how a particular idea of writing for the screen came to be institutionalised, how the screenplay became page-based and how the idea of the script as a 'blueprint' operates in screenwriting discourse. Putting these three notions together, the book traces the way 'writing for the screen', the form of the screenplay and the notion of the script as blueprint define the discursive foundations and boundaries of a contemporary understanding of screenwriting.

Since the late 1970s, film scholars and critics have paid increasing attention to the history of screenwriting, especially early screenwriting. This book draws on that work, but it also wants to open up questions around the kind of history being written. In particular, I want to challenge approaches to history that do not open up issues to do with the conceptualisation of screenwriting. The history writing that concerns me is based on notions of the screenplay and screenwriting that have not been fully examined or theorised, and are projected back onto the past, thus obscuring important aspects of screenwriting history.

It will be useful to briefly describe some of the works in this area.[10] A well-known study is Tom Stempel's *FrameWork: A History of Screenwriting in the American Film* (first published in 1988) – which has its own origins in his 1980 book on screenwriter Nunnally Johnson. Other key works include Edward Azlant's 1980 doctoral thesis, *The Theory, History, and Practice of Screenwriting, 1897–1920;*[11] John Brady's introduction to *The Craft of the Screenwriter: Interviews with Six Celebrated Screenwriters* (1981); Richard Corliss's edited collection *The Hollywood Screenwriters* (1972a) and his *Talking Pictures: Screenwriters in the American Cinema, 1927–1973* (1974).[12] Ian Hamilton's *Writers in Hollywood, 1915–1951* (1990), while arriving later than the aforementioned works, and drawing on them, shares most of their preoccupations in its evaluation of different writers at different periods of Hollywood's development.[13] Lizzie Francke's *Script Girls: Women Screenwriters in Hollywood* (1994) forms a response to the masculinist slant of the history, as does Marsha McCreadie's *The Women Who Write the Movies: From Frances Marion to Nora Ephron* (1994) and Cari Beauchamp's *Without Lying Down: Frances Marion and the Powerful Women of Early Hollywood* (1997).[14]

Pat McGilligan's important 'Backstory' project should be mentioned here. Although its focus on interviews gives it a different standing, it goes some way to investigating conditions of screenwriting at varying times and in particular contexts. As McGilligan explains in the introduction to the third volume (1997), the project started life as a single volume devoted to the stories, reminiscences, craft method and point of view of some of the best screenwriters from the Golden Age of Hollywood. It has evolved into a running series but was never intended to be a scholarly or historical work, and McGilligan characterises it as 'part biography, part historical record, part anecdotage, and part instructional seminar' (1997: 1). Or, as he explains in the introduction to the fourth volume, it is an 'informal history of screenwriting' constituted through the life stories of a representative cross-section of high achievers (2006: 1).

The history-writing around screenwriting that has emerged since the 1970s has an odd relationship to the revisionist film historiography that has been a powerful force in film studies in recent years. Thomas Elsaesser describes a new historicism, largely emerging from the US, but interlinked with research in the UK and Europe, that began to question the received, often anecdotal, history of cinema 'as the story of fearless pioneers, of "firsts", of adventure and discovery, of great masters and masterpieces' (Elsaesser 1990: 3; see also Bordwell 1997: 103). The earlier generation of historians looked at film in terms of demographic, economic, technological and industrial determinants. As John Belton notes, revisionist historiography 'differs from traditional paradigms for the writing of film history in its attempt to understand the cinema as a system and to identify the various practices that define this system' (1997: 226). Revisionist history attempts to synthesise traditionally separated areas such as technology, aesthetics, audiences and business (Popple & Kember 2004: 24). Revisionist film history has had a unique impact in the study of early film, which was particularly limited by a narrow focus on technology, 'great figures' and a division between early and later cinema that cast early cinema in a 'primitive' realm.

David Bordwell characterises revisionist history as 'piecemeal history', because it deviates from the idea of one scholar writing a 'comprehensive history of style across the world', but also because it builds up very detailed accounts of film development from particular investigations into film technique and collective norms (1997: 118–19). 'Focusing on a narrower time span, viewing films in bulk, and tracing shifts in terms and concepts allowed revisionist historians to construct fresh contexts for explaining stylistic continuity and change' (1997: 124). However, as Belton notes, 'revisionist historians have yet to write a history of screenwriting practices' (1997: 226). This is a significant issue, for while it has an interest in practice much (non-revisionist) historiography of screenwriting relies heavily on a biographical, humanist approach to history and the studio. Practice is through questions of who wrote what, for which star or producer, credits and general stylistic issues. For all of the discussion of the passage of the story through the studio, different studios and writers, and the interaction between writers, directors, actors and producers, the historiography of screenwriting has not always paid detailed attention to different modes of film practice and their institutionalisation. It generally remains tied to either an evolutionary account of the development of screenwriting, and narrative, in the studio, or an individual life and times approach.[15]

Few historiographers of screenwriting have explored the implications of the new historicism on their research in the way that Janet Staiger (1979; 1980; 1983; 1985) and Patrick Loughney (1990; 1997a; 1997b) have sought to do. Stempel cites some work by Musser, and Bordwell, Staiger and Thompson in passing. In the case of Azlant's 1980 dissertation – which was written prior to the publication of Bordwell, Staiger and Thompson's work on modes of film practice and classical Hollywood (1985) – his account relies heavily on the standard works in film history that revisionists seek to move away from (see 1980: 114, n. 3). He draws on production histories in order to 'establish the historical presence of screenwriters and their works' (1980: 10). Tracing the refinement of the 'craft' of screenwriting 'within the studios' (1980: 160), he draws on a concept of 'narrative design' to 'pursue the origins of the screenplay through film's evolving complexities of materials, features, schemes of development, and production circumstances' (1980: 58), but this falls short of a full account of modes of practice in the studio of the kind offered by Staiger.

One implication of the new historicism is a much closer attention to practices and their institutional contexts, although the lens through which this practice is analysed can often be very specific. Take, for instance, a common focus on 'economic and signi-fying practices'. This joining of the two forms of practices is one of the strengths of the revisionist approach. In one instance of this approach from Staiger, a culture's signi-fying practices can be said to include 'ideologies of representation, its conventions, its aesthetics' (1980: 12). Within this, a key area of focus has been on 'historically particular representational systems' (ibid.), and in Staiger's case the main concern is with the classical Hollywood representational system of narrative and continuity. Approaching signifying practices in this way is crucial to understanding the interaction between economics and a system of representation in Hollywood. Staiger wants to show how economic processes 'might be related to the development of representa-tional systems' (1980: 13). But other ways of approaching practice are possible – and Staiger herself explains that her focus is the dominant practices not the options which might have been. I would suggest that looking at scripts and scriptwriting as illustrations of the system, and instances of it, as Staiger does, is important; but also that an analysis of screenwriting on its own terms raises different issues. Looking at the discourse of screenwriting shifts the emphasis slightly away from representational systems to the construction of the practice in non-systemic, and less functional, ways. It involves approaching signifying practices from a different direction, in terms of the space of writing and identity of practice.

Staiger's work on the history of the Hollywood system, as carried out through numerous articles, and her study with David Bordwell and Kristin Thompson, *The Classical Hollywood Cinema: Film Style and Mode of Production to 1960* (1985), is of unique importance to the study of screenwriting. While not directly writing in the historiography of screenwriting, Staiger's work is important for two reasons: firstly, for its rigorous account of the emergence of the studio system and the separation of conception and execution. Secondly, her researches into the division of labour in the Hollywood mode of production have led to a careful examination of changes in scripting practices in relation to changing systems of film practice. As Andrew Horton notes (1992: 14), historians of screenwriting could do well to build on Bordwell, Staiger and Thompson's study.

Film scholars and historians have become adept at looking beyond the film as text and appreciating industrial and production conditions as well as technological and trade discourses (especially exhibitor discourses) supporting film practice. They have even begun to talk about screenwriting manuals. But they have been less successful in exploring screenwriting discourse, generally using writing handbooks to elaborate upon or illustrate points of film style or narrative (see Bowser 1990: 257; Thompson 1999: 11, 15, 21).[16] In this context, historical work on screenwriting is obviously important to expanding our understanding of screenwriting practice, and can form something of an antidote to the shortfalls of revisionist film histories. However, the historiography of screenwriting has not always been in tune with 'revisionist' film history approaches that seek a more complex idea of practice and discourse. This book is a contribution, then, towards finding a middle ground between revisionist film history and still-emergent currents in the historiography of screenwriting.

Standing next to, but to one side of, revisionist film history, the emergence of a historiography of screenwriting at a particular point in time is itself a curious phenomenon. It is worth asking, 'Why did it arise in the 1970s?' I suggest that there are two key factors. The first is the rise of auteur theory in the US, and its perceived devaluing of the contribution of the screenwriter (see Froug 1972: ix–xix; Hamilton 1990: vii). Received in the context of a long-standing struggle to gain credit for the work of the writer in the filmmaking process, it has come about that auteurism can only be regarded as a usurpation of the writer's claim to authorship. Thus, for William Goldman, auteurism is taken to mean that 'it is the director who *creates* the film' (1984: 100; emphasis in original). The sense of grievance activated by auteurism has had powerful effects, leading to much debate. In this sense, as William Froug notes, 'the screenwriter does owe a debt of gratitude to the auteurists' (1972: xvii). Sometimes for political purposes, at other times for the purposes of granting long-overdue recognition, this focus on the writer has motivated close examination of earlier periods in which the writer was not so valued. Auteur theory has prompted a more careful evaluation of the work of screenwriting, and also gaps in dominant accounts, such as to do with ethnicity (see Harris 1996). The re-evaluation of screenwriting by women is also related to this ferment around authorship. There is a perception of a double oppression for women screenwriters. As Nora Ephron states: 'It is the writer's job to get screwed ... Writers are the women of the movie business' (quoted in McCreadie 1994: 3, 186).

A second motivating factor is a change in the screen culture of Hollywood itself, placing a great deal of emphasis on the script as a key part of the package. As Thompson notes: 'with the rise of package production since the 1970s ... freelance scriptwriting has enjoyed a resurgence and a flood of manuals has appeared to cater to aspiring authors' (1999: 11). This approach is linked to the emergence of the so-called 'movie-brats' (see Pye & Myles 1979; also Madsen 1975; Hillier 1993). That is, film school-educated, 'cine-literate', directors and screenwriters who engineered a rethinking of the status of ideas, the importance of a good script and the role of creative people (see Stempel 2000: 197). Michael Pye and Lynda Myles associate the emergence of these filmmakers with a change in production conditions and the traditional creative and technical division of labour (1979: 85–6). Although film theorists have been careful not to overstate the differences between 'old' and 'new' Hollywood (see Tasker 1996; Thompson 1999: 6–8; Bordwell 2006: 5–10), this is regarded as a time when the power of the studio executive was fading, the cost of moviemaking was rising dramatically (leading to less production) and proven actors were becoming more discriminatory about their commitment to a project (see Brady 1981: 24). The emphasis on a quality script as a key component of the 'package' during this period extends a much earlier tendency that stresses the importance of story and storytelling as a way of creating 'quality' drama. It has led to curiosity about writers. It has also generated a popular interest in writing 'on spec' – that is, writing a screenplay for speculation without prior commercial commitment – that continues to fuel the publication of countless screenwriting handbooks, magazines and websites on the topic (see Field 1984, 1994; Horton 1992; Fragale 1994; Seger 1994).

Considering both of these developments together, it is fair to say that the 1970s and 1980s were a time for re-evaluation of the role of the writer in US film culture. This has led to the publication of screenplays as books in their own right, and promoted greater public interest in 'America's storytellers', resulting in magazines, books of interviews, podcasts and coffee-table books of photographic portraits (see Lumme & Manninen 1999). Writing issues are more widely discussed. Aligned with changes in the film industry, this has led to the rise of the 'script guru' touring the world promoting their approach to screenplay writing.

It is not my intention to suggest that these two factors had no relation to what came before in the domain of filmmaking, or that they are totally distinct from one another. On the contrary, the auteur controversy has everything to do with the battles over credit that took place in the industrial structure of the 'old' Hollywood: a period that preoccupies many screenwriters of the 1930s and 1940s, through to the present debates over the 'film by' or possessory credit. Corliss is thus able to suggest that 'the effect of auteur theory was to steal back whatever authority (and authorship) the writers had usurped' (1974: xxvii).

Screenwriting and the Separation of Conception and Execution

Bearing on the object-problem in screenwriting is the issue of the separation of conception and execution in film production, forcing particular approaches to practice and creativity. One of the useful aspects of the concept of scripting introduced in the preface is that it is highly processual and thereby resists the prising apart of a product (script) and the practices of composition supporting it (writing). It is a dynamic way to approach scriptwriting that is not solely focused on the end manuscript. But this emphasis on the 'writerly' rather than the product aspect of scripting goes against a dominant logic of the studio system, organised around the separation of the work of conception and execution. This separation tends to see the work of acting and shooting as functions on the 'execution' side of the separation, not the conception side. This arrangement influences how we talk about performance and style. The separation is institutionalised by dividing production into stages (pre-production, shooting, post-production), and introduces a logic that makes it difficult to see execution in terms of scripting (which tends to be posited at an earlier stage of production).

The division of functions and tasks in the studio influences the nature of screenwriting itself. Unlike other forms of literary production, the space of screenwriting can be highly segmented and subject to what Staiger calls a 'division of writing' between creation and rewriting (1985: 190). The work of writing is distributed between different 'subspecies' of writers: gag, continuity, treatment, adaptors, title writers and so on (McGilligan 1986: 1). In the 1930s the distinction between constructionists and dialoguers emerged (see Fine 1993: 74). These developments impacted on the space of conception and influenced relations between writers, directors and producers especially.

The separation of conception and execution permeates our ideas about the script. The script is supposedly written and then shot as planned. One myth surrounding scripts at the Ince studios held that, once approved, each script was stamped 'Shoot as Written' (see Staiger 1979; Bowser 1990: 222), thus formalising a distinction between creative and constructive phases. Today, the script is commonly seen as a kind of blueprint, with production being modelled closely on the building of a house. But the blueprint idea of the script is also being challenged and our notions of screenwriting may need updating.

Not all forms of production rely on a single moment of conceptualisation or scripting, and scripting can happen across the entire process of production. In addition, different technologies are disturbing the separation of conception and execution. Once understood narrowly in terms of digital effects, digital technology is now seen more broadly as an 'alternative production path for solving practical film problems' (McQuire 1997: 37). Reflecting on digital filmmaking, George Lucas speaks of a shift from linear processes to layering (see Kelly & Parisi 1997). According to Scott McQuire, digitally-orientated film production no longer follows an assembly 'line', but rather happens in a parallel development, whereby work that may traditionally have been seen as 'post-production' happens during the shooting phase (1997: 36). Digital filmmaking techniques not only potentially rework the separation of conception and execution, but also the relationship between words and images and the nature of scripting itself (through animatics and pre-visualisations).

If the traditional separation of conception and execution has reached a limit and is mutating, and is today being challenged by filmmaking approaches that do not follow the linearity of the assembly line, then this has important ramifications for screenwriting which now needs to grapple with new forms and sites of scripting. A novel account of scripting beyond the separation of traditional models of conception and execution is needed, as well as new ways of comprehending the shifts taking place. Questions arise, however, around the place of screenwriting in this new environment, and the adequacy of current frameworks. Contemporary discourses of screenwriting were forged in the context of a separation of conception and execution as it impacted on the division of labour in Hollywood studios. There is much to celebrate and value about screenwriting and the efforts or screenwriters to gain both recognition for their craft and improved working conditions. When I write of these matters it is in testament to the real creativity of writers. Nonetheless, careful consideration needs to be given to the impact of the separation of conception and execution on our ideas about writing. In the following I explore the possibility that while some key ideas of screenwriting (such as those articulated by Dudley Nichols) emerge in reaction to the separation of conception and execution, our discourses of screenwriting may also be heavily invested in this separation, and perhaps dependent on it. In a two-fold process, it may be necessary to reflect on the way screenwriting is invested in the separation of conception and execution, but also at the same time consider and revalue forms of scripting that may not be subject to this separation in the same way.

Particularism: Players and Non-players

Walk into most bookshops today and you can find an abundance of material on the practice of filmmaking as understood by filmmakers; books and journals about the practice of screenplay writing; and more specifically screenplays as books (see Horton 1992). A survey of screenwriting manuals in the early 1980s describes a bullish market for scriptwriters, with many universities and colleges offering screen-writing courses (see Leff 1981: 281). This literature plays a key role in promoting screenwriting, but it also provides an insight into the sets of relationships and interac-tions surrounding the 'object', which in turn contribute to ideas about the identity of screenwriting.

From a media industries perspective, it could be argued that the proliferation of books about scriptwriting is incidental or marginal to the process of making films – a kind of secondary industry or publishing spin-off. However, this overlooks the extent to which the script/screenplay does not exist outside of institutions and history, but is fundamentally a discursive entity. The discourse of screenwriting is constituted in the interaction and interference of different formations of creativity, narrative, industry and production, theory and practice. By analysing these formations it is possible to get an insight into the way the industry is imaged and imagined by its practitioners. More specifically, we get an idea of who can or cannot speak with authority about screenwriting, and what forms 'proper' screenwriting practice.

This approach sees 'the industry' itself as a discursive entity. While the conven-tional approach is to define an industry quantitatively and organisationally in terms of its profits and losses and corporate structure, it is possible to view industry as constituted through ways of talking (sets of jargon), and constructed in the interaction and interference of different ideas about creativity, narrative, industry and produc-tion, theory and practice. Approaching industry as a discourse it is possible to gain an insight into the way the industry is maintained, imagined and contested by its members, often through frameworks that are taken as a given, often 'assumed or explained' but not questioned see (Macdonald 2004a: 96; 2004b).

The work of French philosopher Michèle Le Dœuff might seem an unlikely point of reference here, but it offers a useful framework for exploring the 'imaginary' that shapes the film industry. In her analysis of philosophy, Le Dœuff describes a process whereby a social minority or group wraps social discourse around itself, by differentiating between masters and apprentices, 'players' and 'non-players', and manipulating the conditions for access and entry into the institution (see 1989; 1991). For Le Dœuff, this process involves using metaphors and images to construct philosophy as a space in which women have a secondary place. They are allocated the space of simile ('truth is like a woman', for instance), instead of agency. Le Dœuff describes this move as a form of 'particularism'. History with a masculinist bias could be seen as particularist in this sense. However, particularism is not limited to conventional formations of sexism, racism, colonialism or religious intolerance, and the concept can be applied to the world of film production.

Le Dœuff's work on metaphors and discursive 'imaginaries' is useful for describing the operation whereby screenwriting is defined or imagined around the figure of the writer and the blueprint. The theme of particularism is relevant in a study of screenwriting because it helps us understand how one particular group can shape, and speak for, writing defined in a particular way. This in turn gives us an idea about the limits and borders that define screenwriting practice.

As an example I want to turn to famous screenwriter of the 1920s, and Cecil B. DeMille[17] collaborator, Jeanie Macpherson, and her 1922 article 'Functions of the Continuity Writer'. When she writes that 'the continuity IS the photodrama, the very soul of it – preconceived and fully worked out on paper by the photodramatist' (1922: 25), Macpherson is wrapping the discourse of film around the unique labour of the photodramatist, to the exclusion of other film workers and from those not qualified to do the work. The screenwriter emerges from this position as grand 'architect' – knower of the laws of screen drama – and differentiated from the 'amateur' and the 'hack' writer. Drawing on building metaphors, Macpherson explains that the writer, like the architect, is concerned with 'foundations'. The metaphor sets up ways of relating to the director, as 'master builder', handling raw materials and fitting them into place. At the same time, Macpherson addresses the reader in a particular way. The reader is an 'outsider, looking in', seeking to become an 'insider looking out' (1922: 32). This issue is not exclusive to the US. In 1936, Soviet theorist Osip Brik identified a similar problem, and saw the script as a key object of debate between different film personnel and between the arts. 'There is a tendency', he writes, 'to declare the group of film workers a closed caste reigning over the secrets of cinematic expertise' (1974: 95).

It is easy to associate particularist strategies of this kind with exclusion, and a potentially reductive idea of the politics of screen writing in which the writer keeps novices out and co-workers in their place. The more complex reality is that writers have had (and often still do have) a tenuous place in the mode of production. In Macpherson's case, she is trying to define a legitimate space for the screenwriter as craftsperson.

Macpherson's text is one example of a wider phenomenon of works offering screenwriting advice to a public eager for success in the movies. This genre of writing offers a glimpse of the way practitioners package themselves and their craft for the public, but it also provides a way to imagine the industry. Indeed, much discussion of the script invokes a whole protocol for dealing with industry: one that sets up presup-positions for interaction with the craft, and modes of interaction between industry, practitioners and lay-people. Screenwriting, as a space where stories and indus-trial processes intersect, is particularly abundant with regulatory norms and filtering gestures. The fact that the majority of script books speak to novices is particularly important here; the bulk of 'how-to' books are, after all, primers to screenwriting that define writing for the screen, and access to it, in a particular way. This particularism works to define the shape of what qualifies, or does not, as industrial practice, as well as legitimate screenwriting; in other words, it regulates who can speak with authority and who cannot.

Less abstractly, these speaking positions are in fact linked to processes of funding, and narrative theories circulating within funding cultures and agencies are ushered in to bolster or define particular views. Within industry, these perceptions and under-standings work to reproduce particular ideas about the object. As Sue Castrique suggests: 'Producers now sit down at script meetings with three questions: Where's the main character? Where's the through line? And where's the three acts?' (1997: 102). They can contribute to what Adrian Martin calls a 'culture of decisions' in which these decisions are made by individuals heavily invested in particular models of scriptwriting. 'And what are these people saying or writing? Things on the order of: "this script lacks a strong second act" ... "the hero is unlikeable" ... "there is not enough driving conflict" ... "this character has no journey"' (Martin 1999; see also 2004: 84). This culture of decisions, needless to say, has a direct impact on the kinds of films that can be made, and is part of a gatekeeping function. As Erik Knudsen notes: 'the systems created will favour those who speak the same "language" and know how to play the right "game"' (2004: 185). What I call a theory/funding nexus, drawing on particular ideas about screenwriting, thus shapes our screen culture (see Maras 2005).

In this chapter, I have sought to flesh out in more detail the methodology of this book, and its rationale for linking history, theory and practice. I have suggested that each of these terms – 'history', 'theory' and 'practice' – become key sites for rethinking screenwriting in different ways. I have sought to clarify what I have called the 'object problem' of screenwriting, the difficulty of fixing an 'object' of screenwriting, by proposing a different frame linked to the concept of discourse. But, the object problem discussed above manifests itself in different ways on the level of history, theory and practice. In terms of history, the objects of analysis, the script forms and practices linked to it, change a great deal. In terms of theory, it is important to develop frameworks for screenwriting that can accommodate different approaches to scripting. In terms of practice, screenwriting as an object itself needs closer analysis in terms of the way that screenwriting is linked to particular production conditions, forms such as the screenplay and discourses that shape the nature of writing. In the next chapter, I look at a foundational issue in screenwriting, which is how the script is situated in film production.

2.

SITUATING THE SCRIPT
IN FILM PRODUCTION

This chapter examines the issue of the place of the script in film production. This is a topic that has drawn different responses over time, but which is important because it goes to the heart of assumptions about the nature of the script and scriptwriting that underpin different views about screenwriting. Readers might come to this chapter with the expectation that there is a single story of how the script should be situated in production. Here I examine a number of different ways of approaching the problem, from an emphasis on the written plan in the history writing on screenwriting, to debates in the Soviet Union in the 1920s, and also the work of David Bordwell, Janet Staiger and Kristin Thompson in The Classical Hollywood Cinema.

Production Plans and Early Film

Histories of screenwriting often begin with an account of the earliest form of scripts. Of course, this task is difficult because over time nomenclature changes (from scenario, to continuity, to screenplay), film jargon develops and the format becomes more codified – all of which need to be factored into our understanding of the development of screenwriting. I want to resist this tendency, or at least complicate it, by bringing production issues into the picture. Scriptwriting today is understood to have a particular place in the production process; an important aspect of the study of screenwriting therefore has to do with understanding how the script is situated in film production/ film practice, and how it gained this place over time. In one sense this emphasis on 'situating' the script might seem odd. An important early function of the script in the US was to allow for an initial estimate of the footage required for each scene (see Staiger 1985: 176). The script organises production in this sense, seemingly standing above it. But there are a variety of ways to conceptually situate the script in production, just as there are different ways to imagine production itself. One common account runs like this: as the length of motion pictures increases in the 1910s the screenplay comes to occupy a key planning position in production, with the advent of sound in the late 1920s finally solidifying this position (see Sternberg 1997: 7–8). But this account does not necessarily tease out the production aspect. The script can be considered central or marginal to production. It can relate to the finished story or be regarded as just the raw material. It can be considered a management tool or creative object. Understanding how the script is situated in film production involves analysing statements about both the script and the production process.[18]

Historians of screenwriting have not always paid attention to this aspect of screenwriting discourse, partly because they have been busy correcting a tendency in film history that downplays the significance of screenwriting. An example of this tendency is evident in the following passage from Kevin Brownlow:

> When the cinema began ... no scenarios existed. Those primitive one- and two-reelers were shot in a couple of days by directors who had a rough idea of the story and who improvised as they went along. Off-the-cuff directors carried on well into the twenties, having grown highly proficient and capable of rapid invention. D. W. Griffith was the dazzling example. A man who could shoot *Intolerance* without a script has methods that defy analysis. None of the great comedians – Chaplin, Lloyd or Keaton – ever worked from a script until talkies came. But then few silent comedies were ever shot from a conventional scenario; that was their secret. (1968: 270)

This passage reflects a view that screenwriting was a fairly inessential aspect of production, except for 'dramatic feature films' (ibid.). In response, historians such as Tom Stempel have made a point of giving greater detail to Griffith's way of working, and his collaboration on storylines with figures such as Frank Woods and Anita Loos (see 2000: 17–26; see also Azlant 1997: 244; Tibbetts 1977: 48–50, 143). Others have sought to identify pre-Griffith scenarios (see Loughney 1990).

Compounding this treatment of screenwriting is another common misperception that there were no writers in Hollywood before the coming of sound. This view is based around the idea that because a particular form of the craft of screenwriting was not evident pre-sound there was no writing.[19] For John Brady there were no writers in the early years of moviemaking: 'not until sound came to the movies in the late 1920s did studios recognise a need for someone more literate than a title-card scribbler or a "scenarist"' (1981: 11). Pat McGilligan introduces his *Backstory* collection of interviews with screenwriters with the view, 'Before 1926, at least to judge by official credits, there were no screenwriters. The expression *per se* scarcely existed' (1986: 1). Indeed the particular expression 'screenwriter' is not a common one until the late 1930s, although (as discussed in later chapters) other terms were in existence.[20] Even in 1938 Frances Marion refers to the 'scenario writer' alongside the 'screen writer' (two words) (1938b: 32–33). While McGilligan gives these statements the standing of myths to be questioned, his decision to use the non-existence of screen-writers as a starting point for discussion is significant.

Given this state of affairs, it is understandable that historians of early screen-writing seek to make screenwriting and screenwriters as visible as possible. One side effect of this effort to affirm the significance of screenwriting, however, is a particular focus on the script and production in terms of the need for planning. For Stempel, the search for the earliest scripts takes us into the realm of silent film and the use of 'written "plans"' – in one case a blow-by-blow newspaper account of a boxing match, in another case a theatre play (2000: 3). This approach takes history writing danger-ously close to a focus on origins and 'firsts' that has proven unhelpful in film and photography studies. The problem is that the search for firsts and origins can have the tendency to 'fix' the landscape in particular ways, leading to a reductive view of the development and institutionalisation of screenwriting.

Take for example, the view that intentional use of a written 'plan' can constitute an early form of script. What is meant by plan? Closer investigation suggests that the plan=script hypothesis may not be adequate to take into account the genre and pres-entational issues involved. In the case of the boxing match mentioned by Stempel, the Corbett/Fitzsimmons fight, he refers to the way a boxing match was staged for the camera by the Lubin company. The Lubin company did indeed arrange a staged re-enactment of the fight. But this was not the first prizefight on the screen, and as early as 1894 the (actual) Leonard/Cushing fight was filmed for the kinetoscope, in six rounds, each shortened to fit the capacity of the reel (itself extended for the bout) (see Musser 1990: 82). A viewer could thus see the entire fight by moving from kinetoscope machine to kinetoscope machine. In 1897, after protracted negotia-tions, Corbett met Fitzsimmons in the ring in Carson City, Nevada, to be filmed by the Veriscope Company, and great attention was given to capturing the actuality of the event (wide format cameras were developed and producers attempted to make the ring smaller to ensure coverage of the action). So-called 'facsimile' films, such as the Lubin company film, build on a wider tradition of re-enactments (including those at other locations during the fight, with descriptions telegraphed to theatres and boxers touring after the event). In the case of the Lubin facsimile, it was released around the same time as the Veriscope production, but received a mixed reception as not all audiences understood the status of the Lubin film or 'fake Veriscope'.

What is important to highlight here is the presentational mode of early cinema and its standing as a form of entertainment and amusement. As Charles Musser notes, for some audiences, re-enactments in their sometimes dubious quality were legitimate amusements, 'the poor man's way to see the fight' (1990: 202). In the case of the Veriscope production, the commentator *beside the screen* conveyed a strong sense of plan. 'The details and significant moments that would one day be brought out by close-ups were now emphasised by narration' (Musser 1990: 198). In the case of the Lubin facsimile, it does not arise in a vacuum, and as 'a first' should be seen against the backdrop of prior practice and theatrical staging. Technology, as with the Veriscope production, formed a real constraint; action was condensed and camera speed decreased to fit the film within available capacity. All of these factors suggest that Terry Ramsaye's overblown suggestion that 'this was art – the recreation of an event – and the "fight by rounds" column was a scenario, but Lubin did not know it' (1926: 288) should be approached with caution. As a historian, Ramsaye had a special interest in the development of story film and he had an eye for firsts, but even he notes of the Lubin venture that the camera was still merely a reporter. That a newspaper was the writerly source for the re-enactment is worth keeping in mind. For Musser, fight films sit in an interesting space in early cinema, defining new ideas around documentary 'observational cinema' but still having strong links to the presentational and lecture traditions of early cinema.

The other written 'plan' referred to by Stempel is that of the Passion Play of Oberammergau. A script by Salmi Morse had been written and performed in San Francisco but a New York production had been abandoned in the face of religious interests in 1880. It was picked up by film producers in the late 1890s and this gives rise to Ramsaye's claim that 'Salmi Morse's ill-fated script was brought to light, to become the first motion picture scenario' (1926: 370). Edward Azlant is more effusive: 'The current Writers' Guild could do worse than mark the spot where Salmi Morse threw himself into New York's North River' (1980: 64). The circumstances around this play (the existence of a playscript), the scale of its dramatic construction (see ibid.), seemingly give credibility to the idea of a plan, as does a connection to legitimate theatre.

But again the cultural context and mode of what Musser terms the 'screen prac-tice' of the day should be kept in mind. After the controversy of Morse's (abandoned) New York theatre production, travelling lecturer John L. Stoddard presented lectures on the topic that were well received (see Musser 1990: 209). Stoddard's lectures influenced the presentation (with slides, organ music and hymns) of a version based on performances by the villagers of Horitz (see Musser 1990: 210). Another version of the Passion Play was produced for the Eden Musée in New York. As Musser notes: 'the Salmi Morse play was dusted off and generally performed the role of scenario' (1990: 212). But again the idea of the scenario serving as a plan is tested by the conditions of performance of the play. As Musser notes:

THE PASSION PLAY OF OBERAMMERGAU had no fixed form. Because reviews usually focused on the films, the full diversity among programs is difficult to establish fully. At the Musee [sic], a well-known lecturer, Professor Powell, stood beside the screen and accompanied it with a narration. The extent to which lantern slides were integrated into these initial programs in order to create a full-length entertainment is uncertain … Early cinema's presentational elements were powerfully articulated in these passion-play programs. The images were designed as moving illustrations of 'the greatest story ever told'. (1990: 216–18)

It is difficult to imagine how the idea of a 'written plan' operates in a presentational context where spectators respond to both familiar iconography and the narration of the lecturer that links and interprets the images.

It is not our main purpose in this chapter to discover the first or earliest forms of script and screenwriting. It will suffice to mention the efforts of Roy McCardell writing single action/one-take mutoscope plots at the Biograph studios circa 1898 – an extension of his supervision of comic strips at the *New York World* and caption writing for photo-stories in a weekly entertainment magazine, the *Standard* (see Stempel 2000: 5; Sargent 1914: 199) – and also that narrative texts seem to have been used as the basis of film productions in at least 1905 (see Loughney 1990),[21] with 'photoplay writing' proper emerging around 1909 (see Sargent 1914: 199). While the task of locating the earliest forms of screenwriting may have political significance in overcoming an aspect of film studies that diminishes the value of the screenplay and screenwriting (see Azlant 1980: 17), even Azlant concedes that the task of looking for *that* first actual script or scenario may not be a priority (1980: 59). We can agree with Patrick Loughney that 'a great deal of research remains to be done before the history of screen texts – in all their permutations as scenarios, scripts, photodramas and screenplays – can be told' (1997a: 278). But, as this chapter seeks to argue, an important aspect of this research is to be mindful of the place of the script in the production process and film practice more generally. The notion of a 'written "plan"'– which has links to a concept of written pre-production design promoted by Azlant in his thesis on screenwriting up to the 1920s (1980), and which Stempel draws on – serves this function. But while useful in focusing on production practices I would argue it ultimately limits discussion.

Steps Toward Narrative Design: Edward Azlant

For Azlant, early screenwriting is linked to pioneering efforts in narrative design; as the length of film grows the scenario evolves as a means of pre-production design and the pre-arrangement of scenes (see 1997: 228). Azlant notes that the two constants of turn of the century American film were 'increased length and some manifestation of design or pre-arrangement' (1980: 65). With the popularity of narrative films, and the growth in the number of nickelodeons stretching to 10,000 sometime in 1910 (Azlant 1980: 84), production is dependent on the planning associated with the script. Azlant writes:

> Obviously, the pre-production design of narrative films fit well into this evolving studio system, as written design was by its very written nature distinct from other aspects of production. Thus, in addition to the intrinsic factors of the narrative mode itself and the increasing length of films, the extrinsic factors of large-scale production and the evolving studio system surely helped institutionalise screen-writing. (1980: 85)

With the arrival of large-scale production then, the institutionalisation of screenwriting is assured; the demands of complex production and narrative require it.

Azlant's work seeks to establish the screenplay as significant to film study. His main argument is that the 'screenplay functions as a document of design in the creation of the fictional narrative film' (1980: 5). While Azlant's work is important in thinking about numerous pressures on screenwriting – length of film, scale of produc-tion, division of labour, narrative – ultimately the notion of design he relies on, and the way he ties it to written pre-production of narrative film, is narrow in its treatment of film practice. He takes it to be an intermediate step between the materials used and the 'techniques of execution or production' and sees this as part of a planning phase. His understanding of design is underpinned by the image of 'an underlying scheme governing the whole development or function of the creation which is assigned or recognised' (Azlant 1980: 58; see also Azlant 1997: 228). The origin of this vision of film production and practice is not unpacked fully, although Azlant acknowledges it is linked to a tradition of narrative design in the theatre (see 1980: 49) and it also arises out of his discussion of the film studio. But this view is guided by an idea of the film object as self-sufficient product, a stand-alone work, that is out of keeping with the presentational/representational practices of early film. Azlant's conception of design, although linked to traditional theatre, is in a sense 'superimposed' over early cinema film practices. Early film dealt with topics of interest already established in popular culture or the news, and required an intertext for decoding. Also while the development of more sophisticated editing shifted control of the programme to the company, exhibitors could still influence the programme through narration or re-ed-iting of scenes. What does 'pre-production' mean in a practice where editing is done by the exhibitor, not the production house (see Musser 1991: 5)? Azlant does not give us a way to think through this problem. From the outset, his approach to scripting is filtered through the image of the screenplay as design plan or scheme for the self-sufficient narrative film; this explains his own interest in the newspaper summary informing the Lubin facsimile of the Corbett/Fitzsimmons fight, which is interpreted as a 'skeletal description of consequential dramatic actions' (1980: 60).

Azlant's approach to 'film practice', a term which Eileen Bowser succinctly describes as the 'differing circumstances of film production, distribution and exhibition' (1990: xi), is filtered through a particular conception of design. This notion of design is reliant on an idea of narrative and writing, but also particular ideas about the materials used, and execution. These come together in what Azlant calls the 'screenwriting phase of production' (1980: 164). But this concept forecloses a discussion of scriptwriting and production, and of the different ways that materials and execution can be organised. Writing after Azlant's thesis, critics such as Musser and Janet Staiger have explored this more closely. Azlant's approach is primarily focused on the institutionalisation of screenwriting (and alongside it a particular image of the studio system), but in doing so he does not explore the conceptual aspect of situating the script in film production practices. Different arguments and debates about the nature of the script and scripting thus become overcoded by a particular idea of screenwriting for narrative cinema,[22] screenwriting as a phase of production and its future place in the studio.

Azlant's interest in looking at the role of the script in production practice is important, although the concepts he uses have limitations. To provide a contrasting investigation of the place of the script in film production practices I now leap ahead from early cinema to debates in the Soviet Union in the 1920s. What is fascinating about these debates (and this explains why the discussion skips chronologically ahead) is that they explicitly relate to the place of the script in the production process. This work is significant because it gives a rare glimpse into the problem of situating the script in film practice and demonstrates a unique attention to film writing and film material. It also questions the place of plot, which is so central to screenwriting in the US. Later in the chapter, I examine the work of Bordwell, Staiger and Thompson, which offers a more complex idea of the studio and the place of the script within it.

Debating the Situation of the Script: Vertov, Eisenstein, Kuleshov and Pudovkin

In the Soviet Union in the 1920s and beyond, the film script was a contentious topic. Debating the nature of a script – whether it was an autonomous literary work or a 'memo' for the director – had importance. At issue in the debate were the kinds of scripts provided to studios, the kind of training involved and the director/script writer relationship itself (see Brik 1974). Comments by key figures such as Dziga Vertov, Sergei Eisenstein, Lev Kuleshov and Vsevolod Pudovkin can be divided roughly into one of two schools of thinking about the script: those who did not want to situate the script into production (Vertov, Eisenstein) and those who did by developing the idea of the script as a filmic plan (Kuleshov, Pudovkin).

For the radical documentarist Vertov and his 'Kinoki' (cinema-eye people), it is 'wrong, in the beginning work, to present a so-called scenario. In the years to come, the scenario as a product of literary composition will completely disappear' (1984: 35). As expressed in a statement from 1926, 'the scenario is a fairy tale invented for us by a writer. We live our own lives, and we do not submit to anyone's fictions' (1984: 71). Vertov saw the scenario as a kind of short story that stands in antipathy to the system of editing (and shooting) factual material that he was developing. To a significant extent, for Vertov, editing and writing with the camera encompasses writing. Montage means '"writing" something cinematic with the recorded shots' (1984: 88). Vertov on one level would be happy to eliminate the scenario: *Chelovek s kino-appa-ratom* (*Man with a Movie Camera*, 1929) was presented as 'A film without intertitles', 'A film without a scenario' (although this was explained in an opening title).[23]

Eisenstein similarly argued that 'a numbered script will bring as much animation to cinema as the numbers on the heels of the drowned men in the morgue' (1988c: 134). Contrary to what Azlant's view of design might suggest, Eisenstein does not link the scenario to a design phase that fixes how the material will be used. He sees it as just another stage in the development of the material: 'not a staging of raw material but a stage in the condition of the material' (ibid.).[24] In his essay on the montage of attractions in 1924, Eisenstein had sought, except in circumstances where reality required a particular emphasis, to diminish the importance of 'plot justification' in the assembly of shots. As a result, a script could be useful as a 'scheme of refer-ence', one that became important if plot was a necessity, but in general he saw 'the presence or absence of a written script' as 'by no means all that important' (1988a: 46–7). Through to the late 1920s he maintained a 'loose' conception of the relation between script and film. Eisenstein encouraged people of letters 'not to write scripts', but rather stick to their genres and 'force film directors to find cinematic equivalents of these works' (1988b: 98).

In a 1929 piece, 'The Form of the Script', Eisenstein posits a distinct difference between literary language and film language and seeks to leave room for the role of the director as translator between them. For this reason he did not seek to enforce writers to write in a particular format, but favoured a novella form[25] such that the scriptwriter and director could expound their passion 'in their different languages' (1988c: 135). He notes: 'We do not recognise any limitations on the visual exposition of the facts. Sometimes the purely literary arrangement of the words in a script means more to us than the meticulous recording of facial expressions by the writer' (ibid.).

Against the contemporary understanding of the screenplay as offering a blue-print for the film, Eisenstein's view may not be fully appreciated. For Eisenstein, the script is 'but a stage in the condition of the material', not a staging of filmic material itself. He sees the script as one part of a process of conditioning material leading to realisation in images, but this stage is separate to the work on the raw film material proper. Eisenstein leaves room for a difference between literary and filmic materials or languages, describing the script as a 'shorthand record', a 'cipher', the product of an 'imprint', not a plan or blueprint.

Eisenstein is responding here to another current in Soviet thinking that seeks to overhaul the scenario, bring it into the sphere of film production and make it directly useful in the creation of filmic material. In the latter school, filmmakers such as Pudovkin and Kuleshov express a need for a coherent 'filmic plan' or shooting script suitable for use in the production process. The early rhetoric of Kuleshov (circa 1920) suggests that only the director could think cinematographically, and that the script-writer could only be seen as a representative of the alien art of literature seeking to impose literary values on cinema (1987a: 51). In the late 1920s, however, Kuleshov sought to educate writers to the needs of film, and in this sense his views were not too distant from Pudovkin's.

For Kuleshov and Pudovkin, lack of awareness of the filmic material led to a situation where the film acts merely as an illustration of the literary material in the script. The solution to this problem was to introduce a different set of expectations around the script. In his study of film technique (first published in English in 1929), Pudovkin links the scenario to an uninformed 'incident' or plot-based understanding of film content:

> Almost all represent the primitive narration of some given content, their authors having apparently concerned themselves only with the relation of incident, employing for the most part literary methods, and entirely disregarding the extent to which the material they propose will be interesting as subject for cinematic treatment. (1958: 29)

He goes on to argue the importance of knowing the methods of filmmaking and filmic action, particularly the importance of shooting out of sequence or continuity. Pudovkin writes against the 'scenario', with the aim of turning the scenario into a meaningful 'shooting script'. The desire for a coherent 'filmic plan' itself places pressure for the scenario to evolve. Pudovkin notes:

> From this derives the inevitable necessity of a detailed preliminary overhauling of the scenario. Only then can a director work with confidence, only then can he attain significant results, when he treats each piece carefully according to a filmic plan, when, clearly visualising to himself a series of screen images, he traces and fixes the whole course of development, both of the scenario action and of the work of the separate characters. In this preliminary paper-work must be created that style, that unity, which conditions the value of any work of art. (1958: 32)

For Pudovkin, this 'overhauling' of the scenario amounts to an argument for a new format that includes details regarding the various positions of the camera (long shot, close-up, and so on) and the technical means (fades, mask, pan). He acknowledges that such an ideal form would require in essence the scenarist become a director, but nevertheless encourages scenarists to work their scripts out in this way as much as possible. In Kuleshov's statements circa 1929, a similar prioritisation of shooting scripts over scenarios can be found, along with an insistence that film scripts be made to order by script-writers, who from the outset should prioritise the needs of filmic material over literary material (see 1987b: 169).

Pudovkin's understanding is closer to a contemporary 'blueprint' perception of the filmic plan, in which the film is conceived on paper prior to execution. The script in Pudovkin's account is a key part of the 'filmic system', and has a role in shaping 'filmic material': 'It is important to realise that even in the preparatory general treatment of the scenario must be indicated nothing that is impossible to represent, or that is inessential, but only that which can be established as clear and plastically expressive key-stones' (1958: 45). The world of 'filmic' material has been extended in a sense to encompass scripting in words, but at the same time the scenarist is encouraged to think not in terms of written descriptions, or dialogue, but in 'plastic images' (1958: 42). Indeed, for Pudovkin, the words are less important than the 'externally expressed plastic images that he describes in these words' (1958: 55).

The Script and the Factory: Staiger and The Classical Hollywood Cinema

Azlant's focus on the script as a design instrument links the development of screen-writing to the evolution of the studio system. But work published subsequent to his thesis – such as his 1997 article 'Screenwriting for the Early Silent Film: Forgotten Pioneers, 1897–1911', in which he attempts to engage with this work – has arguably explored this more closely. A watershed event for thinking about the way the script is situated in the studio occurs in 1985 with the publication of David Bordwell, Janet Staiger and Kristin Thompson's *The Classical Hollywood Cinema: Film Style and Mode of Production to 1960*.[26] In that work, the authors look at the emergence of the script as an administrative device through which manufacture could be regulated and moni-tored in a studio context. At the same time they develop a useful methodology (based around ideas of modes of film practice) for looking at the script.

Hollywood is often criticised on stylistic-cultural grounds (see Ruiz 1995: 9–23; Bradley 1999), but a culture versus industry dichotomy can stymie discussion. Bord-well, Staiger and Thompson avoid this problem by offering a sophisticated conception of industry as an administrative formation that includes cultural/stylistic elements. A strength of their approach is the way they deal with questions of industry and aesthetics together. While it is possible to read Hollywood in terms of its mode of production, its organisation of labour, capital and material, this approach often provides limited insight into the development of Hollywood as a stylistic entity. Through an account of what they describe as Hollywood's 'mode of film practice', the authors avoid privileging what Marxists call the economic 'base' at the expense of all other elements (see 1985: 87–95; also Staiger 1979), and show how stylistic considera-tions operate alongside decisions about the deployment of labour and technology: 'A mode of film practice ...consists of a set of widely held stylistic norms sustained by and sustaining an integral mode of film production' (Bordwell *et al.* 1985: xiv). Their work highlights the importance of the mode of film practice to changes in the mode of production, and in this sense they resist an account of industrial change that is determined either by economics or technology.

It is common to see Hollywood described as a kind of 'factory', but this notion has limitations in describing some craft and artistic aspects of the industry. As Staiger notes: 'It is useful to classify the Hollywood mode of production as mass production, but that does not explain the disparity between D. W. Griffith at the Biograph Company in 1910 and Dore Schary at Metro-Goldwyn-Mayer in 1950' (Bordwell *et al.* 1985: 92). To address this issue Staiger looks at the detailed division of work and the management systems in the studio. Through these instances Staiger shows how mass production in Hollywood never reached the full rigidity of the assembly line of other industries, and did not always follow the cheapest filmmaking procedure (Bordwell *et al.* 1985: 89). By supplementing the concept of mode of production with that of mode of film practice, Staiger develops a nuanced account of the 'factory', articulating six different phases. These phases include the Cameraman system, 1896–1907; the Director system, 1907–1909; the Director-unit system, 1909–1914; Central Producer system, 1914–1931; the Producer-unit system, 1931–1955; and the Package-unit system, 1955–1960. Each of these phases maps onto a differing set of industrial conditions in which, significantly for us, the script, or absence of the script, plays a defining role. Her approach thus offers a framework for thinking about the situation of the script in production.

Staiger discusses each phase or system in detail, across several chapters of *The Classical Hollywood Cinema*, and I refer the reader to her extended discussion. Here, I shall only highlight aspects of each system, mentioning key factors as they pertain to the script and staging. In relation to the cameraman system, the process was conceivable by one person, and conception and execution of the project was not separated: the cameraman would select the subject matter and stage it as necessary. However, this mode of film practice 'was not able to supply films in mass production' (Bordwell *et al.* 1985: 117). With the director system, craft roles became more distinct: 'In this system of production, one individual staged the action and another person photographed it' (Bordwell *et al.* 1985: 118). In this mode, theatre provided a framework for dealing with scenarios that might be received in the mail. The demand for fictional narrative created a need for an increased supply of plots, and the writing of script outlines developed as a separate function to meet this need. 'Outlines' could range from 'causal [sic] scenario to the more formal play' (Bordwell *et al.* 1985: 119), with the director given significant leeway in the use of 'scenario outlines'. In the director system a logic of manufacture takes hold, as well as the start of a detailed separation of conception and execution and different work functions. The demand for narrative films sees a more formalised function of the 'story writer' emerge, modelled to some extent on the theatre.

Under the director-unit system the division of labour became more detailed, departmentalised and hierarchised; companies expand to encompass multiple units. This period also saw the birth and formalisation of the scenario-script, which enabled both increased production rates due to pre-planning and scheduling, and also scenes to be filmed out of order in particular locations, in accordance with a principle of continuity. The 'story outline' proved inadequate to work as a story plan on this scale of production, and more elaborate 'scene plots' were required (see Bordwell *et al*. 1985: 125). Expectations surrounding quality product also placed pressure on film-makers to develop a coherent narrative within the constraints of a standard distribution length of 1,000 ft. This led to more rigorous preparation.

> Thus both shooting out of final continuity and the standard of clear, continuous action militated for a script written prior to shooting ... A 1909 trade paper article set out the format for the standard script: the title, followed by its generic designation ('a drama', 'a comedy'), the cast of characters, a 200-word-or-less 'synopsis' of the story, and then the 'scenario', a shot-by-shot account of the action including intertitles and inserts. This scenario script could insure that the standard of continuous action would be met within the footage requirement. It also listed all the story settings so that shooting out of order was faster, easier, safer, and, hence, cheaper. (Bordwell *et al*. 1985: 126)

Even with these requirements, however, Staiger notes that directors were given flexibility and some followed the outline approach rather than adopt shooting from the scenario-script.

During the period of the central producer system, films jumped from an average of 18 minutes to seventy minutes. Supply started to exceed demand. The feature film, subject to special advertising and billing, became more commonplace but the multiple-reel film places greater pressure on the script. The continuity script format emerged and became central to the planning process, offering not just a scene-by-scene breakdown, but information about location and specific shots so that the production could be budgeted in advance, according to a precise number of shooting days: 'The producer used a very detailed shooting script, the continuity script, to plan and budget the entire film, shot-by-shot before any major set construction, crew selection, or shooting started' (Bordwell *et al*. 1985: 128). In this period, the language of filmmaking and aesthetic of continuity became more sophisticated. Script departments themselves grew. The script acquires its 'design blueprint' function: 'Following "scientific management" practices, this history on paper recorded the entire production process for efficiency and control of waste' (Bordwell *et al*. 1985: 138). It should be emphasised that within this broad scheme Staiger is careful to note exceptions and alternatives to this mode of practice, especially by key directors.

The continuity blueprint forms a precondition for the producer-unit system, allowing for different producers to supervise units, thus fostering innovation but also rationalisation. This system is seen as a revision of the director-unit system but with the producer in charge and a central staff which planned the work process. The identification of properties, 'the procedures for finding suitable story material intensified' during the tenure of this system (Bordwell *et al*. 1985: 322). Of course, spoken dialogue became a key consideration of scripting during this period. 'Each studio adapted the old script format differently' and in the 1930s new efforts to standardise new continuity scripts were made (Staiger 1985: 192). Finally, the package-unit system arises, co-existing with the producer-unit system, so that independent productions are incorporated into regular studio schedules. The 'package' became crucial; work was organised on a film-by-film rather than firm basis. The package-unit system intensifies the need to differentiate films according to innovation, story, stars and direction.

Staiger's account of modes of film practice provides a useful framework within which to think about shifts in this area, and especially the different way the script is situated in production.[27] Staiger's scheme provides an approach related to, but more nuanced than, Azlant's discussion of design through written pre-production discussed earlier. One of the valuable aspects of Staiger's work is the way it demonstrates how Hollywood develops script formats and invests in continuity scripts (continuities) as a way of securing certain aesthetic standards, which in turn become central to the business.

Staiger's work, both with and without Bordwell and Thompson, allows us to see how different understandings of the script are articulated within, and themselves articulate, different configurations of film practice. Her work has a degree of precision regarding industrial factors that is rare in the historiography of screenwriting. The summary of the different modes above cannot hope to capture all the aspects of her methodology, nor the full context and different factors that come into play in Staiger's discussion of the development of each mode.

Staiger's work with Bordwell and Thompson gives a detailed picture of the way the script is central to management practices and division of labour. In fact, 'emphasising the importance of the script as a blueprint for the film' is one of her key tasks (Bordwell *et al*. 1985: 94). But in terms of research into screenwriting discourse and practice, as distinct from film practice, this also represents a constraining frame. The discussion of writing practice, the discourse of screenwriting, is somewhat overdominated by the focus on the blueprint. Issues to do with writing for the screen, or the relation between scenario, continuity and screenplay, for example, are not taken up in depth.

Another concern is that while Staiger describes a range of factors influencing each mode of film practice, a key theme is different forms of the script. In other words, different modes of film practice are closely tied to accepted (and perhaps even dominant) scripting practice. There is a tendency in her work with Bordwell and Thompson for the script to become a marker – not the only one, but a key one nonetheless – for differentiating modes of film practice. The script plays a key role in defining and distinguishing different modes of film practice, but the relationship between film practice and scripting/screenwriting practice is as a consequence not fully developed. And while Staiger does important work in considering exceptions and alternatives within the mode, looking at both practices of standardisation and differentiation, the overarching work of renovating the theory of mode of production at times takes priority over investigation of scripting and the conditions and problems of screen writing. The focus of Bordwell, Staiger and Thompson's project is after all exploring ways in which the Hollywood style 'cohered and sustained itself over several decades' (Bordwell 1997: 120).[28]

Alternatives to the Sovereign Script

This chapter began with a discussion of scripts as written plans in early cinema, but ends with a much more complex and detailed idea of the filmic plan and film practice, and the relations between the two. An awareness of different modes of film practice is crucial to understanding the practices of standardisation and differentiation highlighted by Staiger. This attention to variation is important, as studies of screenwriting can inadvertently set up normative conceptions of the roles and functions of the script.[29] To illustrate this point I shall use one of the key concepts that this book draws from Staiger's work (which I also look at in later chapters), which has to do with the fact that production in the Hollywood mode is heavily marked by a separation of conception and execution (see Staiger 1979). The script is said to exist on the side of the concept, but guides execution; it is a kind of abstract machine guiding practice. But even here, it can be argued, there is a risk of turning this idea into a prescriptive, normative notion of screenwriting practice.

This separation of conception and execution permeates much writing about film production and screenwriting. The legend that at Thomas Ince's production company scripts were stamped 'shoot as written' (see Jacobs 1939: 206; Mehring 1990: 232) has not been supported by evidence (see Staiger 1979: 20; Azlant 1980: 166; Stempel 2000: 44).[30] However, the legends hints at some reality, which is that once conception and execution are separated 'production' becomes a matter of sheer execution of the written idea (see Staiger 1979: 20–1). Supporting this idea of production is an approach to labour based on a separation of the worker's brain from his/her hands, a separation of creative conception and practical work (see Staiger 1979: 18; Braverman 1974).

The separation has become central to the way screenwriters make sense of production. Margaret Mehring writes: 'Film production is the process of *executing* the choices of film form that the screenwriter has written into the screenplay' (1990: 3; emphasis added). Film jargon accentuates the linear nature of production – pre-production, shooting, post-production – thus securing a particular idea of production based on the 'execution' of the script: from concept to finished work, from script to screen, and so on. The script is imagined as a blueprint, the master plan of a large-scale production operation.

Staiger's careful examination of the origins of the separation of conception and execution, and its institutional purpose, is crucial to the analysis of screenwriting. In approaching Staiger's work from the point of view of scripts and scripting processes, however, a significant issue arises. While reading systems of film practice in terms of their use of the script her work leaves the script subject to the separation of conception and execution. In other words, while highlighting the influence of the separation of conception and execution on production Staiger's account of the script, and scripting, is largely determined by this separation.

In *The Classical Hollywood Cinema*, the need for a broader account of different understandings of the script and scripting becomes evident in one of the final chapters of the book, where Bordwell and Staiger consider 'alternative modes of film practice'. They see this task as important: 'The historical hegemony of Hollywood makes acute and urgent the need to study film styles and modes of production that differ from Hollywood's' (1985: 379). Their chapter looks at a range of typologies for thinking about different modes of film practice, and stresses the importance and difficulty of theorising alternative or oppositional styles to the classical style. As with Staiger's analysis of the systems in the Hollywood mode of production, one section of this account is heavily dependent on the status of the script in the production process 'as a major area of variation' (Bordwell *et al.* 1985: 382). Starting from the proposition that 'because of the world-wide imitation of Hollywood's successful mode of production … oppositional practices have generally not been launched in an industry-wide basis' (ibid.), Bordwell and Staiger examine variations in the status of the script made by individual filmmakers or filmmaking groups. They present a brief summary of a diverse set of examples including working 'by heart' (Jacques Tati), preparing a detailed script and then abandoning it (Jean-Marie Straub and Danièle Huillet), working from notes (Miklós Jancsó), writing shortly before shooting (Wim Wenders), scripting throughout the production process (Dziga Vertov), working against the scenario (Jean-Luc Godard); shooting without a script and then scripting; collaborative decision-making; shooting in continuity (Carl Theodor Dreyer, Straub/Huillet); shooting in long takes (Kenji Mizoguchi); shooting at the time of day and year outlined in the script (Eric Rohmer); and alternative methods of shooting (see Bordwell *et al.* 1985: 382–3).

This account provides a useful reminder of different possibilities of situating the script in production, and raises key issues for any pluralistic account of filmmaking. However, by using the script as a means of articulating alternative modes of film practice to Hollywood, Bordwell and Staiger could be said to 'other' these practices in the domain of the 'alternative'. By framing their analysis in terms of 'variations' of

'Hollywood's successful mode of production', Bordwell and Staiger limit the political and conceptual significance of struggling against the script.

In the section in which they examine these examples, Bordwell and Staiger begin by emphasising Jean-Louis Comolli's point that 'there has emerged a tendency to challenge the sovereignty of the script in the fiction film' (Bordwell *et al*. 1985: 382). While Bordwell, Staiger and Thompson provide a comprehensive account of how the script came to work across the production process as blueprint, Bordwell and Staiger do not elaborate on this notion of the sovereignty of the script, nor the implications for screenwriting and film studies of challenging it. Approaching the issue from a different angle, it is not about 'alternative modes of film practice' but the status of cinema as a kind of writing, and as a form of expression.

While Bordwell, Staiger and Thompson do not elaborate on this notion of the sovereign script, it is useful to try to describe it further. Firstly, the sovereign script is the product of an operation whereby scripting is directed towards a primary object, the manuscript form. (In this operation the script as object becomes separated or treated independently from other forms of 'scripting' including staging or rehearsal.) Secondly, the script is given a transcendental form, such that it stands above the production process, governing a specific area of production or production context. The script dictates what is meant to happen on the set and the screen, and even though it can also be influenced by changes on the set a particular communication loop limits the extent to which different kinds of scripting can influence the script. In this sense, the sovereign script relies on a separation of conception and execution. Finally, the sovereign script underpins what Comolli identifies as a 're-presentational system' tying together representation and production:

> Thus the project of the film is repeated for the first time in the scenario, which is repeated by the cutting continuity which is in turn itself repeated by rehearsals (appropriately so named). The latter are then reproduced for the filming, the editing of which is simply its reconstruction with post-synchronisation, finally closing the cycle of re-presentations. (1980: 239)

Taken together, these three aspects define a particular space of screenwriting and film production.

Having articulated the three aspects of the sovereign script, it can be seen that the latter has a key role in relation to the two senses of screenwriting discussed in the preface. It paves the way for an understanding of screenwriting as the writing of a script that serves as a plan for the film. Any idea that the event of shooting, of writing with the camera, or with light, or with bodies, might function as a system of writing, falls by the wayside. These techniques are subordinated to a logic of 'execution', or as the auteurist critics call it, 'illustration'.

The sovereign script form legitimates particular ideas about reading, writing and interpretation of the script. But at the same time, it can also be said to de-legitimate a broader theory of scripting that includes the script, *mise-en-scène* and other aspects of filmmaking. This is not to suggest that this system of power has gone unchallenged. Indeed, Bordwell and Staiger's account of alternative film practices shows that it has been challenged. But what has received less attention are the modes of interpretation, forms of reading and discursive constructions that become attached to the sovereign script, which are made out to be a 'natural' part of screenwriting discourse. I examine some of these practices surrounding reading the screenplay in the next chapter.

3.

THE SCREENPLAY
AS LITERATURE

This chapter examines a long-standing debate in screenwriting discourse to do with the literary status of the script, and whether or not a script can be considered literature. As well as looking at the views of figures such as Jean-Claude Carrière and Pier Paolo Pasolini, the chapter pays special attention to the work of John Gassner and Dudley Nichols, which raises key issues to do with the screenplay as literature, the completeness of the script, and reading.

For filmmaker-theorists such as Dziga Vertov or Lev Kuleshov, literature represented one of the older arts against which the new art of cinema had to assert itself. Their struggle against literature was part of a commitment to the specificity of the cinematic medium, the expressive character of filmic art and the creation of filmic material. In the realm of aesthetic criticism, film theorists have long reacted against a notion of 'quality' that 'means Literature and the Theatre' (Jensen 1970: 57). But literature does not always need to be considered as a problem area in this sense, and literature often appears in screenwriting discourse in positive terms. The back cover of one volume of screenplays extols: 'This remarkable collection of screenplays could well represent a true expression of 20th-century literature' (Garrett *et al*. 1989). For some, categorising the script or screenplay as literature represents a significant achievement, and as a result it is important to 'recognise and acknowledge that the motion-picture screenplay, at its best, can and should be considered literature in the same sense as a great novel or a great drama' (Thomas

1986a: 1). Epes Winthrop Sargent, in 1912, values literary recognition: 'conditions move rapidly to the recognition of the scenario writer as a contributor to dramatic literature' (1912: 3). In 1915, William C. deMille predicts 'you will see inside of a very few years a certain screen literature, in which the author will begin to come into his own' (quoted in Blaisdell 1915: 258). Sidney Howard is more pessimistic about literary aspirations when he declares in 1937 that 'there is no immediate likelihood of literature on celluloid' (1995: 205). In the 1940s, screenwriters and critics such as Dudley Nichols and John Gassner sought to promote the 'screenplay as literature'.

On one level the debate around the script as literature has to do with artistic status and standing, played out in a struggle between older and newer arts, or established and popular forms. In the US in the 1910s, the struggle between old and new media manifested itself in discussion around the new art of photoplay and its relation to older arts, especially stage drama (see Freeburg 1918). On a different level however, thinking about the script as literature involves grappling with its complex 'literary' status, and the way it has particular ties to a production context that gives it meaning. Thinking about the screenplay as literature involves making a set of assumptions about the script, how it is read and also its relationship to production – what literary theorists might term the 'textual' nature of the script.

The Scripts as Outline versus A New Literary Form: Brik and Balázs

The interconnection between literary status and the issue of the script's textuality is demonstrated in the writings of two key European authors of the 1930s, Osip Brik and Béla Balázs. Writing in 1936, Brik, a screenwriter with Vsevolod Pudovkin on *Potomok Chingis-Khana* (*Storm Over Asia*, 1928), and 'Russian Formalist' literary theorist in his own right, asks 'what precisely constitutes a script?' In answering this question Brik situates the script between two poles: on the one hand it could be considered an autonomous work of art; on the other, 'a memorandum for the director indicating the sequence of scenes and episodes' (1974: 95). Between these two options, Brik formulates the view that the script has a precise function and readership: 'scripts are written for those who will be making the film'. The literary status of a script is subservient to the demands of filmmaking:

> [In fact] ... the script is not an independent literary work, nor some kind of literary manual for the adaptation of a novel or story for the screen. It is not a literary work at all. A script is the outline of a future film, set out in words ... The script is written in words. But this in no way makes the script a literary work, let alone an autonomous one. The script is a system of cinematic images and devices calculated to make the author or author's artistic project open out on the screen in the forms of cinematic art. (1974: 96)

For Brik, a key objective is to find the right means of expression (including film actors and landscapes and soundscapes). Who writes the script is irrelevant as long as they have an understanding of the cinematic means of expression, and indeed the art of script writing. At the same time, Brik does not see this function of the script limited to the paper script or literary language. An 'expressive photograph can give a fuller idea of the future than long pages of flowery literary script' (1974: 96). Counter to those who would celebrate the script as a form of literature, Brik declares that 'the script is not a work of literature' (1974: 99). For him, 'the process of work on the script is far more important than the finished script' (ibid.).

Brik enquires into what constitutes a script at a time when the art of cinema is developing and making new requirements of filmmakers and filmmaking techniques. Hungarian theorist Béla Balázs, who is best known for his *Theory of the Film: Character and Growth of a New Art* (published in Russia in 1945 as *Iskisstvo Kino*), writes within the same problematic as Brik and others but at a stage when many key battles have the appearance of being won. Of special interest is the way that he revises the literary standing of the script.

> Not so very long ago it was still difficult to convince the Philistines that the film was an independent, autonomous new art with law of its own. To-day ... it is also admitted that the literary foundation of the new art, the script, is just as much a specific, independent literary form as the written stage play. (1970: 246)

For Balázs the script has come of age as a literary form, and is no longer a 'technical accessory' to production. In this sense he does not regard it as mandatory to situate the script solely *in* production, or see it in instrumental terms. He sees no obstacle to prevent scripts from being literary masterpieces, drawing on the stage play to underwrite the autonomy of the script.

For him the existence of the script as an independent literary form is closely tied to the development of film language. In the opening of his chapter on the script, Balázs provides a brief account of the historical development of the script thus far: from no script, to 'technical aid' – mere 'lists of the scenes and shots for the convenience of the director' (1970: 248) – to 'literary script'. The emergence of the 'literary script' is significant for Balázs because it marks a change in film language, namely the arrival of the close-up: 'The intensity of the close-up drove out the complicated story and brought a new literary form into being ... There was less adventure, but more psychology. The development turned inward and script-writing was now a task worthy of the pen of the best writers' (ibid.).

The emergence of this new literary form is related to changes in the techniques of the silent cinema, specifically its deployment of the close-up forcing a division of scenes into shots. It is with the arrival of the sound film in the late 1920s, however, that the script as literary form finds its formal logic: a need to go beyond stage play directions to render the audible spectacle of film. Balázs elaborates on this logic through a detailed discussion of the film script relative to the stage play. The two share an obvious connection in the need for dialogue, but the need to render the visual aspect of the action and background – indeed all the elements of the 'audible spectacle' of film – is greater in the script (Balázs 1970: 250).

Balázs's writing on the script is complex and multi-layered. Unlike Pudovkin and Kuleshov, and to a lesser extent Brik, Balázs does not subordinate the art of script-writing to the art of cinema, but gives it a different artistic lineage through drama. While he celebrates the script as a literary genre this does not translate into a minimisation of visual qualities of film. The script is not literary because it is part of the literary side of production, but rather the script *becomes* a unique literary form because of the demands that cinema makes of it. He articulates the paradoxical existence of the script 'which was to present in words the visual experiences of the silent film, that is, something that could not be adequately expressed in words' (1970: 248). By placing the production of 'specific visual effects' and not literary effects at the centre of script-writing practice Balázs overcomes the implications of the paradox of representing visual experience in words.

One final aspect of Balázs's argument is noteworthy. In this early period of cinema, and indeed into the present, battle lines are drawn between film and literature, the cinematic potential of cinema and the literary influence of the script. A defensive attitude prevails, whereby the autonomy of the script is made subservient to the art of the cinema and the demands of the production process. While this argument may be legitimate, Balázs is one of the few critics to open up an alternative road: namely, that there is an interaction between the developing art of cinema and the newer art of scriptwriting *that goes both ways*. He writes: 'up to now the history of the film script has been merely a chapter in the history of the film. But soon the script may in turn determine the history of the film' (1970: 255).

An Autonomous or Intermediate Work?

At first glance, there seem few obstacles to viewing the script as literature. After all, scripts are written down; as manuscripts they are read, published and can be purchased and anthologised like books. 'Spec scripts' can be written and sold without a production deal in place. Scripts can be read, and draw on techniques shared with poetry and novels. Like stage plays, the sound film script involves dialogue and description, and different films can be made from the same script. A long tradition in the scholarly study of the performing arts has managed to separate the play script from the performance, and frequently studies drama off-the-page, as 'dramatic literature', rather than in its theatrical manifestation. Certainly there are differences between screenplays and stage plays, but the 'screenplay and stage play are not as far apart as you might think' (Thomas 1986a: 1). All of these factors contribute to the perception of the screenplay as a 'literary' entity.

Given the linguistic demands that the screenplay forces upon writers, it would be natural to think of the screenplay as a literary genre in its own right. Although this can place some screenwriters in a difficult position, such as when Paul Schrader insists that 'I am not a writer. I am a screenwriter, which is half a film-maker' (quoted in Hamilton 1990: ix).[30] Statements such as this one point to a significant issue when considering the script as literature – discussed earlier in terms of an 'object problem' – which is that the existence of the script is bound to the cinematic medium, and also to the production of films. In practice what this means for many screen-writers is that an authorial or 'moral rights' claim in the written manuscript alone, limited to the literary domain, is not enough. The script is not simply an autonomous work of art, but is what some theorists have dubbed an 'intermediate' work. Barbara Korte and Ralf Schneider suggest that the intermediality of the screenplay is at the centre of concerns over the literariness of the film scenario (2000: 89). They identify a 'strong intermedial link with film' (2000: 93), especially its promotional aspects where screenplays are marketed in the glow of a film. But this intermediality is not just to a finished product; it also has to do with the way the script sits in sbetween different contexts (industrial/artistic), media (word/audiovisual) and processes (writing/ film production). The intermediality of the script complicates the extent to which the screenplay can be considered an autonomous form. As Ian W. Macdonald suggests: 'there is never a definitive version of the screenplay of a film; by definition it must relate to the screenwork, but also by definition it cannot, as more work must precede the final outcome' (2004: 90a).

One general problem with the attempt to see the screenplay as a form of literature is that it tends to take the script out of its production context, restrict this intermedi-ality and treat it as an autonomous work of art. By seeing the script as autonomous from the film, the screenplay as literature approach risks painting a poor picture of the relation between script and film. And yet, for some critics this relationship is paramount to making sense of the specific nature of the script. Jean-Claude Carrière, for example, refuses to dissociate a screenplay from a film: 'Once the film exists, the screenplay is no more … It is the first incarnation of a film and appears to be a self-contained whole. But it is fated to undergo metamorphosis, to disappear, to melt into another form, the final form' (1995: 148).

This line of thinking about the 'vanishing screenplay' is not without its critics in screenwriting circles. Although Carrière is not a film theorist, Edward Azlant identifies a general tendency in film theory to devalue and marginalise the writer's contribution to filmmaking, and also to overlook the linguistic and literary aspects of filmmaking in favour of looking at the film as an essentially visual entity. Azlant notes how, in Hugo Münsterberg's 1916 study of the photoplay, it is only through the actions of the director that the 'imperfect' work of the scenario writer becomes a 'complete work' (1980: 23). Robert and Katharine Morsberger observe that 'cinema journals are inclined to consider every aspect of filmmaking before the script' (1975: 45). They complain that the desire to discuss films as 'film' leads to a situation where the script is considered a 'vulgar ingredient' (ibid.; see also Horne 1992).

In terms of the idea that the screenplay 'disappears', James F. Boyle writes 'in defence of a screenplay as an intermediate art form':

> Many people scoff at the idea of defending the screenplay as a form of literature. Yet it has a sense of poetry about it. Perhaps the problem is that most people have not read enough screenplays to get a sense of the beauty of them ... Serious critics maintain that a screenplay is not an end product. They point out that the finished film is the end product and that the screenplay is only a stop-gap measure ... Admitting that a screenplay is an intermediate form of art, it may be compared to a sketch that a sculptor makes while designing a bronze statue. The actual finished product might be a life-sized statue in three-dimensional form which is comparable to the three-dimensional reels of emulsion in film cans which is the actual release print. Both the charcoal sketch on paper (two-dimensional) and the typist's ink on paper (two-dimensional script) are stop-gaps. But consider that the sculptor might be Picasso or DaVinci or Michelangelo. Then those scraps of charcoal sketches would be on display in a museum. So, too, some Academy Award winning films have their screenplays on display at museums. The day may come when a screenplay does not have to be produced and released to become considered worthy of being included in the museum's collection. (1983: i–iii)

While the classification of an intermediate art form is in itself intriguing, and the screenplay indeed draws on poetic techniques of reading, the museum is a strange choice of institution in this context as it facilitates display rather than reading, and accommodates curios as well as art works. It could be argued that, as with other arguments about the autonomy of the script, Boyle leaves us with a limited understanding of the relations between script and film, focusing instead on 'film cans'.

As a critic of the idea of the autonomous, literary script, Adrian Martin sees the script as a plan or proposition for a film. He is wary of the way focus on the script as an object can take over from, or supplant, the film. Martin also sees the script as an intermediate work (although unlike Boyle he would see the script as a step in the development of the *mise-en-scène* of the film). Martin raises the additional point (one mentioned earlier in the preface) which is that there has been a 'historical drift towards screenwriting as an autonomous activity, breaking apart the ideal unity of script conception and screen realisation' (1999). In this sense, the 'autonomisation' of the script – the becoming autonomous of the script from the process of realisation of the film – has resulted in a division in the scene of creativity. For Martin, the autonomisation of the script is not merely a bid for artistic recognition, but a by-product of a publishing industry. Many commentators have noticed the emergence of what Andrew Horton calls the 'The "How to Write the Best Ever Screenplay" Book Biz' (1992), and the rise of 'story gurus' (Fragale 1994; Coleman 1995; Castrique 1997; Mercurio 1998). For Martin, a 'script industry' has worked to elevate favoured texts to the realm of literature.

Pier Paolo Pasolini also tackles this issue of whether the screenplay can be seen as an autonomous object. He explicitly considers the moment at which the screenplay 'can be considered ... a work complete and finished in itself' (2005: 187; emphasis in original). He admits that it is possible to look at the script in this way, as a new literary genre, but that this would be erroneous. Pasolini argues that a screenplay does have poetry or metaphor, but that this significantly comes from a different language system: that of cinema itself, the potential film to come. He suggests that the screenplay is a 'structure that wants to be another structure' (ibid.). This is not to suggest that the screenplay cannot be understood as an autonomous entity, or that the screenplay cannot be viewed as literature, but that this has risks:

> If there isn't the *continuous allusion to a developing cinematographic work*, it is no longer a technique, and its appearance as a screenplay is purely a pretext ... If, therefore, an author decides to adopt the 'technique' of the screenplay as an autonomous work, he must accept at the same time the allusion to a 'potential' cinematographic work, without which the technique he had adopted is fictitious – and thus falls directly into the traditional forms of literary writings. (Ibid.; emphasis in original)

For Pasolini, there is a unique connection between a screenplay and a language system of the cinema, the imagining of the film to come. The writer may draw on autonomous techniques, and it is possible to see the screenplay itself as an autonomous object, but both perspectives would leave the screenplay in a different language system, that of literary writing. A 'spec script' in this sense would be seen as a 'precursor text' for a film to come, drawing on cinematic codes of reading. If we adopt Carrière's point of view, while the script disappears into the film, it can be read after the film, perhaps for the quality of its writing, but as an object with a strange status (an intermediate status that may indeed enhance its interest or novelty value to a reading public, in the sense that it allows them to compare the script to film (see Korte & Schneider 2000: 94)). But, as Pasolini reminds us, the screenplay as literature approach relies on cinema to provide a code or way of reading scripts. There is a risk of misreading the screenplay if we fail to understand its virtual status in relation to the actuality of film, its role as a particular kind of technology, a structure that wants to be another structure.

Distilling a Literature of the Screen: Gassner and Nichols

Creating a new category called 'a literature of the screen' is not a simple process. The critical and intellectual work that goes into the process is significant. I use the word 'distilling' to describe the process whereby the script is treated in a particular way to become an 'object' of literature. John Gassner (established theatre scholar, and later with Columbia Pictures) and Dudley Nichols (well-known screenwriter and former president of the Screen Writers' Guild[31]) published their influential anthology of screenplays called *Twenty Best Film Plays* in 1943.[32] The two introductory essays to this collection, 'The Screenplay as Literature' (Gassner) and 'The Writer and the Film' (Nichols) are in tune with the politics surrounding the resurrection of the Screen Writers' Guild in 1933. Nichols' writing in particular is a defence of artistic creation against the functionalism of the factory system and the Machine age (see 1943: xxxi; 1946: xxii). Their collaboration is not only significant in terms of the history of publishing collections of screenplays, giving rise to a new genre of sorts,[33] but also marks a key moment in the screenplay as literature tradition of theory. Even if the anthology resisted putting the word 'screenplay' in its title, Gassner's introductory essay began with the declaration that 'There is now a literature of the screen – the screenplay' (1943: vii).

It will be useful to consider the context in which Gassner and Nichols are writing. In 'The Writer and the Film', Nichols presents a portrait of film production in the age of 'the Machine': that system of modernity characterised by large-scale manufacture, specialisation and the division of labour. Nichols posits a direct link between the cinema and the Machine: 'We are all specialised, for better or worse, and it is only natural that the one new art form which the Machine has produced should be the most highly specialised of all' (1943: xxxi). Nichols sees specialisation as a necessary phenomenon in science and art, because 'those fields have grown too enormous for the single mind to embrace' (ibid.). He nevertheless sees a downside to the breaking down of the production process into functions and separate crafts: it is 'detrimental to film as an art form and an obstacle to the development of artists who wish to work in film. It is too much the modern factory system: each man working on a different machine and never in an integrated creation' (ibid.). In the studios a 'widening gulf' between original story and script introduced tensions between writers (McGilligan 1986: 3). And it is perhaps out of this desire for an 'integrated creation', and against a degradation of the nature of work in the Machine age, that Nichols turns to the idea of screenplays as 'blueprints of projected films' (1943: xxxv). Nichols' account of the development of artists and the factory system is particularly apposite in terms of the situation of film writers in the 1930s. As John Brady points out: 'Hollywood in the thirties was assembly-line writing – a closed shop in which studio executives had a stranglehold on their studio's creative talent' (1981: 12).[34] And while for some the arrival of the sound film is a turning point, Pat

McGilligan suggests that 'ironically, the prestige of the craft of screenwriting actually took a dip with the heralded arrival of sound' (1986: 6). The image of the factory system presented in this writing looms large in many accounts of screenwriting and screenwriters. It effects terminology: 'Script writer' and 'Scenario Writer' were seen as designations of subservience (see Dunne 1980: 45). In this context being recognised as a 'screenwriter' and writing 'screenplays' took on special significance. The attempt to construct the screenplay as a kind of literature, and defend the artistic value of the screenplay, can from this perspective be seen as part of an attempt to overcome the alienation of the factory.

From Gassner's perspective as a critic, one of the key arguments in favour of viewing the screenplay as literature is its relationship to a form of writing. This relationship on a fundamental level has to do with the existence of a work on paper, in a manuscript form that can be studied. Of course, a relation to writing can be forged in many ways. It can relate to the existence of dialogue: for Henry Arthur Jones, the drama is literature by virtue of dialogue alone, and the photoplay by virtue of it being 'pictorial' cannot be literature (1977: 53–4). It can also relate to the work of adaptation from 'literary' fiction to film. Another way, and perhaps the most ambitious, has to do with the quality of the writing itself. This is the option Gassner chooses when he argues that 'most of the talking pictures that have given the American film its claim to distinction have been fashioned out of a body of writing that commands respect as writing' (1943: vii).

This attempt to form a connection between film writing and writing cannot be simply viewed as a merely academic preoccupation. Numerous writers, at different times throughout the history of film, tell us that production has little to do with writing. James Slevin in 1912 remarks: 'You will often hear it said that the writing, or literary style, has nothing to do with a picture-play' (1912: 14). Howard in 1937 states bluntly that 'motion pictures are neither written nor acted but made' (1995: 205). Nichols reiterates the point regarding the scenario in 1939: 'It is not written, it is made' (1982: 405). Lewis Herman in 1952 states that while a novel and occasionally a dramatic play are written for an audience, 'a screen play should never be written to be read' (1952: 4). Casey Robinson suggests that the screenplay 'is not written to be read … It is not written to be performed, it is written to be realised' (1978: 6). Charles Deemer in 2002 writes: 'screenplays are not written to be read but produced'. In 1950, Hortense Powdermaker explains how writing was a key point of contention in the studio:

> To make clear the nature of movie writing, it is necessary to replace the usual connotation of the word 'writer' by its meaning in Hollywood. There, the writers are part of the production of pictures rather than authors. A *bon mot* in the community is that 'writers in Hollywood do not have works, but are workers' … In Hollywood, the writer does not write to be read. (1950: 150–1)[35]

From this passage we can see how writing is at the centre of a politics about authorship and control.

While the link with writing opens the door for the classification of the screenplay as a literary object, it should be noted that not every form of writing qualifies as literature, and entrance to the category 'literature' is subject to control.[36] Gary Davis observes that 'the screenplay is not film, the argument seems to go, and film is not literature, therefore, the screenplay cannot be literature' (1984: 90). For William C. deMille, literature is more than just words, and he speaks of 'literary value' (1977: 321). For Douglas Garrett Winston, whose work is discussed below, literature suggests 'the highest level of intellectual achievement attained by a particular people or culture' (1973: 22). In this usage the 'literary' is short for 'literary quality'.

A 'literature' is defined by rules governing a corpus and access to it: these can be membership in a profession, as in a technical literature, or notions of aesthetic worth and taste, as embodied in the idea of a canon of great works (see Waugh 1992: 59). Korte and Schneider emphasise the institutional dimensions of the term, in that 'the "literariness" of a text type is constructed through how it is "treated" by the literary community and the institutions of literature' (2000: 92). A modest conception of literature links the script to all forms of literary expression. Davis presents a less aesthetically loaded assemblage of the terms 'literary' and 'literature' when he argues for wider discussion and acceptance of the screenplay by literary critics: 'By what possible standards could a story told with word-pictures in a linear structure not be considered a literary form?' (1984: 92). Davis goes on to define literature in terms of the relationships of word pictures or word images. Considering the limits of the term 'literature', it is significant that Gassner's argument in favour of the screenplay as literature comes in the context of an act of canon building, a presentation of the 'twenty best film plays'.[37] But not all critics were convinced of this strategy. A reviewer of Gassner's and Nichols' 1945 anthology of screenplays remarked that these screenplays were 'blueprints' and accordingly should not be 'judged as literature. They were never intended as literature' (Paxton 1947: 308).

Gassner's argument in favour of the screenplay as literature relies on the fact that theatre dramas are already regarded as literature. Although he points to the fact that screenplays differ from stage drama, Gassner entertains the idea that 'we can also read the scenarios as plays that happen to be written for the screen rather than for the stage' (1943: viii). He uses the stage drama as a precedent in the case for the screenplay as literature. He also uses the stage drama to counter several critiques that could be made in relation to the screenplay, to do with staging, technical directions and adaptation. For example, that screenplays have multiple authors is recognised as a problem by Gassner, but one that can be sidestepped because of the increasing emergence of writer/producers and single-authored screenplays (despite the fact that in the 1950s Powdermaker still sees authorship as a significant problem in Hollywood). Minimising the problem of institutional authorship in

Hollywood, Gassner suggests that theatre is not without its collaborations, although he goes on to express his hope that the anthology could help secure greater creative rights for screenwriters among creative artists and suggests that studios should themselves publish screenplays.

For Gassner, just as the stage drama once laboured without legitimacy as the actor's text but is now valued, the screenplay will also find its rightful place; his introduction attempts to clear a critical space for this to happen.[38] However, from the outset of his enterprise particular problems emerge with this 'literature'. Gassner worries if screenplays, as functioning industrial entities, 'can be read with gratification' – a quality which he and others deem a key aesthetic value for literature.[39] A difficulty is that as technical objects they are designed for narrow readerships. Gassner's solution is to alter the text:

> The screenplays in this book are neither summarised or novelised, but are complete – in fact more complete then the films as they appeared on the screen – and they retain their motion picture form, their shot-by-shot or scene-by-scene development. All that has been ventured in preparing them for publication has been predicated on the fact that a shooting script is intended solely for use in the studios by those who make our films, and that in this form they do not make pleasurable or easy reading. To assure gratification to the reader, and to enable us to realise the literary qualities of the text, the broken typography of a shooting script, useful only to the director and the camera-men, has been dispensed with ... and, except for a few sufficiently descriptive terms, technical jargon has been omitted, shooting directions being translated into their visual equivalent as 'seeing' directions. (1943: vii–viii)

Gassner is clearly referring to choices, edits and alterations here, and paints his practice as a process of realisation of the literary qualities of the text. His screenplays are not tainted through novelisation or summary (and in this sense Gassner sees his approach as progressive, a move away from crass popularisation or predigestion).[40] The scripts are (emphatically) 'complete' even though it could be argued that the incompleteness of a script is a defining feature. In the alterations Gassner describes, the screenplay is made more readable according to the usual norms of print culture. In the case of the screenplay the integrity of the printed page becomes a primary concern, to be protected from the 'broken typography of a shooting script'. Guiding Gassner in his realising of literary qualities is the requirement for 'pleasurable or easy reading', and the reader's gratification. One kind of reading (in the studio) is thus made secondary to another (by the public).

In the passage above, Gassner distinguishes the screenplay from the shooting script which is 'useful only to the director and camera-men'. In doing so he distances screenplay form from the production context of film: the form begins to transcend the format, with the differences between the two overlooked in favour of the escalation of the screenplay into the realm of a literary genre. The question of format has to do with the interrelation between the literary and the filmic in the working production context. In the case of the screenplay, its literary status cannot simply be taken for granted (which is implied by the fact that Gassner must mount a sophisticated argument to make the case). While the screenplay often interacts with pre-existing literary forms and genres as 'story material' for use in films, it also exists as a functional format, incorporating studio conventions for presentation, enabling planning and communication. As Gassner notes, scripts 'were not originally written with an eye to publication but for "shooting" purposes' (1943: ix). The existence of the screenplay derives from the organisation of a filmic material, which explains the discrepancies Gassner notes between 'the complete texts of the screenplays marked "Final" in the studios and the films as seen on the screen' (ibid.). Looking at these 'final' screenplays, Gassner is speaking of versions prepared as shooting scripts prior to shooting: that is they are final in respect to the pre-production phase of preparation, before shooting and editing.

Such acts of formatting and reformatting of the script as those enacted by Gassner are not unknown in literary studies.[41] Few of us today would read Charles Dickens'. *A Tale of Two Cities* or *Great Expectations* as weekly serials in magazines as his original public did, nor Shakespeare in a form that was not altered to meet the needs of pentameter and standardised typography (see Styan 1984: 4). This typography, introduced in 1793, replaced Shakespeare's own use of spaces to indicate pauses.[42] In terms of the film script, it is the industrial more than the actorly dimensions of the text that can be effaced by presenting the screenplay as literature.

Completion and the Script

The relationship between the form and the format can be explored in a different way, through the question of completion. Completion is a thorny issue in terms of the script. I have already touched on Münsterberg's idea that 'the work which the scenario writer creates is in itself still entirely imperfect and becomes a complete work of art only through the action of the producer' (1970: 83). DeMille sees the director as a collaborator in the way the story is told, and 'that, in its relation to the finished work, the manuscript of a picture cannot be as complete in itself as the manuscript of a play. So much of a picture's value depends on the director's work...' (1939: 121). The critique of the screenplay as an autonomous object carried out by Carrière, Martin and Pasolini, focuses on the ongoing relationship between a script and the film in the process of production, leading to questions about the script's completeness and its intermediate nature. And yet, Gassner discusses alterations to the screenplay alongside an insistence that the screenplays are complete. The problem becomes: how can one reconcile the structural incompleteness of the script with a notion of completeness?

Of course, the completeness of filmic texts can be problematised in a range of ways. Completeness can be questioned by suggesting that the shutter is closed for part of the time a spectator sees the film (see Bergman 1967: 183), or that the spectator can be distracted or restless in their viewing (see Patterson 1921: 114). The similarity of one viewing of a film next to another can also be questioned on the basis that sequences may have been cut according to different censorship requirements, dubbing or colourisation may have occurred, print and projection quality may be inferior, or superior (see Brunette & Wills 1989: 191–2). Directors themselves released films with multiple endings, treating them effectively as open texts (see Koszarski 1990: 137). Recourse to the negative as 'the original' is no guarantee of a definitive text, as this eliminates the phenomenological dimension of film viewing (changes in screen ratio, audience interaction, theatre conditions, and so forth). As William Routt notes, few film scholars detail the nature of the prints they study. He suspects 'that even in these postmodern days most film academics would be uncomfortable with the idea that films are textually unstable as a [sic] implacable consequence of the circumstances of their production, distribution and exhibition' (1997). For Routt, 'the textual analyst's lack of interest in the specifics of specific prints has the effect of transforming a mundane and imperfect physical thing into an imaginary and perfect "text" ("the film") which is/could be accessible to all readers/ viewers'.

In Gassner's case, he has to continually do work on the script text to support his idea of completion. A note in the third anthology reads:

> The texts used in this book are the final shooting scripts. Necessarily, however, in the nature of film making many changes and deletions occur in the shooting and film editing. Whenever a brief sequence occurs which did not appear in the realised film, it has been enclosed in heavy brackets. When it seemed absolutely necessary, shooting scripts were collated with dialogue and continuity transcripts of the film. (1945: xx)

When discussing the discrepancy between the scripts marked 'final' in the studios, and the films as seen on the screen, Gassner favours the former as they are 'more representative of the authors' intention and more illuminating, and more forthright too, as they had not yet been completely subjected to the taboos with which Hollywood has been saddled' (1943: x). By focusing on the 'final' shooting script Gassner is seeking an ideal authoritative text, one that can be linked back to authorial intention. However, even a shooting script can be the product of story conferences and directorial intervention – one phase in an ongoing process. Sam Thomas notes: 'by the time a script achieves the status of "final screenplay" ... [that script has] had input not only principally from the writer but also from the director of the film and the producer, and ofttimes from the stars of the film itself, good or bad as that may be' (1986a: 10). Gassner's assertion that the screenplays 'are more complete than the films as they appeared on the screen' works as a response to the unpredictable and often collaborative nature of production. Yet he also stresses that the screenplays have been 'neither summarised nor novelised'. Through the construction of texts conducive to 'pleasurable or easy reading', and the reader's gratification, Gassner finds himself in the paradoxical situation of both acknowledging and obscuring the question of completeness of the film script.

The question of completion is addressed in a different way by Gassner's screenwriter collaborator Dudley Nichols. While Nichols ponders the possibility of the screenplay becoming a 'fascinating new form of literature', this is conditional on works being written 'directly for the screen' (1943: xxxii). More significantly, however, and as if correcting Gassner, Nichols casts doubt on the 'enjoyment' of the screenplay 'as a literary form in itself':

> There is one other circumstance which makes it difficult for the screenplay to be enjoyed as a literary form in itself: it is not and never can be a finished product. It is a step, the first and most important step, in the process of making a film. One might also say that a play is not a finished product for the theatre; yet a play relies entirely on the word; idea, character and action are projected by means of the word; and a skilful playreader can enjoy wonderful performances within the theatre of his own imagination. The screenplay is far less a completed thing than the play, for the skilled screenwriter is thinking continuously in terms of film as well as the word. The filmwriter must be a film-maker at heart, and a film-maker thinks and lives and works in film. That is the goal, the end-result – eight or ten thousand feet of negative patched together to reproduce, upon its unreeling, an illusion of a particular kind and quality. It is that illusion which the film-maker – and in this instance the filmwriter – is pursuing when he begins to gather together his first nebulous conception. (1943: xxxii)

Two points can be made about this passage. The first is that at the same time as raising questions of reading, Nichols emphasises the production situation of film and its implications for the screenplay and the screenwriter. The blurring of the idea of the filmwriter and filmmaker is fascinating in this sense. In his reading of the apparatus of cinema the finished product of screenwriting is not the screenplay, but the film. Projection 'by means of the word' is not sufficient for the filmwriter, for which the end result is 'eight or ten thousand feet of negative patched together to reproduce, upon its unreeling, an illusion of a particular kind and quality'. Nichols draws a link between the question of completion in relation to the screenplay and the question of the production situation of film itself. For Nichols the creation of the screenplay is one in a 'series of creations' (1943: xxxii). The screenplay is full of alterations and elisions, precisely because it is not a 'completed thing in itself' (1943: xxxix). By insisting that the screenplay is not the end result of a (pre)production process, but rather part of the process of filmmaking, Nichols goes against the tendency to view the screenplay as an autonomous work of literature.

The second point that can be made regarding the passage is that, like Gassner, Nichols opens up questions of reading, enjoyment and completion. Nichols links completion directly to performance in imagination which ties completion to a form of reading: 'A skilful playreader can enjoy wonderful performances within the theatre of his own imagination', but this is only possible through a word-based practice of reading, a form of projection 'by means of the word'. Gassner invites readers to consider screenplays as 'plays that happened to be written for the screen rather than for the stage' (1943: viii). Significantly, Nichols does not feel this form of reading to be automatically available to the screenplay, largely because of the need to think in terms of 'film as well as of the word'. As I suggest in the next chapter, later writers build on Nichols' work and actually define such a form of reading (see Mehring 1990: 238–40). But historically there has been significant concern over differences between dramas and scripts on the level of reading and performance. Defending the notion that movie scripts are unlikely to make good reading, Erwin Panofsky asserted that the '"screen play" ... has no aesthetic existence independent of its performance, and that its characters have no aesthetic existence outside the actors' (1947: 16–17; emphasis in original); although Davis observes that this comment is harder to support today than when it was written (1984: 92). Korte and Schneider note how while the stage play can be performed again and again, the film scenario is entirely 'burnt up' in the production process, directed as it is towards a special audience of filmmakers (2000: 90). For Claudia Sternberg a drama is written for multiple performances as an open text, while the screenwriter 'is likely to design his or her text specifically for one performance' (2000: 154).

Gassner's and Nichols' collaboration extends over several years, and they worked to create three anthologies in total. These were published in 1943 (reprinted in part in 1959 and 1977), 1945 (also reissued in 1977) and 1946. Given the duration of their work together, and the contrasting positions they hold, it is worthwhile noting how in a 1951 article titled 'Film and Screenplay' – which although written solely by Gassner introduces Nichols' script for *The Informer* – Gassner modifies some of his earlier views, but also restates others. Firstly, while in his earlier work he is prepared to argue a strong similarity between screenplays and stage plays, in his later work he tries to clarify a 'confusion' by saying that the screenplay is 'a species of play', a 'libretto for a different kind of theatre than the stage' (1951: 82). His argument that the screenplay was literature, and had become a new literary medium, is put less strongly:

> It is apparent, too, that although we must acknowledge the screenplay to be a distinct, if rather recent, literary form, it is at least one step further removed from pure literature than a stage drama ... Until such a time as screenwriters compose

their film directions, as well as dialogue, in imperishable verse or prose, few critics will validate claims for the literary eminence of the screenplay. (1951: 82)

The question of the literary quality of the description becomes a key issue here. This leads Gassner to imagine a situation when 'screenwriters come to regard themselves as men of letters writing for publication as well as for the picture studio, they may write down their final draft, or the copy they wish to preserve, in the best language at their command' (1951: 83). This passage recognises a limit to the analogy of the screenplay with the stage play; but it also fits in with the tendency described above to distil a pure form from the format. Gassner's dream of the 'final draft' both acknowledges and ignores the complexity of completion, and the industrial aspect of the screenplay and, even at this later stage, Gassner maintains that 'judicious editing of directions' in the shooting script can rectify many problems.

In a preface to a 1959 edition of the *Twenty Best Film Plays* – which is in fact a revised version of his first introduction – Gassner sums up his new position by modifying but not giving up on the idea of a literature of the screen, although he takes it as an 'assumed' position or assumption of his argument. 'We assume here that there is now a literature of the screen – the screenplay' modifies the earlier and more emphatic 'There is now a literature of the screen'. He concedes, 'Perhaps I should have called the screenplay a new *dramatic* rather than a new *literary* form, although my sometimes too-logical mind tells me that if the drama intended for the stage can be called a form of literature, so can a screenplay' (1959: iii; emphasis in original).

It is not by accident that the screenplay of the 1930s, replete with dialogue, becomes the basis for a concerted attempt to articulate the screenplay as literature. The 'literary screenplay' (Gassner 1943: xviii) is only one variety of script however, and Gassner, for example, does not explain the difference between scenarios, 'screenplays', 'continuities' or 'film plays', despite the fact he uses all of these terms. This supports an argument that the screenplay as literature formation of criticism works in fact with a limited account of scripting.

While Gassner and Nichols are co-editors, their contributions are at times at odds with one another. Gassner takes the view that screenplays are basically 'narrative and dialogue'. His approach focuses on the 'screenplay as dramatic literature' (1943: x). While he demonstrates some interest in the industrial dimension of film, and the screenplay as script rather than as literature, this is mediated through his interest in narrative and dialogue, and the 'literary screenplay' (1943: xviii). We have already heard Nichols disputing the idea that the screenplay is a complete object; he takes a different view of 'writing for the screen', and his piece can be read as an attempt to define what this phrase means as part of a project with a wider purpose. He situates it first and foremost in the context of a filmmaking process, and questions the possibility of projection 'by means of the word'. Nichols' approach prioritises craft issues, a practical engagement with the screen, and the medium, over stylistic abstractions. He entertains the idea that the screenplay is literature – 'the screenplay might become a fascinating new form of literature' (1943: xxxii) – but the word 'might' cannot be ignored here. His engagement with literature is in the end strategic and premised on the idea of writing for the screen. These differences in approach between Gassner and Nichols become significant in the context of Winston's approach examined below, which utilises Gassner's work but fails to mention Nichols.

New Conditions of Scripting: Winston

In 1973 the 'screenplay as literature' phrase formalised by Gassner is reinvented for a new era in Douglas Garrett Winston's *The Screenplay as Literature*. Interested in the European new wave of cinema, and aided by the publication of the scripts in English, Winston seeks to look at the innovations and techniques of these films. What is odd is how he uses the category 'screenplay as literature' to talk about some very 'cinematic' works. Thus it is a paradox that Winston can cite Ingmar Bergman's quote 'Film has nothing to do with literature' (Winston 1973: 96, also 114–15), and discuss Federico Fellini's frustration with the 'literary level' (1973: 143), and still treat the film and screenplay as literature. As a result the screenplay itself has an ambiguous position in his work: 'the claim that screenplays are actually literature is based not so much on the recent trend to publish them (along with the fact that many of them do make good reading), but on the new status that cinema itself has attained – that of art form' (1973: 14). His categorisation of screenplays as literature is based on three factors: the fact that scripts are now being published, that the post-World War Two cinema reaches the artistic standard of any literary form and that new conditions of screenwriting enable the writer/director to write the scenario. Drawing on Alexandre Astruc, Winston notes that 'Direction is no longer a means of illustrating or presenting a scene, but a true act of writing' (1973: 16), and in this sense he creates a new link between the screenplay and writing. For Winston, this development allows filmmaker/writers to be considered artists, whereby previously script assignments of famous writers were regarded as 'hack' assignments (1973: 14–15).

Winston is among the first critics post Gassner and Nicholls to re-examine the work of scripting around new production conditions. On his account, while traditional Hollywood production divides the process into distinct stages, with each stage overseen by a specific figure – writer, director, editor, with the producer in a supervision and co-ordination role – in the new system filmmaking constitutes a continuous creative process typified by increased interaction between writing and directing (thinking and shooting) in particular. He uses examples of filmmakers such as Fellini and François Truffaut altering dialogue on the set, Michelangelo Antonioni editing the script on the basis of the reality of the location and actors' capabilities, and John Cassavetes allowing actors to improvise.

Despite seeing the filmmaking process in continuous terms, Winston nevertheless focuses on writing or scripting in the earlier stages of the process: firstly, because he is interested in the formation of ideas; secondly, because looking at the script can give greater understanding of directing and editing; thirdly, because he is interested in the interaction between the 'visual' aspect of films and the writing side of filmmaking. While Winston is aware of new conditions of film production – and his work in general is very open to new ways of thinking about the role of the scriptwriter in contemporary films (1973: 201) – his is not a study of screenwriting or scripting with a wide-ranging focus. Winston spends little time on the textual status of the format or shooting script itself (1973: 56), and there is a sense that the screenplay is useful only insofar as it is a study tool in the analysis of the film (1973: 95, 98). Winston explains that it is an avowed purpose of the book to study the creative process of filmmaking, especially as it relates to the screenplay (1973: 142), and the working methods of Fellini and Bergman come in for special attention. However, it is the creative process that takes precedence over the screenplay. A chapter on 'The Classic American Screenplay' refers to the script only as an expression of dramaturgical ideas (point of attack, conflict). The screenplay instead becomes a way of talking about 'the first stage of the filmmaking process – the writing or thinking stage – as embodied in the screenplay' (1973: 22).

Winston does not entirely detach the script from its production context like other critics, and thus does not rely on an idea of the autonomous script, but his approach still sets up a particular idea of the screenplay form. He suggests that 'the best-known and most influential form of the narrative screenplay' is 'the American film script' (1973: 64). What becomes apparent is that while Winston gives an account of story material through the studio (1973: 55), and sees the screenplay as a hybrid of the silent cinema and the theatrical play script (1973: 64), he focuses on the 'classic American screenplay' in essentially dramatic terms as being defined by conflict that can be expressed visually. Admittedly, the classic American screenplay is not Winston's only focus, and he is tuned into changes to the conditions of screen writing, but the conceptual framework he uses to talk about these developments does not fully break with the tendency to segment production, divide filmmaking roles and separate conception and execution.

Winston's activation of the screenplay as literature idea is motivated by his sense of direction as a true act of writing. His work does not have the political urgency of Nichols' writing, partly because, for Winston, the European art cinema has cemented cinema as an art form and opened up a style of filmmaking different to, and critical of, traditional Hollywood methods of production (1973: 17). For Winston, the Hollywood system is rapidly breaking down, 'which in the long run can only be a good thing' (1973: 52). Reading Winston, one could be forgiven for thinking that Nichols' dream of a filmmaker's cinema has been fulfilled. Much of the screenwriter's struggle for writing original material for the screen is defused in Winston's work. He makes an interesting contribution to screenplay aesthetics, but his is a highly circumscribed approach. The novel is his key-touchstone of narrative analysis. His tendency to focus on a particular form of the screenplay, the impact of the publication of screenplays and his focus on a particular mode of film practice frustrates the attempt to track the emergence of the screenplay as a particular kind of poetic and industrial form, or situate it in relation to a broader and more detailed account of screen writing.

As Winston's work illustrates, the critical effort embodied in Gassner and Nichols' work has had long-standing effects. Larry Ceplair and Steven Englund cite them in terms of an attempt to address the anonymity of screenwriters (see 1980: 12–13); Tom Stempel identifies himself as a student of Gassner's in the acknowledgements to *Screenwriting* (1982); Gassner and Nichols' publishing programme was picked up by Sam Thomas (1986, 1990) and is a precursor to the many publishing ventures to do with screenplays today (see Morsberger & Morsberger 1975). The literary standing of the screenplay continues to be an issue raised in screenwriting circles. Charles Deemer notes that the attempt to approach the screenplay as a form of literature gained momentum in the 1990s with the emergence of the journal *Scenario* (2002), but as evident in the discussion above, the issue has a much longer history.

Having looked at the efforts to define the screenplay as a form of literature in the 1940s it would be reasonable to expect that this would form the basis of a period of sustained scholarship of the script, or at least the screenplay. This, however, did not eventuate. Certainly, Gassner and Nichols' work found an audience, particularly among screenwriting theorists and craft practitioners. But scholarly study of the script has not advanced to the same extent, or as quickly as one might have thought. In 1984 Gary Davis writes: 'though some critics and many English departments are beginning to study film from a literary perspective, no one seems quite sure what to do with the screenplay' (1984: 90). In 1997, Sternberg feels that research into the screenplay remains 'peripheral' (1997: 1), and more recently Jill Nelmes has called for 'more attention to scholarly research around the feature-length screenplay' (2007: 107) – a call that is becoming louder with more undergraduate and post-graduate teaching in screenwriting emerging (see Dunnigan 2004).

In a sense, the 'screenplay as literature' problem has taken different paths. The issue of literature and film relations has been expanded hugely and taken up in academic circles, initially via adaptation theory and discussions about the novel and film (see Bluestone 1957).[43] It is only relatively recently that efforts to re-evaluate the screenplay as a form in its own right have emerged (see Horne 1992; Korte & Schneider 2000; Sternberg 2000), some of these efforts drawing on contemporary textual theory (for example, Kohn 2000; Macdonald 2004a). Perhaps the most significant area in which the screenplay as literature issue continues to evolve has to do with reading the screenplay, and it is this issue that I turn to in the next chapter.

4 .

READING THE SCREENPLAY

Closely linked to debates about the screenplay as literature is the question of reading screenplays. Whereas discussion of reading the screenplay as literature is often directed at the general public, and to a lesser extent literary critics, a different discourse focuses on reading the screenplay from a practitioner's point of view, as a key aspect of screenplay form, and the creation of a certain experience for the reader. Going beyond the idea that screenplays can be read with gratification, in this chapter I look at the way different screenwriting teachers imagine reading as a particular skill. This chapter also approaches the theme of reading the screenplay from another angle, which has to do with the way the script is often constructed in literary analysis as a surrogate for the film.

In the previous chapter, 'completion' of a text was linked to an act of reading, of performance in imagination. But, as noted, Dudley Nichols felt this form of completion was more suited to stage plays and he was pessimistic about performing the screenplay in this way. A more recent echo of this view comes from Robert McKee: 'A literary work is finished and complete within itself. A screenplay waits for the camera' (1997: 394). Reading is at the centre of arguments to do with the literary standing of the screenplay. William Goldman suggests that conventional screenplay style makes the screenplay 'unreadable' (1983: 53). For Stanley Kubrick the 'screenplay is the most uncommunicative form of writing ever devised' (in Thomas 1973: 24). Going against the view that the script can reward reading, Adrian Martin suggests that 'scripts rarely hold up as literary objects, because they are mere skeletons without flesh, tales without poetry or metaphor, figures without life' (1999).

Reading is a sore point in screenwriting circles, the central complaint being that 'precious few people actually know how to read a screenplay' (Azlant 1980: 210). As Ian W. Macdonald suggests: 'this is a form that requires training (and/or experience) to use it' (2004: 89a). Another complaint is that due to time pressures or lack of training, studio executives do not give the script a proper read. Richard Fine relates how many writers new to the studios in the 1930s 'were shocked to learn that most producers didn't read' (1993: 113).

Of course, what constitutes a proper read is subject to debate. In her discussion of quality control in the Hollywood studios Kristin Thompson describes a situation whereby overburdened readers check the script against Syd Field's formula, skimming 'pages 25–30 and 85–90 to check whether something resembling a "Plot Point" occurs. If it does not, the script may receive no further attention' (1999: 364). Macdonald in his survey of UK screenplay readers suggests that 'there is no wholehearted endorsement of a "right" way to write screenplays ... though there is a significant level of enthusiasm for techniques grown and articulated in the USA' (2003: 34). Nevertheless, Thompson's example highlights a potentially disturbing meeting of a highly particular model of narrative with financing structures. The potential for exclusion of different forms of storytelling in this system is high. For Thompson, these practices work as part of a drive to 'quantify the quality of a screenplay' (1999: 364). While on the one hand this works against a literary conception of reading, on the other hand, as discussed in a later section, the script can be seen as a mechanism for balancing technical and literary or poetic protocols of reading, and is thus designed to marry 'quantity' and 'quality' issues.

Another hot topic in discussions of reading is the rise of the short verbal 'pitch' as a selling technique. Writers can be wary of a process that boils beautiful writing down to memorable verbal phrases. Tom Stempel recounts that studio boss Louis B. Mayer would have his scripts read to him, reminding 'Mayer of the time his mother read stories to him' (2000: 70; see also Fine 1993: 115). Writers, protective of their creative efforts, are sensitive to misunderstanding because with 'Hollywood's ravenous appetite for story, scripts are often picked before they are ripe' (McKee 1997: 7). Indeed, in recent years, the act of reading has become intertwined with the question of creative control in the production process. A view has emerged that the secret to creative control is a well-developed screenplay experience. Margaret Mehring writes:

You hear the words your characters are saying and you see the things they are doing in a particular setting, surrounded by specific people, things, and sounds. It's the *total* image that contains the full meaning of your ideas, and as images appear in your mind they'll ultimately and effortlessly appear first in the screenplay and then on the screen ... When form and content are truly wed in the screenplay, they cannot readily be torn asunder ... THIS IS THE SECRET OF A SCREENWRITER'S

POWER! THIS IS THE WAY TO INSURE THAT THE SCREENPLAY IS PRODUCED AS WRITTEN – TO RETAIN THE ORIGINAL VISION. THIS IS THE SOLUTION. THIS IS THE WAY TO DISMANTLE THE BRICK WALLS – TO CLAIM THE POWER OF THE SCREEN-WRITER. (Mehring 1990: 6; emphasis in original)

This passage (and its liberal use of upper case) reminds us that, in screenwriting discourse, reading is political. While this politics has to do with creative control, and directing the film from the page, it also has to do with integrity: 'unfinished work invites tampering, while polished, mature work seals its integrity' (McKee 1997: 7). Lewis Herman goes further and suggests that 'a professionally written screen play can be, to all intents and purposes, a predirected screen play' (1952: 173).

Mehring has a strong faith in the power of visualisation as central to the power of the screenwriter; but there are signs also that visualisation can break down, and that practices of visualisation may not be shared equally by those involved in the evaluation of screen ideas. To illustrate this point: Macdonald reports that in the UK the screenplay has become a key component in the evaluation of a screen idea and forms a crucial part of the proposal process, and on a conservative figure approximately one per cent of screenplays read go into production. Readers attempt to read the entire screenplay but significantly 44 per cent do not always finish the script. Against the argument that it is through crafting the 'total image' (Mehring) that one can retain the original vision, Macdonald notes that '83% of readers often or always find the screen idea in front of them unattractive' (2003: 32):

> There is a clear rejection here of a large number of screen ideas and screenplays as clearly workable 'finished' products, and an expectation that it will be difficult to visualise them as films. This is in itself not a condemnation of the quality of screen ideas or screenplays; it reflects both the status of these documents as 'hints fixed on paper' ... and the reader's expectation that there will be some difficulty in visualisation. (Ibid.)

Little surprise then that since 2002 'the [UK] Film Council and Skillset have identified screenwriting and reading training as a priority' (Macdonald 2003: 34; see also 2004b: 261).

Despite the possibility of a lack of consensus around what visualisation means and how it works, recognising that the script as screenplay is closely linked to an act of reading is important for two reasons. Firstly, it allows us to appreciate the unique format of the screenplay, which facilitates a certain kind of reading. (Although it should be noted that overemphasis of this form can lead to problems, such as the notion that if you can work in the format you can write a script (see McKee 1997: 410); and McKee reminds us that there is a long tradition of writing extended prose treatments in screenwriting – that is, not screenplays – 'often two hundred to three hundred pages long' (1997: 415).) Secondly, recognising the screenplay as a format that makes specific demands on particular kinds of readers enables us to affirm, in a non-reductive fashion, the importance of poetry to the technical processes of production – indeed, the way the screenplay produces imagistic effects has become a significant strand of research (see Davis 1984; Korte & Schneider 2000; Rush & Baughman 1997).

Screenplay Form and the Status of Description

Although there can be disagreements around specifics (see Lent 1998), and many films that do not fit the mould, for many practitioners the screenplay has precise aesthetic dimensions, consisting of around 120 pages,[44] three-act structure with set-up, confrontation and resolution, a central character conflict and plot points on particular pages. While accusations of writing by recipe can be heard in the world of screenwriting (see Castrique 1997), these conventions are at the same time held to embody time-honoured dramatic principles that are often restated to justify the format- or template-driven nature of the work. Syd Field stresses that his work is about a 'paradigm' which explains the universal 'foundation of dramatic structure' (1994: 16).

The screenplay can be seen as a regulated format. It is defined by rules of pacing and page design: 'a well designed script flows with the reading and accentuates the pacing' (Boyle 1983: iii). For Boyle, the screenplay has aspects of visual or 'concrete' poetry to it, the placement of words on the page contributing to impact. The organisation of the screenplay into scenes also forms the basis for a technical way of reading the script, breaking it down into locations, numbers of actors, props and so forth (see Miller 1986). Boyle articulates three rules or axioms regarding the screenplay:

i) that the screenplay is paced, that one page of writing represents one minute of screen time;
ii) one may write down the page in short sentences rather than write across the page in a paragraph as in fiction;
iii) there are different versions of the script, ranging from presentation screenplays to production screenplays or shooting scripts, that vary in the amount of technical information presented. (1983: iv–v)

The existence of different versions of the script can have significant impact on how closely the script matches a produced film, or how distant it is from the screenwriter's version, and how much input from other figures in the filmmaking process might be included. For Lew Hunter, the recognition of different versions forms the basis of thinking strategically when applying three-act rules about running times, which apply more to a 'selling draft' than the 'shooting script' (quoted in Thompson 1999: 339).

The conventions outlined by Boyle inform a particular set of ideas about what constitutes the distinctive poetry of the screenplay: the marriage of content and expression. These conventions have a direct impact on the way description and detail is handled, for example: by linking page space to screen time sentences must show action and not simply dwell in the minds of characters. For example, the noun 'we' might suggest an 'omniscient' rather than subjective shot; the degree of detail might imply a particular shot size (see Rush & Baughman 1997: 30).

The unique aspect of the script as screenplay is the way it functions as an audio-imaging machine, a playback device or registration device specific to the page. Boyle observes that 'reading a script is a bit like viewing a film. The pages should be turned constantly and uniformly the way the film is projected smoothly without ever turning back' (1983: v). As such the screenplay is a fascinating invention, performing a function that is different to other script forms. While the scenario-script, which listed each scene in sequence, was used in production to count footage (the length of each scene as shot), it did not in many cases support 'playback' in the same way. By contrast, the screenplay facilitates a personal preview of the film to come, a process McKee calls 'putting a film in the reader's head' (1997: 94).

With this emphasis on putting a film in the reader's head obvious pressure is placed on delivering an experience that is undisrupted, seamless. Description plays a key role here, and historical changes to the descriptive mode of the script are interesting from this perspective. The status of descriptions has been contentious, largely because it is an area where the writer can potentially take on the director's role. There is the strong view that the script should include only minimal production instructions, so as not to impinge on the work of the director (see Mehring 1990: 232).[45] Jeanie Macpherson notes that some 'childish' directors are insulted by too many instructions (1922: 28–9), although she argued that the director ultimately 'WANTS the complete, detailed script' (1922: 29). William C. deMille recounts that one director faced with a script with too much business stated: 'You're supposed to be writing the story, not directing the movement' (1939: 121). Mehring suggests that this view assumes a particular defensiveness on the part of the director and writer, and finds a better justification for this practice in the need not to disturb 'total "living" experience' of the read (1990: 240). Such considerations do not only impact on explicit cues, but result in changes in the style of description around the idea of the read.

Screenwriting discourse has not always been concerned with the read. William Lord Wright tells readers that 'Clear English is important, and the use of adjectives that mean something is desirable. There is no room in photoplay for "word pictures" and dialogue is not wanted' (1914: 191). Leslie T. Peacocke advises: 'Do not attempt to be "literary"', adding that the reader 'cares nothing about literary style' (1916: 20). Indeed, his suggestions for covering big scenes involve written advice to the director in brackets in the scene description: 'Have three cameras on this scene...' (1916: 34). In his discussion of Thomas Ince's production practice, Tom Stempel observes the detail of his scenarios, filled with notes for the directing of the scene, so that the proper mood is achieved. Take the following passage from an Ince script:

SCENE 1: CLOSE UP ON BAR IN WESTERN SALOON
A group of good western types of the early period are drinking at the bar and talking idly – much good fellowship prevails and everyman feels at ease with his neighbor – one of them glances off the picture and the smile fades from his face to be replaced by the strained look of worry – the others notice the change and follow his gaze – their faces reflect his own emotions – be sure to get over a sharp contrast between the easy good nature that had prevailed and the un-natural strained silence that follows – as they look, cut. (In Stempel 2000: 41)

In this passage, the script addresses questions of direction, mood and action without any concern for the visual picture being built up in the scenario. This is not to deny the presence of 'visual' or descriptive writing such as, 'one of them glances off the picture and the smile fades from his face to be replaced by the strained look of worry', but the emphasis here falls on what is in, or not in, the picture. The production context overwhelms any idea of an illusion or world being built up on the page. The principle of suspension of disbelief here is not applied to the reader of the scenario. Even earlier, Patrick Loughney describes a practice in Biograph Company scripts of 1905 of using 'redundant' passages, where each scene is given two descriptions, one a general outline of narrative action in the scene for preparation purposes, and the second a detailed description of the business on the screen for staging purposes, noting that 'The division of narrative levels probably facilitated scene rehearsals' (1990: 217).

The origins of the read are not straightforward. In some respects it emerges not from the final shooting script but from prose-based treatments that sought to be as 'cinematic' in style as possible. For Tamar Lane in 1936, a key issue for treatment writing is 'pace and movement … If the leisurely pace is chosen, the writer may use fewer and longer scenes, fewer and longer sequences … If the moderate pace is decided upon, the more and shorter sequences are desirable … With the fast pace, the whole telling of the story is quickened' (1936: 37). A precursor to this approach exists in early photoplay handbooks, which stressed 'values and emphasis'. Epes Winthrop Sargent discusses holding or slowing down action in the writing of the script (1916: 233). As judged by Boyle's insistence that one should turn the page uniformly when reading a screenplay, it could be argued that a condition for this to happen (and therefore a prerequisite for the read itself) is a standardised tempo for shooting and projecting the film – a standard that did not arise until the sound film. In early cinema shooting speeds could diverge markedly from projection speeds (see Koszarski 1990: 56–7). But the standardisation of speed that accompanied the sound film had an impact on screen writers: 'The scenarist who could formerly write his script with a certain amount of roughness, knowing that titles and action could be altered later

if desired, must now endeavour to create his script with the smoothness and precision that will be demanded of, and seen in, the finished photoplay' (Lane 1936: 7).
Smoothness can be seen as an effect related to fixed projection speeds, which in turn
work to create a uniform experience of and for the read, whereby a page can begin
to approximate a minute.

Jeff Rush and Cynthia Baughman explore an example of a form of reading that is
not based on suspension of disbelief, namely shooting scripts in the studio system.

> Under the studio system, a contract writer produced shooting scripts – that is,
> scripts whose slug lines, the lines in all caps proceeding the bodies of description,
> identified shots rather than scenes … Any descriptive material under the slug line
> functioned adjectivally to modify the slug line, not to represent the shot itself.
> (1997: 29)

In this mode, slug lines constitute directions for the camera, right down to shot
sizes and movements. They 'prescribe the relationship between camera and subject'
(ibid.).

This should be contrasted with more recent screenplay practice, which increasingly seeks to facilitate visualisation, 'screen' the film on the page, and attempts to
present 'vivid action in the now' (McKee 1997: 195). This involves taking a master
scene rather than shot form of organisation, and allows the reader to define the
relationship between camera and subject. The format advice pages of various screenwriting journals, both past and present, make interesting reading here. As David Trottier suggests, the purpose of proper formatting is to present a story in readable form.
'"Readable Form" means the reader can easily visualise the action of the story, hear
the characters in his or her head, and feel the emotion that underpins the story'
(1997: 14). In advice that would no doubt frustrate Ince, Trottier observes: 'many
writers believe this means including camera angles, editing instructions, and other
technical directions, but doing all that is exactly the wrong thing to do. Why? Because
it intrudes on "the read"' (ibid.).

The movement towards minimal directions is about preserving a practice of reading
that simulates the practice of viewing in the cinema: 'active verbs, strong nouns, and
only a few but very emotional adjectives and adverbs' are thus favoured (Mehring
1990: 239). 'A good script is like a good poem … It is economical – meaning is elic-
ited in few and evocative words; it has rhythm, like music; its images are powerful'
(Carmichael 1998: 1).

The Act of Reading as Image Building

Screenplays require not only an act of filming, but also an 'act of reading'. For
Mehring, the screenplay is 'where you translate your images into words so that

people can read them, "see" them in their heads, and then recreate them' (1990: 231). The fact that the screenplay can be so fully visualised in the reading can lead to conflict with the argument that the script is structurally incomplete. John Truby's view that writers 'start with nothing, and from nothing produce the entire world the audience enters' (1994: 86) seems based on a strong concept of mental visualisation. It stands in potential conflict with Jean-Claude Carrière's emphasis on the vanishing screenplay, the way it dissolves into the film, or McKee's notion that 'a screenplay waits for the camera'.

This link between the screenplay and an act of reading allows us to engage with the 'literariness' of the screenplay in a precise way. Before exploring this link, I should hasten to add that this is not to suggest that there is only one way to read a screenplay. On the contrary, Pat P. Miller details a complex process of reading the script performed by the continuity supervisor. For Miller, this means breaking the script down into its major elements (locale or set, action or business, and dialogue), underlining each Master Scene (a continuous action staged in a specific locale), times of day and night, names of characters, the characters' physical distinctions, overt action and props (1986: 18–23). 'Primarily, breaking down the script consists of marking each page with notations that will enable you to spot salient details at a glance during pressured shooting hours' (1986: 18).

This form of reading as 'break down' can be distinguished from a different understanding of 'acts of reading'. From a phenomenological point of view, the literary work is a 'scheme' to be built up in the practice of reading. The scheme or blueprint is 'concretised' in the course of reading, which is envisaged as a single uniform act that constitutes the work of art as a whole. Wolfgang Iser refers to this process as 'image building' (1978: 35–6).[46] This term highlights the way in which concretisation is linked to the visualisation of 'aspects' of the work; and thus proper actualisations contribute to a construction of a fully functional image or picture of the scheme. A concretisation is 'precisely what is constituted during the reading and what, in a manner of speaking, forms the mode of appearance of the work, the concrete form in which the work is apprehended' (Ingarden 1973: 332).

Pier Paolo Pasolini has analysed this process of image building in relation to the screenplay in more semiotic terms. For Pasolini, the screenplay reads as a literary work, but in the process forwards the reader to a film that is yet to come. 'In other words: the author of a screenplay asks his addressee for a particular collaboration: namely, that of lending to the text a "visual" completeness which it does not have, but at which it hints' (2005: 189). In this sense, the reader is an accomplice, a collaborator, a translator: constantly connecting written signs (graphemes) to visual ones (kinemes), and producing an interaction between the language system of words and the cinematic language system that shifts the screenplay beyond the realm of the literary, or at least written-spoken language. The screenplay asks the reader 'to see *the kineme in the grapheme, above all, and thus to think in images, reconstructing in his own head the film to which the screenplay alludes as a potential work*' (2005: 192; emphasis in original).

To suggest that the script as screenplay is characterised by acts of reading is to make room, within technical understandings of the script, for more artistic processes. It allows us to explore how a screenplay is closer to poetry than a plan, evoking rhythm and powerful images. As Helen Carmichael writes:

> to read a script properly is a craft that takes years to develop. It's hard work … the reader has to be able to see and hear the film on the screen of the mind's eye. Therefore anything that makes it difficult for the reader – anything that distracts or pulls them away from the script's special world – is to be avoided. (1998: 1).

For Mehring, 'reading the screenplay is a total "living" experience':

> This demands the reader's immersion in the continuous creation of mental images of layered and progressive plot and characterisation events … If excessive camera placements and movements and set and/or location details are present IN THE FORM of instructions, the reader is pulled away from the living experience. (1990: 240)

The idea of a reader seeing and hearing a film 'on the screen of the mind's eye', in a kind of immersive experience, is an important aspect of the screenplay. But one wonders if the claims made about this aspect of the screenplay can be overstated. These claims are sometimes invoked when screenwriters argue (in many cases justifiably) for greater creative recognition because they lay down the fictional world, essentially inventing scenes word by word. Leaving to one side the issues of creative recognition (which I shall discuss in a later chapter) at its most excessive, this notion can make the screenplay out to be like the film projector itself, throwing images on the (mental) screen. Or it gives rise to the expectation that a properly visualised script accurately registers what is seen on the screen. This raises a significant issue with the notion of image building as applied to filmmaking, which is that it should not be seen as a singular act. Film production, while heavily geared towards image building, only partly relies on mental visualisations; other forms of 'concretisation' (that of the design team, for example) co-exist with it.

The emphasis on successful audio-visualisation via the screenplay can have the effect of obscuring the way the screenplay is bound to the page through the use of particular language and design of the page. Indeed, the 'rule' discussed by Boyle, that one minute of screen time is the equivalent to a page (see also Mehring 1990: 233), is a good illustration of this. The correlation of screen time to the page has been an important part of contemporary screenwriting discourse,[47] and has been a significant way in which the screenplay has been 'quantified'. It allows screenwriters to refer to page x of a properly formatted script to minute x of the film. Indeed, much of Syd Field's advice on plot points and turning points are in the form of page recommendations. In this way, the written screenplay is able to work as a proxy for the film. But this relationship is established through practices of reading, and such practices can be manipulated and ignored. In terms of manipulation, it is possible in screenplay writing software to squeeze more on a page through the magic of formatting, thus getting that plot point on the right page through the art of typesetting.[48] In terms of being ignored, Kristin Thompson – citing the case of *Meet Joe Black* (Dir. Martin Brest, Writ. Ron Osborn, Jeff Reno, Kevin Wade, Bo Goldman *et al.*, 1998) which was a three-hour remake of a 78-minute film – highlights that the page/minute equation is a product of convention, and as such it can be disregarded:

> [It] probably only works when there are further constraints at other stages of the production process. Most notably, there are good indications that if the director does not cooperate, the page/minute equation means little … Thus the script can only provide one way of controlling film length, and the idea that its most crucial dramatic moments can be pinpointed well in advance solely by page number seems dubious. (1999: 367–8)

Of course, disruption of the page/minute equation need not be cast in negative terms of uncooperativeness. The equation has always been dependent on the mode of coverage of the scene, the kind of action (emotional, stunts) and directorial/acting style.[49]

Not all screenwriters focus on the screenplay as a medium of audio-visual playback or mental visualisation. Rather than focus on screening the film on the mind's eye, William Goldman proposes a more modest idea of the screenplay as a kind of carpentry: 'it's basically putting down some kind of structural form that they [the actors and director] can then mess around with. As long as they keep the structural form, whatever I have written is relatively valid; a scene will hold, regardless of the dialogue. It's the *thrust* of a scene that's kept pure' (Goldman in Brady 1981: 116; emphasis in original). But other critics go further in challenging the place of the film script as a structural form. John Fawell argues that 'the contribution of the filmscript to a film is often overestimated. Of course, one cannot discount the contribution of literature and drama to film but the script is only one of several elements that make up a film. It does not represent the central girding or support of the film. Its success depends on how well it plays with other elements' (1989: 47).

Balancing the Technical and Poetic Functions of Screenwriting

A distinctive feature of the screenplay is that while it is open to technical forms of reading that break the script down, it also demands forms of reading that are literary in orientation, but which can more accurately be described as poetic. The 'technical' and 'poetic' aspects of the script cannot readily be placed in opposition or separated. A lighting director, for example, may find some evocative part of the poetry of the script crucial in the lighting of a scene. Attempts to reduce the screenplay to a form of notation, or a blueprint for (re)construction, works to the detriment of a fuller understanding of the screenplay as a literary genre (Rush & Baughman 1997: 36). In an important sense the notion of a 'blueprint' undersells what is happening with a screenplay. Yet the opposite can also be true; an approach that focuses exclusively on the screenplay as literature, and forgets its origins as a production document, risks overlooking important aspects of scripting.

Technical and poetic forms of reading the screenplay do not exist in neat opposition. Different forms of reading come into play at different stages of production, and poetic details can often work in a technical fashion to convey a sense of a mood or effect. In this way, as Rush and Baughman suggest, 'inferential or evocative language functions to determine meaning and focus in screenplays' (1997: 28). Stepping back from the idea of directing from the page, Rush and Baughman look at the way screenplay language, properly interpreted, 'embodies the nuances of directorial style'. Claudia Sternberg makes a similar point when, rather than focus on the predirected screenplay, she speaks of the screenwriter as 'hidden director'. What she means is that the interplay between scene text, dialogue text and other elements guides realisation, and demands 'a certain degree of cinematic-technical imagination' from the reader (1997: 231).

The notion that poetry can function 'technically' disturbs a separation in screenwriting which deems that *shooting scripts* might be read as 'denotative blueprints or instructions' while *screenplays* 'can be understood only as a form of writing that communicates much of its meaning through the connotative nuances of language' (Rush & Baughman 1997: 28). Any clear-cut distinction between 'instruction' and 'meaning' is complicated in the space of the screenplay. Through an examination of narrative voice in screenplays, Rush and Baughman show how the reader is in a particularly important position in relation to the screenplay, since it is they who must interpret the relationship between camera and subject, and all the nuances of that relationship: 'the implied camera directions under the slug line'. It is for this reason that while some readers feel scripts are not easy to read because of the format, others insist that 'screenplays are written to be read' (Sternberg 2000: 155; see also Davis 1984: 91).

But despite the importance of reading, it is only one in what Nichols might call 'a series of creations' (1943: xxxii). Given the tendency to see the script as the primary blueprint for production, it is interesting to pay attention to how some critics handle the idea that not only is the screenplay part of a much broader, ongoing process of production, but that it is a form in which technical concerns and literary expectations, instruction and meaning, ideally find a balance. Take the following passage from Sternberg:

> A screenplay serves as an *instructional outline* for the transformation of a particular material into the target medium of film. It must be seen as a literary product that is foremost, but not exclusively, pragmatic. This pragmatic or functional side might account for a lack of literary subtlety. Thus, looking for literary or linguistic refinement means moving in the wrong direction. As film consists of sound and vision, purple prose that does not 'translate' into film 'language' is used sparingly in scripts. Readers of screenplays thus have to develop a *cinematic competence* and look out for information that will materialise in acting, directing, cinematography, editing, set and production design, sound, image composition, and, last but not least, in plot and dialogue. (2000: 155; emphasis in original)

Here, Sternberg shows the precarious mode of being of the script. Existing between 'instructional outline' and 'literary product' it is a pragmatic entity. At the same time, her focus on materialisation is one way to think through the broader process of production in a more intricate way than just seeing the script as a blueprint.

Our reading of John Gassner and Dudley Nichols in the previous chapter focused largely on the difficulties in constructing the screenplay as literature. Reading, nevertheless, is of central importance to the concretisation of the screenplay. But this is a particular kind of reading, itself linked to production conditions; through the use of language the screenplay hails the reader not simply to decode story information and events, but also cues the reader as to how the story should be realised in cinematic form (see Korte & Schneider 2000: 99). As Sternberg puts it, the 'screenplay contains information not only about the characters and film story, but also about the way these events are to be presented' (1997: 231). In this way the screenplay can work to indicate and represent effects beyond the page. These effects, embedded in 'the read' of the screenplay, require imagination. If the screenplay were simply a plan, it would be possible to make the point (which Rush and Baughman themselves consider) 'Why not come out and tell us how to take these images?' Rush and Baughman respond by pointing to the importance of ambiguity and irony in the reading of screenplays, and the way the narrative explores different possibilities and stylisations. Different subtexts or ironic modes can be revealed through the language and the way the topic is treated. In this manner, the screenplay supports and engenders interpretations that will become the basis of collaboration.[50] As Rush and Baughman observe, on one level the screenplay teaches us how to read, who and what to trust and the significance of different situations (1997: 31).

Thinking about reading, visualisation and the screenplay, it is possible to over-emphasise 'the read' as though it will provide a 'complete' picture of the film, but this in an important sense is an illusory completeness, and this concept needs to be further developed along the lines suggested by Rush and Baughman, in terms of the interpretation process that occurs throughout the process of film production. This leads some critics to speak of cinematic competence or 'film-reading competence'. 'As the screenplay is an essentially intermedial text type, a verbal text originally written as a blueprint for a production using another medium (which is itself multimedial), an intermedial competence is essential in grasping the screenplay's special artistic demands and artistic merits' (Korte & Schneider 2000: 97).

For writers, balancing the technical and poetic aspects of screenwriting can lead to interesting insights. Nichols idealised a longer, 500-page script, which 'would contain detailed notes on moods of lighting, lenses, filters, notes on set and music' (1942: 772).[51] Much earlier in 1914, William Lord Wright expressed frustration at the 'machine set rules' behind the form of the photoplay manuscript, and noted the development of 'a very complete synopsis including all the important points in the plot and climax' (1914: 61; see also 1914: 177). In 1913, J. Berg Esenwein and Arthur Leeds imagined a script of the future that would be longer, but provide motive for every action of the character (see 1913: 145). It would be vastly superior to a script simply describing external action. They raise concerns, however, at overexpansion and the 'indiscriminate introduction of extraneous details', and value brevity and conciseness. Interestingly, they fall back on the idea of the importance of visualisation, the 'picture eye', to convey the most important action.

Rather than follow the idea that increased information in the script leads to better technical information for all, some screenwriters see the two as distinct and work to accommodate other film workers. Ian McEwan imagines himself as an intermediary, 'crossing and re-crossing the border' between script and film, accommodating producer's thoughts and what the director thinks they may want to shoot (see Korte & Schneider 2000: 97).

Reading the Script as Surrogate for the Film

Having looked at different ways of reading the screenplay it is worthwhile dwelling briefly on a different problem of reading to do with the way literary studies leaves the script in a position of secondary importance, or as surrogate for the film. The intermediality of the script means that it sits uneasily between fields of study such as film studies, media studies, theatre or performance studies and literary studies. In the case of literary studies, which is our focus here, the script is often used as an instrument of literary analysis (a utility that has fuelled publishing of scripts), but in the process has not been carefully studied in its own right.

For example, for Lawrence Baines and Micah Dial (1995), screenwriting provides an ideal tool to reinvigorate the English curriculum by drawing on students' knowledge of (and preference for) the moving image and redirecting their interest back towards the page, reading and writing. But theirs is a highly normatised conception of screenwriting, derived to a large extent from Syd Field's work. Screenwriting becomes a curriculum vehicle, a way to deal with the negative effects of electronic media and disinterested students. Arguably, it becomes a way to discuss film production and the screenplay format, and debates around different forms of scripting and production are de-emphasised.

This gesture of drawing on the script in partial ways is evident in the collection *Film Scripts* edited by George P. Garrett *et al.*, where a programme for bringing film into literature departments is laid out in order to end an 'unfortunate' neglect of film, a key aspect of twentieth century culture. Garrett *et al.* argue for an aesthetic approach to film 'with the same care and thoroughness as a novel or a poem' (1989: 11). To do so, however, some access to a final negative or master-print is required for consultation: 'if film is to be given its proper place in the study of modern culture, then viewing must be supplemented by use of scripts' (1989: 12). As well as functioning as a portable surrogate for the film that can be annotated and reviewed, another benefit is that by using 'shooting scripts' one gains an insight into 'the first critical phase in the process of filmmaking' (1989: 15). Garrett *et al.* are not the only critics interested in the script as surrogate for the film. Robert and Katharine Morsberger seek to use the script as 'objective documentation' (1975: 54). William Horne reacts by suggesting that 'passionate pleas for access to screenplays in published and non-published form is nothing more than a veiled lament for a lack of access to films' (1992: 51).

Garrett *et al.*'s vision of film study involves educating the reader about the place and use of the script, 'the relationship between a shooting script and a finished film' (1989: 14). The use of script as surrogate for the film has an interesting side effect, which is that the need to explain the place and use of the script opens up a new discursive space in which filmmaking and screenwriting, and the relationship between the two, has to be explained. In this discursive space the reader is informed of the relationship between different versions and formats of the script, and stages of film production. To meet this need Garrett *et al.* include a section on the process of filmmaking (see 1989: 18; see also Nichols 1982). On the one hand, this involves educating the reader about screenwriting, but at the same time there is a process of normalising the space of screenwriting, of packaging it for a particular readership, of institutionalising a particular way of working that is 'standard'. Axioms are formulated, such as the writer makes the 'blueprint' for the film.[52]

Another example of an approach that centres on the script but which in fact leaves it in a position of secondary importance is the work of George Bluestone, a foundational figure in adaptation theory. Bluestone's work takes place against the background of significant changes in literary studies in the post-World War Two period.

Chris Baldick argues that at this time the canon was reorganised to allow for 'a flourishing of critical interest in the novel' (1996: 144). The novel has played a central role
in both the institutionalisation of film and the script in the US education system. It is
not a coincidence that when Bluestone begins to examine film, the primary object is
not the analysis of the script, but of the relationship between novel and film, particularly focusing on the filmed novel, and issues of character, metaphor and symbol.
Writing in 1957, before the widespread institutionalisation of film studies, Bluestone's
approach can be read as a response to television and film impacting upon the literary
audience. The novel becomes a primary vehicle for the examination of 'root-problems'
in the industrial organisation of production to do with the economic, technological
and educational position of literacy (1957: 32).

In Bluestone's *Novels into Film*, it is remarkable that while he looks at the 'limits
of the Novel and the Film', in a section on the raw material of film he looks at camera
and editing but not the script (1957: 14). While he notes that popular denigration of
screenwriting by novelists has led to a 'neglect of scenario-writing as an independent
art form' (1957: 35), he does little to directly engage with scriptwriting concerns
except through a discussion of censorship codes and commercial constraints. Scriptwriting is overshadowed in his work by the novel. This is evident in Bluestone's description of his method of analysing films and novels:

> Essentially, the method is a way of imposing the shooting script on the book.
> By evolving an exact record of alterations, deletions and additions of characters,
> events, dialogue, I was able to reduce subjective impressions to a minimum. The
> method calls for viewing the film with a shooting script at hand. During the viewing,
> notations of any final changes in the editing were entered on the script. After the
> script had become an accurate account of the movie's final print, it was then
> superimposed on the novel. Passages in the book which in no way appear on the
> screen were deleted; descriptive scenes which show up in the film were bracketed.
> Dialogue which was carried over into the film was underlined, added characters
> noted in the margin, and so on. Before each critical evaluation, I was able to hold
> before me an accurate and reasonably objective record of how the film differed
> from its model. (1957: ix)

It is interesting to note the absence of any detailed analysis of the script as a literary
object in this formation, except in terms of its rendering of the novel. Also noteworthy
is the way in which the ties between the shooting script and production situation
are minimised in favour of a novel/film relationship. Bluestone effectively constructs
what is termed in the studios a 'cutting continuity' that summarises editing decisions following changes that emerge in the shooting process; although in this case
his 'continuity' is not a document of the studio but his own construct. This continuity
becomes a surrogate for the film which is then imposed on the novel; and in this way

Bluestone's method can be seen as a mechanism through which to manufacture a page-bound version of the film.

It should be made clear that in questioning the role of the novel in this context I am not suggesting that exploring the links between novels and films is an illegitimate or unproductive exercise. Bluestone justifiably details the extensive use Hollywood makes of the novel form as the basis for feature films. Yet, by focusing on the process of turning novels into films, and on the novel as a subject matter for film, this form of adaptation theory provides only a partial account of the institutional mechanisms and logics whereby a mode of production accumulates material, and processes one kind of material onto another. Bluestone certainly shows that the novel had a special place at Hollywood story conferences (see 1957: 3). The focus however is on the transposition of novel to film, where novel and film are seen as 'different aesthetic genera' (1957: 5). Textual analysis is geared towards the novel. No history of scripting practices or scripting techniques is provided, and it is only relatively recently that the screenplay is being approached as a kind of text in its own right (see Kohn 2000). Critics have begun to become enthused by the plurality of the screenplay, in which the locus of meaning is constantly shifting. 'Deciphering the screenplay would therefore mean both establishing a coherent set of meanings by (and for) the individual reader, and agreeing a coherent set of meanings for the group of readers [who are also *de facto* writers involved in the production]' (Macdonald 2004a: 92). It will be interesting to watch how these approaches might begin to make their way into mainstream screenwriting discourse.

5.

THE INVENTION OF
THE SCREENPLAY

The screenplay has a key place in our contemporary understanding of screenwriting. It has become an important form of script and historians have begun the process of excavating the earliest screenplays. This chapter looks at the invention of the screenplay not so much in terms of the first kinds of scripts, but in terms of a language game or discursive struggle in which the term 'screenplay' emerges. This approach allows us to appreciate the screenplay in a new way, in terms of its place in screenwriting discourse.

Ours is the age of the 'spec' script: of the written screenplay sold without prior studio investment and offered for development on a 'speculative' basis. William Goldman heralds this era when he writes: 'Right now, with movie companies fragmented and dying and with money coming from all kinds of strange new sources, it is a golden time to write screenplays' (1983: 52). Given the plethora of published scripts and handbooks in our bookshops it is easy to fall into the trap of thinking that the screenplay has always been there. A form of 'screenplay-centrism' in which the screenplay is considered to be the only kind of script, or the most significant (or only) kind of scripting, is difficult to avoid, and with it a tendency to approach film writing exclusively in terms of the screenplay.

The term 'screenplay' in fact only emerges at a particular point in the history of scripting – it is not there at the origins of screen writing. Here, I try to examine the conditions under which the screenplay has become an important form, and a key concern, for screenwriters. My approach is to look at the way the discourse 'of' and 'around' the 'screenplay' has changed. A discursive approach works against the idea of empirical study of a particular object existing outside language. The screenplay is not some object that is discovered pre-existing in reality, so much as constructed or 'invented' in language. This focus goes against the grain of some approaches to historical research. Common sense might say that the first script was the first screenplay. Some film historians might argue that locating the first design documents or written compositions used in filmmaking is the key objective of any such study, and as a result what these documents were called is of secondary importance. Furthermore, until the organisation of the studios was sufficiently advanced to produce a standardised notion of the script there is little that can be said to be truly standard or typical about the script and the way it was used.[53] With respect to these views, I argue that it is still important to engage with the screenplay as a discursive construct. Why should we be attentive to how we use the term 'screenplay'? I would like to put forward three responses:

(i) because screenwriting represents not simply an empirical practice, but a language game, a discursive regime for talking about practice out of which practice is formed. In what follows I argue the script as screenplay was a site for discursive struggle in which written compositions were framed and argued for in different ways: in short, the term enables a different discourse on screenwriting. As I suggest below, even when the script was standardised as a 'blueprint' this discursive struggle continued. The fact that 'screenplay' is a compound word (made up of 'screen' and 'play') is important here, as compound words are usually formed as a result of social and cultural forces.

(ii) changes in terminology are related to changes in film culture. Using the term 'screenplay' to refer to writing practices that were not understood as screenplays by practitioners of the day can obscure important historical and discursive changes. Ignoring the invention of the 'screenplay' means ignoring important aspects of film culture.

(iii) if we ignore how the term 'screenplay' emerges we risk neglecting a key problem in screenwriting studies, namely, how did the 'screen play' move from being an image-orientated entity to a word-based one? The term 'screen play' was used in the 1910s to describe the filmed performance of a drama – a very different meaning to that used today. In other words, how and when does 'screen play' cease referring primarily to a picture play and become attached mainly to a manuscript?

Screenplay-centrism in the History-Writing Around Screenwriting

Contemporary accounts of the history of screenwriting frequently fall into a 'teleological' account of the development of the script. A purpose or 'end' (from the Greek *telos*) is put forward as a key to unlock the phenomenon at hand. In this case, the 'end' is the writing of screenplays, which becomes the primary form of screenwriting. In his thesis on screenwriting in the period between 1897 and 1920, Edward Azlant writes: 'the writing of some format of the screenplay is perennially reported to be the first creative phase of filmmaking proper' (1980: 2). Azlant's phrase 'some format of the screenplay' suggests that the screenplay is the predetermined end point of the script. He examines the treatment of the screenplay in early film theory and practice, even though that specific term is rarely used. This teleology is not questioned in his work. The complex and shifting terminology of screen writing in the 1910s and 1920s – 'plot of action', 'scenario', 'photoplay', 'continuity', 'treatment', 'screen dramatisation', 'cinema play', to name a few terms – is seen in relation to the development of the screenplay. In the process, past practice is overcoded with present day terminology and understanding. The problem is not restricted to Azlant's work. Margaret Mehring in her account of the evolution of the screenplay sees the scenario and continuity script as the 'first screenplays' (1990: 232). Referring to the screenplay might be a 'slip' in these works, but they have a broader significance. Through inaccurate or loose terminology the emergence of the screenplay, its invention, becomes obscured. Because the history is poorly understood, the screenplay becomes a transcendent, ahistorical format; and the question of the emergence of the screenplay itself becomes lost and is rarely, if ever, posed. The search for the earliest forms of script is treated the same as the search for 'early cinema screenplays' (Raynauld 1997: 257).

While this chapter raises the issue of 'invention', it seeks to put a different twist on the idea, nudging it away from a focus on firsts and geniuses. Research into the history of photography has challenged the notion of a single moment of invention associated with a particular apparatus (see Batchen 1991). In film studies, scholars have contested the fetishisation of origins, births and newness involved in such accounts (Musser 1990: 1). They have questioned the emphasis on individual pieces of technology (lens, stock) and the ideology behind a focus on techniques (see Comolli 1985). A more complex story of invention and cultural convergence has emerged that recognises an assemblage of factors including cultural discourses, individuals, technological concepts and experimentation with a range of different apparatuses. In light of this scholarship we should approach the matter of the invention of the screenplay with caution, wary of any magic date, founding father (or mother) or single moment of conception. In terms of the screenplay, at issue is a change in vocabulary, but also a form of scripting and other practices shaped by discourse, and this complexity needs to be kept in mind.

1916: The Screen Play as Exhibited Entity

It is difficult to affix a specific date to the invention of the screenplay, and much depends on the historical period being looked at. The first usage of the term I wish to discuss dates from 1916, when the term 'screen play' (two words) was used to describe the film as visual performed object, or exhibited entity, much like its earlier counterpart term 'photoplay', while the script itself was most commonly linked to the 'scenario'. The *Oxford English Dictionary* cites as part of its entry on 'Screen' the first reference to 'screen play' in 1916 as *N.Y. Times* 7 February, 'Anna Held's debut in a screen play'. *Photoplay* magazine announce in 1916 that 'We stand at the threshold of the full-length screen play' (see Higashi 1994: 28). Leslie T. Peacocke writes: 'The really good screen play is the play written by trained screen play writers especially for that most uncharitable thing in the world, the motion picture camera' (1916: 97). This usage continues into the 1920s. Referring to one film, Terry Ramsaye notes: 'it was something between the embryo of a screen play and a mere photographic repro- duction of an excerpt from the stage play' (1926: 420).

Competing with other terms such as 'photoplay' and 'feature', the 'screen play' was not the dominant term – which makes the task of tracking its use in this period difficult.[54] Nevertheless the term 'screen play' was used to describe the feature multi- ple-reel drama on the screen up to the 1930s. In the teens, with the screen play referring to the produced film, Peacocke's 'screen play writer' was not a common term. More common was 'photoplaywright', 'photoplay writer', 'photoplay dramatist' or 'screen-playwright'.

This understanding of the screen play sees it as the drama brought to the screen – thus my emphasis on the screenplay being an entity that is filmed and performed – and the link with the stage is an important one (see Higashi 1990).[55] The term 'screen play' allowed one to conceive of theatre and film in a continuum, and signifi- cant figures were using this link to forge a 'new technic of story-telling' (deMille 1939: 61). In 1921 William C. deMille states that 'I have come to the conclusion that the screen must create its own literature. It is not enough that we steal novelists and play- wrights for short periods each year. We must interest them so profoundly that they will seriously devote themselves entirely or almost entirely to the screen' (quoted in Smith 1921a: 36). He goes on to make a direct link between the screen and stage play when he writes: 'we will see playwrights turning out a number of original screen and stage plays each year, just as we now have them simultaneously producing magazine stories and novels or novels and dramas' (ibid.). The notion of screen play allows deMille to consider the film under the rubric of drama and dramatic literature.

Listening to discourse around the 'screen play' one is struck by how the under- standing of screen play as produced filmed performance overlaps significantly with discussion of the script as written object. The close relationship between the idea of the 'play' as performance and 'playscript' as manuscript opens up a complex and ambiguous textual space in which to discuss the screen play. As early as 1912 James Slevin explains to his readers that he is including a picture-play in his handbook, 'a play completely written' (1912: 65). Clara Beranger comes close to a 'manuscript- based' reference to the screen play when she takes offence at 'the almost unanimous presupposition that all authors of books and plays are good, and all authors of screen plays and workers for the screen are bad' (1923: 11). Frances Marion could be read as referring to a written entity when she observes that 'a number of things may serve to complicate the writing of the screen play' (1938b: 37). These passages are interesting for the way they still make sense if either understanding of screen play (performed dramatic work on the screen or manuscript) is held in mind.

Following on from this first usage of the screen play, a shift in the textuality of the screen play from a screen-based entity to the screenplay as a page-based script occurs. Gradually, the screen play became exclusively a kind of manuscript, subject to particular reading protocols and principles of 'proper' construction. The screen play did not simply or instantaneously switch from being a performed and filmed object to a written one. The appropriate conditions needed to arise for a shift in textuality from image to word to happen. Some of these are linked to changing understandings of the art of the photoplay (examined in a later chapter); others relate to credit practices and institutional politics.

1920–1932: Localised Company Production Credits Leading to the Writer-Producer Code of Practice

If the Screen Play begins as a way to describe the exhibited film, from around 1920, and possibly earlier, localised company or production-unit references to the 'Screen Play' as a form of credit begin to appear. These can be found in copyright records, screen credits and publicity materials.

The existence of these credits is at times difficult to verify. For example, the Catalog of Copyright Entries or CCE (US Copyright Office, Library of Congress, 1951) lists limited descriptive information for particular titles, which include an apparent 'screenplay' credit for some films between 1912 and 1920.[56] But on closer inspection this use of the term 'screenplay' for films from this period dates from the 1951 edition of the catalogue, and is not supported by inspection of supplementary sources (such as applications, descriptive deposits or material, annual versions of the catalogue or record books in which extra information is recorded). Indeed, the earliest verifiable credit of this kind is for the film *The Little 'Fraid Lady* (1920): it is listed with a 'screenplay' credit in the 1951 CCE, but in the record book is recorded as 'Screen version from the Novel "The Girl Who Lived in the Woods", by Marjorie Benton Cooke. Screen-Play by Jos. W. Farnham. Directed by John G. Adolphi. Photoplay in 6 parts by Marjorie Benton Cooke of United States'.[57] But note even in this case the credit is two words rather than the compound 'screenplay'.

Through the 1920s the credit appears more frequently. Famous Players-Lasky Corporation films such as *Grumpy* (Dir. William C. deMille, Writ. Clara Beranger, 1923), *The Breaking Point* (Dir. Herbert Brenon, Writ. Edfrid A. Bingham & Julie Herne, 1924), *Triumph* (Dir. Cecil B. DeMille, Writ. Jeanie Macpherson, 1924), *Bluff*

(Dir. Sam Wood, Writ. Willis Goldbeck, Josephine Quirk, 1924), *Code of the Sea* (Dir. Victor Fleming, Writ. Bertram Millhauser, Byron Morgan, 1924) and *Peter Pan* (Dir. Herbert Brenon, Writ. Willis Goldbeck, 1924), are examples.[58] Many films from the 1920s are no longer viewable, so verification against prints is difficult. However, it is possible to inspect some of the script department records for these films, held in the Paramount collection at the Margaret Herrick Library.

A typical dossier from these Famous Players-Lasky films will consist of items such as a synopsis of the original story or play if relevant; a short or sometimes detailed synopsis or treatment; a continuity or scenario; a location plot; a list of spoken titles, intertitles and subtitles or 'title continuity'; a cover page listing the cost of the play, the negative and the key production cost figures; and a 'cutting continuity' briefly describing each scene of the finished motion picture and its duration in feet. In some instances, a story report from the 1930s or 1940s is also present, and while this refers to the screenplay it is from a much later period. Different files vary in terms of which of the above items are present.

This documentation is revealing. On the one hand, all of the cutting continuities consulted list a 'Screen Play' credit (in the form of two words). On the other hand, the documentation shows a less than systematic use of the term in the production process. On the cover page of the 'Scenario' for instance, the words 'continuity by' will regularly appear. On a covering production sheet that lists details of the property, one line reads 'Name of Photoplay' and another 'Author of Scenario'. These are the institutionalised terms through which the business of the studio is carried out. The credit 'Screen Play' in this context seems limited to the domain of exhibition, a way of adding cachet to the product by highlighting the literary and artistic (in the 'high art' sense) work of the writer. The integration of the term 'screen play' into the administrative processes of the studio seems at best partial.[59]

An explanation for this partial integration can be teased out using terms from dramatic criticism, and the distinction between plays and playscripts. For Roger Gross '"A Play" is the name of a kind of occurrence. It does not exist; it happens. A play has no "body"; it is the behaviour of bodies … A playscript [is] the name of a kind of thing, a symbolic notation on which certain kinds of plays are based' (1974: 4). Working within these definitions, it can be argued that writers can receive authorship credit for a Screen Play, just as they could for a Play. But this does not necessarily signify that the Screen Play here has the same meaning as the 'playscript'. In other words, credit practices do not necessarily have to result in a shift in the textuality of the Screen Play from visual to written entity. That said, the term 'play' in the theatre has gained sufficient ambiguity to relate to both 'play' and 'playscript' in Gross's terms. (The term 'play' sometimes works as a diminutive of 'playscript'.) As a result, the idea of a Screen Play can contribute to a redefining of 'screen play' as a term referring exclusively to the written script. Thus, in 1934, Gouverneur Morris can suggest 'Plays are written primarily to be played. Screen plays [two words] are written to be photographed' (1934: 4). Here the orientating of the screen play towards the written object is clear.

While initially the Screen Play credit operates at the local or company level, a key event in relation to the development of 'Screen Play' as an industry-wide writing credit is the negotiation of a 'Writer-Producer Code of Practice' established by the Writers' Branch of the Academy of Motion Picture Arts and Sciences in the early 1930s. Conventionally, despite some notable exceptions (see Ross 1941; Wheaton 1973), accounts of the struggle for recognition of the craft of screen writing focus on the birth of the Screen Writers' Guild in 1933. However, an earlier incarnation of the Screen Writers' Guild was formed as an official branch of the Authors' League of America in 1920 (see Schwartz 1982: 14; Wheaton 1973: 20).[60] While the Writers' Branch of the Academy and the Guild (mark one) were distinct organisations, a complex set of exchanges existed between members of the Guild and members of the Writers' Branch, who were often Guild members (see Ross 1941: 57). As many as half of the members of the Academy Writers Special Committee negotiating the Writer-Producer Code of Practice in 1932 had been members of the Screen Writers' Guild from 1923.

With a general standard contract for writers unlikely to emerge after several years of negotiations (and it would not emerge until 1942, although it was backdated to 1940), producers and the Writers' Branch addressed three of the most important problems in a 'Writer-Producer Code of Practice' established on 1 May, 1932. As Murray Ross notes:

> With the possible exception of the Academy Free Lance Actor Contract, this writer-producer code was given more conscientious study and discussion than any other agreement ever made between creative employees and the studios. It was signed without reservation by nine studios and more than two hundred established screen writers. The Screen Writers' Guild called it a 'great step forward in relationships between writers and producers'. (1941: 59).

An ongoing problem with the code of practice (and other agreements reached by the Academy) was that it could not be enforced under Federal US labour codes, and this has led to a view that the Guild (mark one) had its industrial function usurped by the Writers' Branch (see Ceplair & Englund 1980: 18–19).

The three areas addressed by the code were notice of the termination of the employment of a freelance author, payment provisions for freelancers not employed week by week and, finally, credit to screen authors. It is this latter issue that interests us the most in terms of the invention of the screenplay and the broadening out of the credit across the industry.

It is worth reiterating that a screen play credit is not the same as calling the written script a screen play. The Writer-Producer Code refers to the script in several ways, as 'treatment' and 'continuity' (see provisions of Paragraph 2), never screenplay. It is in the provisions of Paragraph 3 relating to credit to screen authors, however, that the 'Screen Play by ____' is institutionalised as the credit an author or group of authors is given, and which is printed on the release prints of the photoplay. If the photoplay is based on an original story or work of the author the credit 'By ____' is granted.

It is likely that the introduction of the 'Screen Play' credit into the code was a contributing factor to the first use of the term in the Academy Awards in 1934 for 'Best written screen play (adaptation)'.[61] It was only in 1936 that 'Best written screen play' became the name for the general category in writing alongside the 'Best original motion picture story award', which is described in the rules as applying to 'those pictures in which the integrity of an original story written especially for the screen has been preserved in the completed production'. The significance of the award categories is firstly that they are not simply credits, and secondly that the early categories specify 'written screen play', thus furthering the link between script and screenplay, although specifying that the screen play is written still suggests that the screen play was not exclusively considered in manuscript terms.

1937–1949: Writings by Practitioners

Possibly the first usage of 'screenplay' as compound is in the Academy Awards categories of 1940, when the space between the two words disappears in formal documents. Can too much be made of the space between two words, in this case 'screen' and 'play'? Is there a danger of overinterpreting what might be a printer's mistake? In the approach taken here, the melding of the two words into the signifier 'the screenplay', signals a normalising process in discourse. It is linked to a broader discursive act or process; part of a transformation in the nature of practice. The practice of writing scripts starts to move closer to the process of writing screenplays, and gradually a new object is made natural. Slowly the polysemy of the term 'screen play' narrows around particular understandings of the written object.

In the history of screenwriting the use of the term screenplay, and understanding of that entity, evolves at different speeds. This is evident in writings by practitioners working in the 1930s and 1940s such as Sidney Howard (who we shall discuss in more detail in a later section), Dudley Nichols, Raymond Chandler and John Howard Lawson. In these writings the role of the screenwriter is constantly being negotiated in relation to the dominant story machinery of the studios. What is interesting about this body of work on the screenplay is that the authors in question expend a great deal of effort relating the screenplay to the production process and the position of the writer in that process.

In his 1943 introduction to *Twenty Best Film Plays*, 'The Writer and the Film', Dudley Nichols explains that the compartmentalisation of filmmaking into different specialisations is an unavoidable aspect of the modern motion picture, but at the same time it is detrimental to film and the work of the writer because of the lack of an 'integrated creation'. In an attempt to reclaim this sense of creation, Nichols prioritises the work of writing directly for the screen (and we shall look more closely at this idea of screenwriting in chapter eight). It is as part of this project that he promotes the screenplay as a way to reintegrate the work of the writer and also raise the standards of literary quality in the studio. An earlier 1942 essay by Nichols, 'Film Writing', is interesting here, because of the way the 'profession of writing for the screen' is established as the key framework from the outset. After an introductory section in which he contextualises film writing, Nichols links 'screen-writing' (in the hyphenated form) to 'the perfect screenplay'. He characterises the work of early film directors, learning through their efforts and mistakes, as barely 'writing' at all. Eventually they did 'become writers in a sense' ('they "wrote" their translations directly in film'), but he differentiates their efforts from that of 'word writers' (1942: 771).

The idea of the 'screenplay' (1942: 772) eventually takes on a key role in his working out this new sense of writing, which Nichols presents as being 'new under the sun of literature' (ibid.). He differentiates between one understanding of the screenplay he previously held ('the complete description of the film') and a newer one which is the product of his research ('the complete description of a motion picture and how to accomplish the thing described') (ibid.). In proposing this distinction Nichols is making room for the script to be recognised as a key element in the realisation of the motion picture, and of the screen writer as one of its creative authors. He is keen to create the script as a document relevant to 'the functions of other people engaged in the making of any film' (ibid.), and construct the author as a part of the production team. This leads him into a debate about the technical and artistic status of the 'script'. A conventional view desires a succinct technical object, filled with ordinary description, while Nichols promotes an alternative kind of script, a document describing detailed feeling, 'three times as long as the ordinary script' (ibid.). Nichols goes on to tell how a producer rejected such a script. This conflict is typical of Nichols' time, in which screen-writing as an aesthetic activity struggles to emerge from beneath a technical understanding of the script as a complete description, a continuity or blueprint, central to the administrative processes of the studio; which is perhaps why Nichols' understanding of screenplays as blueprints of projected films can be considered strategic (1943: xxxv).

In Nichols' work the writer is cut off from the process of filmmaking not just by a suspicion on the part of other film workers of those who create with words, but also due to the specialisation of the process – 'too much the modern factory system' (1943: xxxi) – that makes it difficult for writers to write 'as a camera'. Following an era in which the continuity was regarded as the 'blueprint' for production (see Staiger 1985), Nichols suggests that writing should not be referred to condescendingly as 'paper-work'. It is worth noting that, in Nichols' framework, the idea that the 'screen play' could be both a written entity and a picture play becomes harder to sustain.

His is a conception of writing for the screen based on the script and specifically the screenplay; the screenplay is a form of script deployed in the production of motion pictures.

This is a novel view – even in the context of Nichols' own work. Just a few years earlier, in 1939, even though many of Nichols' concerns were similar to those raised in his 1940s writings, the discursive conditions were quite different. In one 1939 article, 'The Making of a Scenario', in which the term 'screenplay' does not appear, the 'scenario is the blueprint of a film rather than a written work' (1982: 405). The conditions of writing here are different to his 1942 essay; his main focus in 1939 is the scenario, not the screenplay, although he does refer to 'the writing of the play itself', and uses an old-fashioned sounding formulation of 'screen playwriting' (1982: 409), giving the impression that writing for the screen is a subset of playwriting.

Reading Nichols and other authors, one gains a sense of the invention of the screenplay as happening not in the flash of an instant, but rather in a slow, incremental process of changing values and understanding. By 1945, the 'screenplay' (one word) has a key role in debates, but there is a fragile aspect to the term, a crisis of recognition of the art of the screenplay. Raymond Chandler writes: 'for the basic art of motion pictures is the screenplay; it is fundamental, without it there is nothing' (1945: 50). Motion pictures are written, conceived in screenplay form and then made: 'Everything derives from the screenplay' (ibid.). However, after surveying the position of writers in Hollywood, and the lack of any control over their labours, Chandler is compelled to conclude that the way the system works means that 'there is no such thing as an art of the screenplay' (1945: 51). The system is geared towards exploitation, and denies the writer 'the right to be a talent' (ibid.) and the sense of independence and finality that goes with it. Chandler also posits another view:

> If there is no art of the screenplay, the reason is at least partly that there exists no available body of technical theory and practice by which it can be learned. There is no available library of screenplay literature, because the screenplays belong to the studios and they will only show them within their guarded walls. There is no body of critical opinion, because there are no critics of the screenplay; there are only critics of motion pictures as entertainment, and most of these critics know nothing whatsoever of the means whereby the motion picture is created and produced on celluloid. (1945: 53)

Chandler shows us why the kind of work Gassner and Nichols carry out in their anthologies was urgent, but his comments also suggest that Gassner's and Nichols' work, published in 1943, did not represent a miraculous or instantaneous change.

John Howard Lawson's *Theory and Technique of Playwriting and Screenwriting*, published in 1949, can be viewed as an attempt to develop a handbook for the art of the screenplay: 'The screenplay has so little standing as an art that until recently it was rarely considered worthy of publication' (1949: 367). Lawson acknowledges the work of Gassner and Nichols, and his discussion draws on their anthology, but he is also concerned that their heavy editing of shooting scripts and omission of technical jargon is not helpful (1949: 368). But there exists a wider issue. For Lawson:

> Public and critical underestimation of the screenplay may have its origin in the underestimation of the writer's role in the American studios. The failure to recognise the importance of the script is one of the major weaknesses of American production: it has had an effect on the form of the screenplay, which has developed in a haphazard manner. (Ibid.)

In his work Lawson no longer feels compelled to recompose shooting scripts into film plays in the manner of Gassner and Nichols, but presents a detailed account of the shooting script. At the same time, however, change is slow. In Lewis Herman's *A Practical Manual of Screen Playwriting: For Theater and Television Films* the older form of 'screen play' is still evident, and he seems to step back from a focus on the writer to define the 'motion-picture screen play' as 'a written composition designed to serve as a sort of work diagram for the motion-picture director' (1952: 3).

Scenario, Continuity, Screenplay

Our investigation up to this point leaves us with a new problem. Namely, how should we describe the development or emergence of the screenplay in relation to other formats such as the continuity or scenario?

Despite the ubiquity of its current usage, the term 'screen play', once it gets attached to the manuscript, gets used initially in a very uneven way. At times it is almost as though the screen play as object of authorship and credit is distinct from the object being written. A curious aspect of the *Screen Guilds' Magazine* of 1935 is that while a best 'screen play' of the month was named from July onwards, the section in which the magazine reported the work of various writers did not have the screen play as a category. Instead, it organised work in the categories of original story, adaptation, continuity, dialogue, lyrics and music. In a summary brief of the draft Writer-Producer Code presented in the February 1935 issue of the *Screen Guilds' Magazine*, the statement appears that 'no producer shall agree with a writer that the writer shall write any original story, adaptation, treatment, screen play, continuity, dialogue, or any combination of these, except under a written contract...' (Anon. 1935: 3). There is a sense here that the screen play is only slowly being inserted into the industrial logic of the studios and the craft identity of writers.

This process is largely hidden from view by a common practice of imagining an 'evolutionary' link between formats. Mehring, for instance, writes that 'the traditional screenplay format has evolved from its original function as a production blueprint'

(1990: 232). But there is an absence of detail here. Mehring clouds the issue by speaking of evolution, and stating that 'originally the screenplay was called a scenario, or continuity script, and consisted of a list of scenes that described the silent action and camera angles' (ibid.). Yet, as discussed below, there is some debate around the definition of a scenario which leads us to question a direct evolution of script form from scenario to continuity to screenplay.

To attempt to shed light on this aspect of the history of the format it is important to examine in more detail the major change from the scenario script to the continuity script as discussed by Janet Staiger. She draws on a 1909 trade paper description of the scenario script to ground her understanding of that format. It consisted of a 'title, followed by its generic designation ("a drama", "a comedy"), the cast of characters, a two-hundred-word-or-less "synopsis" of the story, and then the "scenario" – a scene-by-scene account of the action including intertitles and inserts' (1985: 177). By 1914, however, the continuity script became standard practice. She describes the format as follows:

> Each of the firm's production scripts had a number assigned to it which provided a method of identifying the film even though its title might shift. A cover page indicated who wrote the scenario, who directed the shooting, when shooting began and ended, when the film was shipped to the distributors, and when the film was released. The next part of the blueprint was the 'Complete Picture Report' which summarised production information in more detail. Following that was a list of titles and intertitles and an indication of where they were to be inserted in the final print ... At the end, the entire cost of the film was broken into a standard accounting format ... A location plot preceded the script. This plot listed all exterior and interior sites along with shot numbers, providing efficient cross-checking and preventing lost production time and wasted labour. The cast of characters followed. After a one-page synopsis of the action, the shot-by-shot script began. Each shot was numbered consecutively; included were the shot's location and a brief description of sets, properties, and costumes. Camera distances were specified, as well as any unusual effects in the lighting or cinematography. Scenes were broken into separate shots, and cross-cutting was fully detailed. (1985: 189–90)

A major identifying difference between the scenario script and the continuity script – in reality a dossier of documents – is that in the former, scenes are listed as 'scenes', whereas in the latter a 'scene' consists of a number of shots, each of which are listed in the script.

One interpretation of the change of scripting practices described by Staiger would see the scenario script as evolving directly into the continuity script. This would be plausible as both script formats involve breaking action down into segments for filming. However, given different usages at different times, the situation may not be so straightforward. Frances Marion indicates a blurring between the terms scenario and continuity: 'in the studios, the word scenario, often used more loosely elsewhere, refers only to the continuity, the "shooting script", or as it is designated on the photographed film, the screen play' (1938b: 29). She defines scenario as 'a continuity ... a shooting script' (1938a: 372). In 1921, Frances Taylor Patterson's description of the 'scenario' as covering the cast of characters, synopsis, scene plot and plot of action or continuity, matches Staiger's description of the continuity (see 1921: 96–7). A difficulty here is that the term 'scenario' was ambiguous. As Frederick Palmer notes in 1924, a number of different views existed:

> there has been and still is much difference of opinion as to the use of the word 'scenario'. Some insist that it should be applied to the continuity only; others hold that the synopsis is the scenario, while still others use the term in connection with the complete manuscript, inclusive of all its parts. (1924a: 3)

Tamar Lane similarly suggests the term covers a wide scope and is loosely used, 'meaning anything from an original story to a continuity' (1936: 122). The ambiguity of the term scenario I want to suggest complicates an 'evolutionary' idea of its development directly into the 'continuity'.

Another complication for the evolutionary narrative has to do with the notion of a 'synopsis', and its link to the term 'scenario'. Informing Palmer's observation of a link between the scenario and synopsis is a notion of the 'detailed synopsis': 'In some cases a story may be told in four or five pages of paper ordinarily used in the preparation of manuscripts (8.5x11), and in others it may be necessary to greatly expand this number. In any event the telling of the story should not consume more than 7,500 words or about twenty sheets of manuscript paper, double spaced' (1924a: 8). Here the notion of the synopsis far exceeds the one page allocated to it in Staiger's description of the continuity script. Lane speaks of reader synopses of between 300 to 1,500 words; but also author synopses of between 6,000 and 8,000 words (1936: 84, 88). The detailed synopsis is an understudied format. Yet for Howard T. Dimick, writing in 1922, 'the present period might be called the era of the detailed synopsis, which has evolved out of the era of the scenario' (1922: 14).

The continuity script is part of a broader impulse, that of the organisation of production according to a total filmic plan. But to read the scenario solely in terms of the development of the blueprint (and then beyond that in terms of the screenplay) would be an error. The scenario, rather, has a 'life' of its own. There is evidence to suggest that contrary to a linear hypothesis the scenario does not merely 'evolve' into the continuity script, or part of it, but informs the still-emerging notion of the 'treatment'. With increased codification of the continuity, the extended synopsis/treatment/ scenario (the interconnection between them varying in different cases) came to be of importance in developing and evaluating a project; and a process of 'devolution' seems to occur where the scenario draws back from highly technical form containing camera angles and other information (see Patterson 1921: 126). So, while maintaining an interest in the blueprint, it is important to remain alert to an interaction between terms such as 'treatment', 'scenario' and 'extended synopsis'. In 1929 Beranger refers to the treatment as 'the first long synopsis' (1977: 141). Earlier, Patterson describes an extended synopsis of 2,500 to 5,000 words. Significantly the aim of this document is 'to tell the story vividly ... in terms of action. The synopsis must create in the mind of the scenario editor who reads it the same picture which is later to be seen upon the screen by the spectators' (1921: 127–8). This is very similar to the emphasis on 'the read' discussed in an earlier chapter, which is usually associated with screenplay form.

This other life of the scenario has significance for an account of the invention of the screenplay. Kevin Brownlow draws a direct link between the two:

> the word 'scenario' – later to be replaced by the term 'screenplay' – did not mean shooting script. It was a sequence of scenes, the story told in visual terms, originally devised to explain as clearly as possible what its author had in mind. From the scenario was written the continuity, or 'shooting script', as it is known today. (1968: 271–2).

Could this idea of a scenario or screenplay in a sense be an 'extended synopsis' or treatment? In any case this comment suggests that the scenario was not simply replaced by the continuity. It is interesting to compare Brownlow's perspective with comments on the scenario made by prominent scenarists John Emerson and Anita Loos. In their definition of 'the scenario' the term 'is now held to mean a detailed synopsis of the plot in ordinary short story form. Originally it referred to the continuity, but this meaning has recently gone out of date' (1920: 19). In both of these accounts the extended prose treatment form is seen as central. Azlant also offers some support for this view: 'By the late teens this format [scenario or plot of action] will come to be called the "continuity", like the modern shooting script in segmenting by units of shots and designating camera directions, and the scenario will come to mean a highly detailed synopsis, like the modern treatment' (1980: 259).

An overemphasis on linear development has greatly confused matters in relation to the scenario, and too much effort can be expended on tracing a direct lineage between the scenario and continuity. In the process, however, crucial entities such as the detailed or extended synopsis and the plot of action (written to various degrees of formality) have been marginalised. Positing a direct linear relationship between the scenario and continuity poses another problem, which is that it makes it hard to see how the screenplay would be situated in production.

Situating the Screenplay in Production

Since the 'Screen Play by' credit did not always map directly on to institutional-ised categories for writing, what is the situation of the screenplay in the production process? This question reprises a problem examined in chapter two, namely how to situate the script in production. Should the screenplay be aligned with a prepara-tory document such as the treatment synopsis or the 'shooting script'? How should we imagine the relationship between the screenplay and the continuity blueprint? Or, put differently, having invented the screenplay, how did practitioners situate it in production, and what were the terms of the arrangement?[62] The brief answer is that film workers did this in different ways, and one needs to be attentive to variations in screenwriting discourse as a result.

Sidney Howard's 1937 essay, 'The Story Gets a Treatment' (first published in an anthology edited by Nancy Naumburg), forms an interesting case here. He describes the passage of a story through the studio. In broad terms the story moves from treat-ment stage, through to the first draft of the picture script, during which story confer-ences and collaboration with the director are key, leading to a 'second draft collabora-tion' which then goes to the producer. The script from which the picture is made – 'it may be the second or the fiftieth, according to the type of producer' (1995: 213) – is deemed the shooting script. Following censorship approval the script is sent to 'tech-nicians' for 'breakdown' into days and dollars (ibid.). But at what point does Howard discuss the screenplay? He talks about completing the treatment and writing the 'first draft of the script itself' (1995: 208). He links this process with the reworking of the story property (in his case a novel) into picture form, 'sequence by sequence and scene by scene, including in it as many picture ideas as may occur to me, but making no particular effort towards a finished script' (ibid.). He later refers to this as 'my first draft of a picture script' (1995: 211). Howard describes a further step in the writing process whereby the script takes the form of a motion picture: 'there are still direc-tors who like their manuscripts divided into many hundreds of little scenes; close-up, medium shot, long shot. The more modern director, however, prefers a manuscript which reads simply as a play' (ibid.). Howard's comment echoes a contemporary distinction between a presentation screenplay with un-numbered scenes (or master scenes) and few angles and a shooting script or production screenplay with more detail (see Cole & Haag 1983: ix–xi, 102–10). But although he seems to be referring to a screenplay-type script, he does not give it that name at this point.

Howard describes a situation that is very prone to producer intervention. He depicts the function of the writer as being secondary in the process, 'a job of adap-tation hack writing, cut to the dimensions of a director's demands' (1995: 205). Following his description of the passage of a story he turns to discuss key issues impacting on authorship: a snobbery against writing for pictures, and a tendency to team up the screenwriter with 'a continuity writer', an expert to whom he does not give much sympathy. He feels that 'the money which builds and equips studio plants and motion-picture theatres can neither build nor equip a talent for writing' (1995: 215). 'Too many authors, of talents both rising and matured, are delegated by studios to rewrite the works of other men and thus kept from writing on their own account' (1995: 216). It is in the context of thinking about conditions of authorship that Howard introduces the term 'screenplay', one word in the 1995 version, and two words in the original piece from 1937. The spacing is significant here as when Howard writes: 'the fact remains that the hundreds of screen plays turned out each year by the Hollywood studios contain few if any more items of real excellence than are to be found among the few dozen stage plays of the New York or London theatrical season' (Howard 1937: 50), he seems to be drawing on our first usage of 'screen play' meaning filmed/performed object. Interestingly, the passage works perfectly fine in the later version where 'screenplay' is the form used (see 1995: 215). What is curious about Howard's text is that while he refers to the picture script at several points he does not call this a screen play. It is only when he speaks of authorship, and in particular the process of 'original creation', or 'original screen material' and the pressing 'need for original screenplays', that the screen play emerges. This is part of realigning the screen writer with work 'written directly for the screen':

> The original screenplay ['screen play' in the 1937 version] represents a knotty problem to both the studio executive and film distributor. A successful stage play or a best-seller novel is each a known quantity and bears a thoroughly advertised title. The unknown work written directly for the screen is a mystery to the public except as a vehicle for a popular star. (1995: 216)

Fortunately, another account of the production process from the same period exists in an article called 'The Producer Makes a Plan' by Jesse L. Lasky. He hints at his understanding of the screenplay when he states that 'a treatment is an intermediary step between the raw material of the story and the screen play or shooting script' (1937: 8). In contrast to Kevin Brownlow's aforementioned observation about the screenplay not being a shooting script, it would seem, for Lasky, that the (final) screen play was understood as a quasi-shooting script, existing one step beyond the treatment stage and the province of a specialist – although his language below leaves room for an understanding of the screen play as exhibited entity.

The unique achievement of the 1930s was the studio as processing plant. The screen writing literature of the 1920s and 1930s is littered with reference to the story as a primary material or 'raw ore' that is processed, and the need for more, or the right kind of, stories (see Ceplair 1996: 39). The script as blueprint is one expression of this ideal, but the issue of the processing of story material goes further. As Lasky points out:

After a story conference, in which the producer imparts to the writer his ideas for the treatment of the story, he proceeds to mould it into shape. When this treatment satisfies the associate producer, the next step is the screen play itself. This may be assigned to the writer of the treatment or, in most cases, to another writer who is a specialist in screen plays. As many as two or three writers may now be put on the screen play, one an expert in construction, one a specialist in the particular type of dialogue required, and perhaps a continuity writer or one qualified in camera shots and camera transitions. (1937: 9)

Here, the story material is thoroughly malleable, with writers merely the instruments by which the producer moulds the story. The system of specialisation described by Lasky helps explain why Dudley Nichols begins 'The Writer and the Film' by examining the idea of the 'specialist' (1943: xxxi). It outlines a power structure that concerned many writers. Chandler can be read as responding to this situation when he hopes for a new uplift for writers. 'There is a hope that a decayed and make-shift system will pass, that somehow the flatulent moguls will learn that only writers can write screenplays and only proud and independent writers can write good screenplays' (1945: 53).

What the comparison of accounts of story development from Howard and Lasky reveals is that even in the late 1930s the screen play was still being bedded down in the production process. Against this background, the contemporary understanding of the screenplay can be read as a challenge to the material dominant logic of the studio, and as a way to craft an object with a different sense of material and aesthetic value specific to the screenwriter. The sense of material and property promoted by the studio process was too passive or inert to suit screen writers.

In this context, a politics of the format, drawing on the craft discourse of the technique of screen writing that had been in development since the 1910s, as well as a powerful set of arguments around writing for the screen, in addition to analysis of labour conditions, led to a reworking of the script as a different kind of textual object and sense of material. Part of this strategy involved renegotiating the aesthetic conditions surrounding the shooting script. The screenplay becomes the special province of the screenwriter. It becomes possible to refer to a 'completed screenplay' (see Lawson 1949: 368), the product of a 'literary activity'. The 'completed screenplay' becomes something of a badge of recognition (see Dunne 1980: 45).

A flashforward to 1952, and Lewis Herman's work, provides us with another opportunity to see the language game and textual politics of the screenplay in action. To begin with, Herman maintains a strong link between playwriting and screen play writing, as evidenced in the phrase 'screen playwriting'. Herman details the continuance of a strong division of labour, with various specialisations such as 'ideas men', 'situation men', 'gag men' and 'polish job' writers (1952: 5, 8). He goes on to make the point that of the 1,500 members of the Screen Writers' Guild in Hollywood at that time, 'less than one fourth actually write screen plays' (ibid.). For Herman, the link between the screen play and the prose treatment form is well and truly differentiated, as those that write screen plays write 'master-scene scripts, without camera shots and angles indicated' (ibid.). This is not the final shooting script that passes through many other hands, and specifically those of a director who adds shots and angles. While the master-scene script is a kind of blueprint, it is still distinct from the shooting script. But it is at this point that the screenplay sits once again at the centre of a textual politics, because Herman sees it as a way to gain control in the creative process, especially in relation to the function of directing:

> Given a screen writer who knows his craft – one who can visualise as well as verbalise, who can create the appropriate visual symbols and then translate them into revelatory dialogue and action, who is cognisant of all techniques of screen-play writing – the director can receive a shooting script, with camera angles, which he cannot help following. (1952: 172–3)

For Herman, 'a predirected screen play' helps the writer retain control. He points to numerous difficulties in getting fully elaborated shooting scripts/screenplays accepted by the studios, but nonetheless points to it as an ideal.

Lest this description of Herman's position give the impression that all writers were of a similar point of view, it is interesting to note that Dalton Trumbo makes a similar observation to Herman in 1933:

> The writers have had – and still have – the power to write scripts directly for the screen with such clarity and exactitude that every motion, every expression, every thought of the actor is outlined on paper. If they chose to write such scripts they would force the director into the minor position of a drill sargeant executing commands given by the author. They would, in effect, become directors themselves. (1933: 118).

But Trumbo ultimately found this argument unconvincing, and felt that Hollywood writers had a vested interest to focus on the importance of stories at the expense of 'the manner in which the story is told' (ibid.). He was also unconvinced by a call for new and original story material. Instead, he wanted to change the system through analysis. Trumbo was well aware of the controversy of his position, and that it would be interpreted as playing into the hands of directors. His main point, however, is to challenge a division of labour, a system that 'would sap the vitality of a Shakespeare' (1933: 118).

6.

AUTEUR THEORY

Auteur theory often gets a bad reception in screenwriting discourse. In this chapter I try and navigate through the tensions surrounding this approach and suggest that there is some common ground between screenwriters and the original proponents of the politique des auteurs, and that both parties can be understood in relation to similar underlying issues.

Few issues provoke as much emotion in screenwriting discourse as the auteur theory; the topic has seen a great deal of polemic. Controversial hot-spots include the importation of the *politique des auteurs* from France, its 'Americanisation' and transformation into a 'theory',[63] critical bias and excess (see Dunne 1980: 46), the way it privileges the 'non-writing, non-conceiving director' (Froug 1972: xiv), its inappropriateness for complex industrial modes of production (see Goldman 1984: 100) and the use of the auteur for marketing (see Thompson 1999: 7), not to mention controversial cases such as authorship in *Citizen Kane* (Dir. Orson Welles, Writ. Herman J. Mankiewicz, Orson Welles) (see Carringer 1978). Literary critics and theorists have pointed out that authorship is an ideological category (see Foucault 1977). Some, picking up on a long-standing conflict between individualistic and collectivist perspectives on creativity (see Arnheim 1958: 12–13), have expressed concern about how the theory misrepresents the collaborative nature of most film production. For William Froug it 'goes against all logic and verifiable fact, particularly when applied to the American motion picture' (1972: xi).

This chapter does not seek to carry out a comprehensive survey or history of the figure of the author (see Caughie 1981), or a defence or critique of the 'validity' of the theory (see Sternberg 1997: 14). Auteur theorists themselves have been diligent in pointing out how an inadequately formulated auteur theory can lead to short cuts in scholarship and lazy criticism (see Sarris 1962: 2; Bazin 1968). Nor do I try and make sense of the way issues around writing, auteurs, collaboration and Hollywood circulate in the magazine sections of newspapers and other popular media, often retracing or aggravating worn out battle lines.[64] Dana Polan (2001) has character-ised auteur criticism as a complex desire, an urge to outline the desire of the director and a desire for the director. As Polan suggests, it is a critical impulse that can take many varied forms: from tracing the primary obsessions and thematic preoc-cupations of this or that creator and the dialectics of freedom and constraint in the Hollywood system, to the study of how the filmmaker works materially with the tools and materials of his/her trade, to looking at how the 'authorial voice' can extend to sources of creativity other than the director, such as the producer, cameraperson, actor or screenwriter.

Rather than map out the landscape of auteur criticism, this chapter attempts to change the dynamics of discussion surrounding the auteur theory. It does so by focusing on the impulse behind the original *politique* (before its transformation into a programme of criticism). Of special interest to us is the discussion of auteur theory by screenwriters, who are often antagonistic towards it. This reaction can overlook the ways in which the *politique des auteurs* was itself a response to a deeper problem that still has implications for film workers today: namely, the separation of conception and execution, and the way that this separation structures filmmaking. By focusing on the *politique des auteurs* as a response to the separation of conception and execu-tion, and linking this with screenwriter struggles against the separation, I am trying to shift the terms of debate.

There is a long-standing view that thinking about the figure of the auteur, especially in filmmaking, cannot be separated from thinking about social, cultural and institutional conditions (see Buscombe 1973: 176). I am building on this view, but my focus is not primarily on the way auteur theory installs in the cinema 'a figure who had dominated the other arts for over a century: the romantic artist, individual and self-expressive' (Caughie 1981: 10). My view is that there are further issues to be addressed here beyond the point about Romantic ideology; thus my interest in the separation of conception and execution as a problem. Lack of appreciation of the significance of this problem has meant that the discussion gets bogged down in unproductive terms of debate, caught in a double-bind in which directors are pre-positioned and screenwriters ironically repeat and rework the terms of the separation of conception and execution in their attack on the auteur theory.[65] Thinking beyond the strong emotions around the auteur theory, I suggest that screen-writers and the original proponents of the *politique des auteurs* in fact share some common ground.

Credit and Control: Reactions to the Auteur Theory

It is not an overstatement to suggest that many screenwriters relate to the auteur theory in a hostile manner. Few have been willing to accept or build on Andrew Sarris's view that 'most American film criticism is directed toward the script instead of toward the screen' (1962: 5). Instead, it has become intertwined with a process of intro-ducing 'creative personality into the Hollywood cinema' (Buscombe 1973: 177). Philip Dunne refers to it as the 'pernicious auteur theory', which 'holds that the director is the author of something he didn't write' (1980: 46). William Goldman suggests that the word auteur has come to mean that 'it is the director who *creates* the film' (1984: 100; emphasis in original). Two terms are central in understanding this reaction: credit, and creative control. Credit arose as an issue for scenario writers as early as 1910, when *Moving Picture World* pondered 'is the moving picture public interested in the personalities of the writers of film scenarios?'. The magazine observed that 'there does not appear to be any scenario writer who is making name and fame so that his work is extensively requested [by the public]' (Anon. 1910: 370). In 1913, J. Berg Esenwein and Arthur Leeds note that 'only a few manufacturers print the author's name on the film beneath the title of the picture. Some do, however. The Edison Company always does; the Lubin Company has recently begun the practice … and one or two other companies have lately commenced giving the author credit on the screen' (1913: 209–10). Esenwein and Leeds feel that it is certain that the time will come 'that all films give the writer's name after the title' (1913: 255). For William Lord Wright in 1914, the crediting of the author of the photoplay is 'the one ethic of the literary world that has been systematically violated in filmland' (1914: 19).

Some of the reactions from screenwriters should be assessed with an awareness of traditional discourses of literary authorship in mind. From a literary studies perspec-tive on authorial credit, the screenplay is unique: 'it is generally acknowledged that established literary genres have a single, known author. This is not the case with the screenplay' (Sternberg 1997: 7). This places pressure on attribution, which is further complicated by practices of team writing and rewriting. But attribution remains impor-tant because of the way credit operates as a key form of 'currency' or symbolic capital within the industry. Credit arises as a key issue because of the sense of outrage felt by screenwriters when the director assumes credit for the work, which is taken to be collaborative in nature. Dunne neatly ties these two concerns together when he states: 'I have no wish to begrudge any director the credit he deserves; I only deplore the fact that the Auteur theory enriches him in prestige while it robs the writer of the credit he has earned' (1980: 47). Australian screenwriter Ian David takes the point further:

> Calling yourself an auteur in film, the most communal of art forms, is so vain it's almost a clinical condition … Auteurism at its narrowest is a miserable, one-dimensional way of looking at the creative process of filmmaking and yet auteur

theorists would have us believe it is the only way that works of value come into existence ... In fact, apportioning all the creative responsibility and credit to the director is a symptom of our increasing desire to simplify complex processes of collaboration and collective responsibility down to bite size. (2000: 36–7)

David links auteur theory to the devaluing of the work of different collaborators in the filmmaking process. However, it should be noted that his anti-auteur response to this phenomenon is only one possible reaction. In an attempt to shift the terms of evaluation, Richard Corliss promotes a *politique des collaborateur* (see 1974: xxiii), as well as the study of the 'author-auteur', or the screenwriter as auteur (ibid.). This was seen as an elaboration of the auteur thesis, that 'a movie could have two, three, many authors' (Corliss 1992: 11).

This brings us to our second term, that of creative control or 'control of material' (Dunne 1945: 3). Here, the issue relates to credit, but this time in the context of a long struggle conducted by writers to gain greater creative recognition of and control over their work, part of what Dunne calls 'the screen writer's problem of recognition and prestige' (1980: 42). Absence of control can equate to lack of authority or clout, and numerous accounts exist of the way the writer is at the bottom of the pecking order in the studio (see, for example, Goldman 1984: xii; Froug 1972: xi). The emergence of the hyphenate, the writer-director or writer-producer, is significant here (see Froug 1972: xvi–xvii). As Richard Fine notes: 'writers did not suffer the indignities of Hollywood ... without protest' (1993: 141). They attempted to assume control in a variety of ways over the scripting and production process: 'Writers employed three principal strategies or gambits to increase their control: insisting on solo assignments; affiliating with an important director or producer; and becoming producers or directors themselves' (ibid.).

Concern over credit and creative control are intertwined. They emerge for instance in this account of 'assembly-line writing' in the 1930s:

A producer would often have a script written and rewritten by different writers, or have several writers working on the same script – each without the knowledge of the others – and he would choose the one he liked best for filming. Writers worked in the worst offices at the studio and under time-clock conditions ... Finally the producer made his choice from the half-dozen final scripts in front of him. With screenwriters often working in pairs, as many as ten could be in the battle for credits once the script was off to production ... There was often much confusion as to who did what – a greedy director could step in and claim part or all of the writing credit, and who could argue? (Brady 1981: 12–15)

This industrial context helped define credit and creative control as issues for screenwriters. The Screen Writers' Guild, especially through the 1930s and 1940s, played a key role in placing these issues on the table and keeping them there (see Dunne 1945). The auteur theory tends to be written into this history as a form of theft, a way of stealing the writer's hard-won credit away (see Corliss 1974: xxvii). Is this, however, the only interpretation possible? A significant aspect of this reaction to the auteur theory is the way it has become built upon discourses of disenfranchisement. In his study of 1930s writers, Fine relates how the discourse can serve as legend: 'In the studio system, the legend relates, writers were bound like indentured servants ... The writers themselves often fostered this impression' (1993: 91). But Fine goes on to note that working conditions were not always so rigid. Views such as this suggest a need to move beyond the sense of insult and grievance that defined, and still defines, the situation for many screenwriters.

A Different Lens on Auteur Theory: the Separation of Conception and Execution

So what does a different perspective on auteur theory look like? I want to suggest that the separation of conception and execution forms a useful lens here. In a system where there is no separation, conception can change in the doing of the thing; the exact plan or shape of the project is not foreclosed. Where a separation exists, however, conception is fixed in a process of design, and execution becomes the implementation of that design. There is, in other words, no writing in the 'shooting'; one can only 'shoot as written'. The separation rules out the notion of the 'writing' of movies outlined by Adrian Martin: a writing 'in colour, movement and sound, using the materials before the camera of light, environment, and (above all) the physical presence of actors' (2000: 94).

A key reference point in any discussion of the separation of conception and execution within the industrial context of Hollywood is the work of Janet Staiger. In her analysis of the Hollywood mode of film practice, Staiger illustrates how the Hollywood mode has developed through various systems of film production and management (which were discussed in chapter two). In its earliest years, film manufacture was orientated either around the cameraperson or the director. In the first method of production, generally applied to documentary subjects and news events, 'the cameraman conceived and executed the filming of a sequence of actions. Advance planning was minimal, and a script as such was seldom – if ever – written down' (1985: 174). In the second method of production, orientated around the director and cameraperson, filmmaking 'approximated theatrical production with the exception of the cameraman's insertion into the division of labour. Scripts, if written, were bare outlines of the action' (1985: 175). Various factors combined to make these approaches inefficient in the eyes of industry. First was the practice of shooting out of sequence, or continuity, in order to shoot all scenes set in the one location on the same day. This practice usually required a prepared script, and it was disadvantageous not to have a guide to 'efficient shooting order' (ibid.). A second factor was a change in expectations of quality, including photographic excellence, narrative continuity and coherence, and continuous action involving pertinent events linked 'linked causally through time and space' (ibid.). A third factor was the fixing of films at a standard length of one reel for convenient distribution and handling by the exchange system. 'Without a script, it became difficult to provide a narrative with the requisite beginning, middle and end' (ibid.). The first two factors, in the context of the third, placed pressure on the mode of production to reform its pre-production activities in order to achieve quality and efficiency in a restricted duration of product. As Staiger notes: 'the solution was to pay more attention to preparing a script which provided narrative continuity prior to actual shooting' (1985: 176). This allowed for estimation of footage and pre-checking of scenes by rehearsal.

A new set of pressures in the period 1908–1917 led to more attention on the script. Expectations around continuity, verisimilitude, narrative dominance and clarity all increased, thanks in large part to the effort of trade papers and reviewers. At the same time, movement towards the multiple-reel 'feature' film meant that achieving quality in a project of more than one-reel length required even more planning. This set the stage for the appearance of the detailed shooting script, or continuity script, which according to Staiger was standard practice by 1914. The continuity script was perfectly in tune with corporate structures and scientific ideals of the day.

The detailed continuity script was a dossier of documents, cover page, titles, costings, location plot, synopsis and then shot-by-shot description. 'These continuities provided a scene-by-scene description of the proposed film: camera angles and distances, action, dialogue, and additional information for production crews' (Staiger 1985: 173). The emergence of the continuity script prised apart activities of conception and execution in the process of filmmaking in order to deliver greater control to management; it allows control over uniformity and enables efficiency measures. The practice of referring to the script as a 'blueprint' contributed to this state of affairs, as the metaphor strongly suggests a separation of planning and construction governed in a centralised way according to principles of scientific management. As Staiger highlights, the continuity script is related to the written form of stage plays but 'their relationship to the finished film was much different from that of the drama script to a theatrical performance. The continuity was a precise blueprint of the film for all workers' (1985: 173). A blueprint facilitates the interchangeability of parts, organisation of standardised production operations, and efficiency of assembly (see Staiger 1983: 38). 'The continuity script, as a blueprint for production, and a structure of divided labour controlled this standardised mass-production system' (Staiger 1983: 34). Staiger describes a new distribution of tasks that resulted thus:

> The story department soon took over the director's authority for much of the story selection, writing and rewriting. In 1913 and 1914, the shift began seriously to reduce the director's input in those areas. Lawrence McClosky, a scenario editor

for Lubin in 1913, said that 'now the director does not see the scenario, until it is handed to him for production, complete in every detail … Under our system a script goes to a director in perfect form.' … McClosky emphasised that a director could argue about and have the script's material changed before it went into production and that the director still had power to shape the project. He called the purpose of the procedure 'to pave the way for the director'. (1985: 191)

Wright supports Staiger when he writes in 1914 that 'It is now the rule in most of the well-regulated editorial offices to present a complete "working script" to the director for whom it is intended, and he is supposed to produce the script practically as written for him … Since [the early days when the director was the Czar of the studios] the director's powers have been considerably curtailed' (1914: 14–15). This is a significant development away from an arrangement in which the scenario editor simply sorts through ideas for the director (see Staiger 1983: 40) – of course, not all companies worked in this way and there were variations (see Staiger 1983: 36; 1985: 177).[66]

Lest it be assumed that the writers had free reign in this period, concurrent with this development was a division of labour in the story department. Staiger cites a range of divisions and sub-divisions in writing responsibility: 'A separate set of technical experts began rewriting all the stories. Although the companies might hire famous writers to compose original screenplays, their material was turned over to these technicians who put it into continuity format' (1985: 190). Staiger characterises these roles circa 1914 in terms of a 'tame' or 'caged' writer, kept on staff, dealing with original plots, and a continuity writer who would rework them: 'The two functions might be combined into a single individual but more often were split among several employees' (1983: 35). On top of this, title and subtitle specialists were common. Caged authors held no rights in their work, thus 'the caged writer gave up hopes of any surplus-value from the work in exchange for a secure income. Furthermore, the employees could also lose any further profits if the story were sold to another firm' (Staiger 1983: 42).

Informing these changes to filmmaking were changes to management practices organised around principles of the division of labour and scientific management. Whereas accounts of early filmmaking often demonstrate a great deal of sharing of tasks and a flexible division of labour (see Staiger 1979: 21), increasingly various functions are bracketed out and treated as particular tasks. For Thomas Ince, these were writing, directing (when he ceased doing that work himself) and finally cutting. In this system of management, the segmentation of tasks restricts workers to a particular part of the production process. The initial segmentation resulted in what Staiger calls a two-stage labour process: 'the work's preparation on paper by management followed by its execution by the workers' (Staiger 1979: 21). At the same time, workers became associated with their function: lighting, camera, directing and so on. For Staiger, the effects of division of labour and scientific management 'were multiple – all leading to the separation of the planning phase and the execution phase' (1979: 18). The role played by the continuity script in these developments should not be underestimated, but nor should the industrial forces at work. As Staiger notes: 'the continuity script works because it is an external manifestation of a more fundamental structure inextricable from modern corporate business – the separation of the conception and production phases of work and the pyramid of divided labour' (1979: 23).

The separation of conception and execution affected all film workers, and increasingly so as the studios' commitment to centralised management increased during the period 1914–1931 (see Bordwell *et al*. 1985: 134). However, different film workers or craft-groups can respond to it in divergent ways, and this is the case for screenwriters and directors. What is required in this context is an understanding of the differences between approaches, one that takes into account the situatedness of these perspectives in the broader problematic of the separation of conception and execution. What follows is an initial attempt at such an understanding, focusing on statements by Dudley Nichols and François Truffaut.

A Shared Problematic

For some screenwriters, the process of 'handing over' the script to the director is associated with anxiety. For Dunne this is a trauma akin to the father of the bride handing his darling daughter to a perfect stranger (1980: 68). The anxiety has to do precisely with the issue of loss of control and concerns about the integrity of the project and creative effort. Film-lore has it that auteur directors often had little to do with editing in the studio (an illustration of the separation of conception and execution in action), and sealed the integrity of their projects by limiting the number of takes supplied to the editor. Also interested in integrity Robert McKee advises screenwriters to resist picking their story before it is 'ripe' in order to stave off changes on the set (1997: 7).[67]

The anxiety of the handover is intrinsically tied in with the separation of conception and execution. This can be felt in the space where screenwriters hand over a screenplay for elaboration into a shooting script. Addressing issues of how much information to give in a screen-play, Lewis Herman suggests:

> There is nothing to prevent the screen-play writer from 'directing and cutting in the script'. To yield more and more to producing only the bare bones of a picture, with a master-scene screen-play, is tantamount, for the screen-play writer, to relinquishing his inalienable esthetic rights. If he is to fulfil all the potentialities of his creativity, he must add the sinews and flesh and surface patinas, so that the finished product is his as he originally created it. (1952: 193)

Here, Herman is reacting to a conception of the screen-play that would freeze it at master-scene stage; alienation here is tied to creating a scheme, the 'bare bones'. He is also reacting against 'the destructive influence of "too many cooks"' (ibid.). In some respects Herman's position builds on earlier ideas of writing 'complete' screen-plays and integrated works. His affirmation of the role of the individual writer, and thinking about the master-scene screen-play, also anticipates some of the debates around the 'spec' script.

The theoretical work of screenwriter Dudley Nichols forms a useful link between the screenwriter's struggle for creative recognition and control, and the separation of conception and execution. In his 1943 essay, 'The Writer and the Film', Nichols attempts to redefine the role of writer in the face of the specialisation of the studio. He seeks to change our understanding of the filmmaking process so as to make room for a conception of film not simply as an assembly-line product but as an art form. In confirmation of Staiger's work, Nichols' main concern is the subdivision of arts and crafts into 'specialised functions': 'writing, directing, photography, scenic designing, optical printing and camera effects, cutting and assembly of film, composing music, recording, mixing and re-recording, the making of *dissolves* and *fades* and other transitions ... an immense field of works which require the closest and most harmonious collaboration to produce excellent results' (1943: xxxi; emphasis in original).

In this context, Nichols sees this subdivision as 'detrimental to film as an art form and an obstacle to the development of artists who work in film' (ibid.). His objective is to reintroduce a sense of 'integrated creation' back into the factory system. The lack of integration 'tends to destroy that individuality of style which is the mark of any superior work of art. Individual feeling gets lost in the complicated process and standardised products of the assembly line' (ibid.). For Nichols, this sense of integrated creation is tied up with the screenplay form as a vehicle for introducing criteria of literary and intellectual value into the factory system. His argument does not deny that filmmakers are compelled to specialise because of the scale of the work; rather he reframes this specialisation as a collaboration built around the screenplay, which are 'not complete works in themselves, they are blueprints of projected films' (1943: xxxv). The main path towards recognition for the writer becomes in Nichols' work the composition of original material specifically created for the screen: 'The serious film-writer cannot resign himself to Hollywood's barriers against original work designed for the screen' (1943: xxxviii). Dunne gives us a glimpse into the politics surrounding the original screenplay when he suggests that 'if the Hollywood producers were limited to original screenplays, the screen writer, by controlling the source of material, would undoubtedly have won by now a far greater degree of recognition and respect than he has' (1945: 5).

It would seem that this focus on the screenplay would sit at odds with the auteur theory. However, the two approaches are not unrelated on the level of the separation of conception and execution. In his well-known 1954 article, 'A Certain Tendency in the French Cinema', Truffaut's interest in the cinema as a medium of expression different to theatre and literature leads him to criticise the then-dominant notion of adaptation: a theory based on fidelity between film and novel. Truffaut (who incidentally was not averse to using novels as the source for his films) opposes the idea that film and the novel are equivalents for one another. As such, he contests the links between a French 'Tradition of Quality' and French Literature: 'A film is no longer made in France that the authors do not believe they are remaking *Madame Bovary*' (1976: 232). This is one of his strategies; the other is to defend cinema as a means of expression. Here, Truffaut is building on critical work previously done by Alexandre Astruc when he affirms the idea of cinema as a 'means of expression' that allows the writing and translation of thoughts (Astruc 1968: 17). Truffaut's article works against a backdrop of prior debate and discussion; as David Bordwell notes: 'for several decades French critics had argued about authorship in the cinema; during the 1930s the film's auteur was often assumed to be the scriptwriter' (1997: 76). In his article Truffaut opposes the idea that the film is complete once the scenario is written. This idea reduces the director to a mere *'metteur en scène'*.[68] '*Scenarists' films* ... When they hand in their scenario, the film is done; the *metteur en scène*, in their eyes, is the gentleman who adds the pictures to it' (1976: 233; emphasis in original). In the approach Truffaut criticises, 'execution' (the work of directing, shooting, editing) is reduced to a mere 'illustration' of the script. Evident in Truffaut's criticism is a struggle against the separation of conception and execution similar to that endured by writers in their quest for writing original material for the film. The response in this case, however, is different. It is to celebrate those figures – auteurs – who overcome the separation of conception and execution. Refusing the position of *metteur en scène*, the auteur defines a dynamic relation to *mise-en-scène* – one that is not necessarily specific to the director or denied to the writer.[69] Today, critics argue over the terms of this relation. However, what should not be forgotten is that the rejection of the *metteur en scène* – one common in later auteur writing (see Buscombe 1973: 171) – is a move against the separation of conception and execution defined by the notion that when the scenario is written, 'the film is done'. This does not mean that auteur theory is totally unmarked by the separation of conception and execution, and Martin notes a link between the concept of *mise-en-scène* and 'an inordinate emphasis on the moment of shooting' (1992: 96). This fetishisation can be read as a reaction to the placement of shooting in a category of mere 'execution'. This reactivity plays a role in the denigration of what Martin describes as 'practices of filmmaking centred more on the script, the direction of actors, and less showy forms of staging' (ibid.).

Looking at Nichols' and Truffaut's work together it is apparent that both screenwriters and auteur theorists have directed their energies towards undermining or overcoming the separation of conception and execution. When Peter Decherney highlights the celebration of the screenwriter as auteur at Columbia University in the mid-teens to 1920s, and 'the possibility that the screenwriter would prevail as the dominant film artist' (2005: 44–5), he is picking up on a particular interest in authorship. But his work also highlights, I would argue, how the problem of separation of conception and execution was being experienced in screenwriting discourse, leading to an interest in auteur theory specific to US conditions. Columbia theorists and teachers such as Victor Oscar Freeburg and Frances Taylor Patterson can be seen as precursors to Truffaut and Astruc to the extent that they were interested in a finished creation 'stamped indelibly with the personality of the maker' (Patterson 1923: 4), but they were also precursors to Nichols in articulating the need for a 'controlling mind' in a context that made this idea difficult. A key article by Patterson begins with concern over the notion of 'industry', and the problems with '"canned" entertainment made on the cooperative plan' (ibid.). As Patterson writes: 'the only imprint that the finished creation bears is the imprint of the machine' (ibid.).

Nichols' work shares three main characteristics with the auteurist tradition. Firstly, like Astruc, another key writer, Nichols seeks to liberate film as a form of expression. For Astruc, 'cinema is becoming a means of expression' (1968: 17). Nichols worries about the way 'individual feeling gets lost in the complicated process and standardised products that come off the assembly line' (1943: xxxi). He suggests that 'the filmwriter must be a filmmaker at heart, and a filmmaker thinks and lives and works in film' (1943: xxxii). In this mode, both figures draw on the idea of film as a kind of writing: Astruc in the form of the metaphor of the *caméra-stylo* or 'camera-pen', and Nichols in the form of the figure of the 'filmwriter' who breaks through the separation of functions in the studio.

A second point of commonality between the *politique des auteurs* and Nichols is the struggle against the practice of bringing adaptations to the screen and the recycling of literary classics. For Truffaut, this is because adaptation became a crutch for an impoverished way of writing for cinema that is overdetermined by the separation of conception and execution. Truffaut admires those 'auteurs who often write their own dialogue and some of them themselves invent the stories they direct' (1976: 233). Nichols acknowledges that 'serious writers in other fields, dramatists and novelists, have given great aid to the development of the cinema' (1943: xxxviii), but insists on the need to write original works designed for the screen as a way of overcoming the division of labour of the studios. Truffaut struggles against 'scenarist's films', and Nichols struggles against the reduction of the filmwriter to mere scenarist, the elaborator of someone else's original material.

Finally, the notion of the signature appears in both Nichols' work and the auteur theory, which is linked to the goal of seeing film as a form of expression. For Andrew Sarris, a key premise of the auteur theory is 'the distinguishable personality of the director as a criterion of value. Over a group of films, a director must exhibit certain recurring characteristics of style, which serve as his signature' (1962: 7). In 'The Writer and the Film', Nichols acknowledges the importance of the personality of the director who combines the contributions of writers and actors (1943: xxxii–xxxiii). In a later essay, 'Writer, Director and Film', he makes the remarkably auteurist state-ment that 'the signature of the great film director is in every frame of his film' (1945: xxii–xxiii). It has become commonplace in the debate over auteurism to see issues of signature in terms of ownership and property. There is, however, another perspective, which has to do with affirming the cinema as an expressive form. Sarris notes that:

> now that the radioactive dust has settled somewhat, it becomes clear that the orig-inal outbursts over 'auteurism' were not concerned so much with auteurs as such, or directors as such, or screenwriters as such, but rather with the proper mode of expression to be used in the discussion of Hollywood movies. (1974: xi–xii)

Indeed, I suggest that this insight has relevance today, and that more attention needs to be paid to the way in which cinema is constructed and framed in debates (as art, as property), as well as the task of seeing cinema as a form of expression.

Sarris, Corliss and the Screenwriter Auteur

My aim is to affirm and reframe the *politique des auteurs* for screenwriters while leaving to one side the issue of director-centred criticism.[70] The question might be asked, is this possible? A key and potentially contentious figure here is Andrew Sarris, who has been heavily identified with the auteur theory and who has also been vocal about screenwriting. Because of this, the piece he writes (by invitation from his former student) as a preface to Richard Corliss's *Talking Pictures: Screenwriters in the American Cinema, 1927–1973*, is worth discussing briefly. In this preface, Sarris makes three main points that I shall highlight here because of their importance to understanding the debate around auteur theory as it relates to screenwriting. Firstly, as someone with a long association with the discourse around auteur theory, Sarris corrects a misperception that critiques of the auteur theory led directly to a revaluing of the screenwriter. He recalls that 'none of the original anti-auteurist diatribes went to bat for the poor, neglected Hollywood screenwriter' (1974: xii). He claims instead that it was a series of serious studies of directors leading to a renewed appreciation of old Hollywood movies, that prompted a response from screenwriters and interest in screenwriting (see also Corliss 1992: 11): 'So let us not forget that it was auteurism and not anti-auteurism that established the very existence of an artistically valid field of study' (Sarris 1974: xii). Here, Sarris resists the tendency to throw the baby out with the bathwater by failing to recognise the important way in which auteur theory contributed to a revaluing of expression.[71]

Sarris's second point has to do with a view commonly promoted in screenwriter critiques of auteur theory, which is that the director is the author of the film. Sarris regards this statement as abstract and meaningless: 'How can anyone say *a priori* that any director is automatically the author of the film for which he is credited as a director? We are then simply making two words do the job of one' (1974: xiii). Sarris sees the conflation of the terms 'auteur', 'director' and 'author' as confusing in regards to a 'separation of functions' important to film; but most significantly the semantic confusion gives the misleading impression that a non-directing author is impossible in auteur theory. Sarris's clarification leaves room for 'nondirectorial auteurs' in the theory.

Thirdly, and continuing on from the second point, Sarris suggests that when it comes to authorship there is a 'no man's land of narrative and dramatic structure. And here I think the balance of power between the director and the screenwriter is too variable for generalisation' (1974: xv). In making this point, like other critics such as Douglas Garrett Winston and F. W. Murnau, Sarris puts directing and writing on a continuum (which is a key aspect of the way the *politique des auteurs* uses the term 'writing'). 'I tend to agree with Joseph L. Mankiewicz that every screenplay is a directed movie and every directed movie a screenplay. That is to say that writing and directing are fundamentally the same function' (ibid.).

This kind of response to the issues raised by auteur theory, where the writer or director are considered more or less equivalents, can raise some difficulties of its own. Some of these difficulties are basic to 'standard' auteur criticism (to do with evidence, the reduction of expression to personality and issues of collaboration) and in this sense are also of interest to any study of screenwriter auteurs. Sarris's preface (along with Corliss's Introduction to *Talking Pictures*) is a primer in some of the issues facing any project focusing on the nondirectorial auteur, and it is worth highlighting a few key difficulties.

A first set of (methodological) difficulties exists around the practicalities of considering the screenwriter as auteur, alongside a number of other possible auteur claims. As Claudia Sternberg notes, while auteur critics concede the importance of contributions by other film workers, they do not always get celebrated in the same way (see 1997: 15). Moving away from the director as main focus can open up debates to do with all of the other significant roles and their input in filmmaking, and a celebration of cinematic expression can quickly turn into craft rivalry. Sarris worked around this problem pragmatically by developing a 'tentative auteurism' focusing on the director as the 'hypothetically dominant figure in the filmmaking process until a pattern of contributions has been established' (1974: xiv). But the underlying problem persists for any screenwriter-focused auteur theory, which has to confront the theoretical and practical problem of how to account for a writer's contribution to film in general and specific films as well.

Another set of issues exists around the qualities and traces that amount to a supposed 'signature'. A fully operational approach focusing on the screenwriter as auteur would hopefully apply norms that can operate across a range of cases and examples – and this is where considering the screenwriter as auteur can represent a significant challenge. Since we have dealt primarily with Dudley Nichols' theoretical writings, it is convenient to use him as an example of how contested this space might be. In a discussion of *Scarlet Street* (Dir. Fritz Lang, Writ. Dudley Nichols, 1945), George Kurman looks at Nichols as a 'screenwriter auteur'. His main focus is on Nichols' adaptation practice and the way that names of characters and places change from the original literary source, which contributes to the structural dynamics between characters in the film, and social conflict. The story is thus 'embellished with a texture created by the screenwriter' (1990: 114). Nichols as a screenwriter (like his collaborator John Ford) is known for his approach of focusing on a small group of people in stressful circumstances. Paul Jensen views Nichols as a curious mix of conservative and intellectual, with a tendency to work in literary and theatrical ways rather than cinematically. In other words, his work falls short of a cinematic ideal because of his interest in theatre and a critical disposition that made him 'more famous than important, more verbose than perceptive' (1970: 61). Corliss deems Nichols a 'spell it out' kind of writer who produced 'rigidly schematised scripts' (1972b: 21–2). Interestingly, some of the characteristics celebrated by Kurman are less than cinematic for Jensen – what counts as 'texture' is thus open to dispute.

This returns us to the issue of intermediality of the script and screenwriting. Is 'texture' a script or film element, or both? Corliss suggests that 'It's possible ... to treat the screenwriter as an auteur who, through detailed script indications of camera placement, cutting and acting styles, virtually "directs" his own films' (1972b: 19). But substantiating this claim requires close analysis of the script and something of an ethnographic account of the filmmaking process and film performance. There is a basic problem here of how to conceptualise or envisage the relationship between the script and the texture of the film. This relationship is complicated by the idea that the best directors are those 'with an unconscious – who, presumably, speak from the soul, and not from the scenario' (Corliss 1974: xx). There are various ways to work through this issue. Corliss draws on a word/action distinction: 'one restraint on the poetic tendencies of a screenwriter-oriented critic, as opposed to those of an auteurist, is that the screenwriter *makes* words and situations occur, while the director *allows* actions to occur' (1974: xx; emphasis in original).

Corliss's own work is illustrative of the problems of putting his suggestion into practice, which leads us to a final set of difficulties to do with the dangers of just reversing the dominant bias. Rather than just shift the focus of attention from the director to the screenwriter, it is important, as Polan suggests, to 'interrogate the very need to look at film production in terms of individuals' (2001) – and I would suggest a more intense focus on screenwriting and production discourse could be useful here.

Corliss's work seeks to revalue the work of screenwriters in the context of auteur theory. It is of interest for the way he does not simply succumb to rivalry and dethrone the director in favour of the screenwriter (despite the fact that Sarris teases Corliss about his revisionist enterprise aimed at enthroning screenwriters). In *The Hollywood Screenwriters*, an edited work that emerged from a special issue of

Film Comment, Corliss resists the drive to set up a new form of auteur theory around the screenwriter by affirming what he calls a collaborator theory. In the process, he goes further than most critics in developing a framework for appreciating the work of screenwriters in terms of theme, tone and composition. Corliss's *Talking Pictures* continues this work, looking at screenwriting in terms of 'dominant theme or style or plot or mood – some strong personal trait of film authorship. After all, film is ... essentially a dramatic medium; and the screenwriters are the medium's dramatists' (1974: xxiii) – although part of the controversy over auteur theory has to do with the kind of drama and notion of style being discussed. The book is presented as a critical survey of Hollywood screenwriters emerging in response to Sarris's asser- tion that the director is the author of the film (1974: xvii). This work forms a more sustained attempt to build on the undeveloped potential of the auteur theory, avoid its critical traps, as well as the 'systematic slighting of the screenwriter' (1974: xxi). For Corliss, auteur theory is essentially a form of theme criticism, which is why he grants the writer greater attention. But Corliss also writes to rescue something important about auteur theory and its promise to focus on visual style, and in doing so he seeks a more complex account of film authorship (and collaboration). The structure of the book reflects this. Focusing on the careers of 36 writers, Corliss categorises them as 'author-auteurs', 'stylists' and writers working primarily with social comment and 'isms', for whom the 'message was the medium' (1974: 215) – note that auteur relates to only one category. Corliss's aim is to resist the tradi- tional neglect of screenwriting, and show, despite declarations of impotence, how vital the contribution of the screenwriter can be. But this is one step in a broader synthesis, focused around the idea of the 'multiple auteur', a re-synthesis of the filmmaking functions which (whether through studio politics or craft debates) have found themselves pitted against one another: 'Once the contributions of all these crafts – individually and collectively – have been accepted and examined, studies of other vital film collaborators could begin and be meshed into a giant matrix of coordinated talents' (1974: xxviii).

Creation and Interpretation

If there is a lesson to be drawn from reading Sarris and Corliss on screenwriting and the auteur theory, it is that when it comes to auteur theory it is important to grapple with the nature of the process and of writing/scripting. On the surface, this fits with a screenwriting perspective that 'the single most important ingredient of any picture is the writing of it' (Dunne 1980: 42). Beyond this, however, stands the question of how to define writing and decide who does it. Dunne, for example, distances himself from the view put forward by 'those critics and editors of avant-garde publications' who seduce film students into thinking that 'movies are written in the camera rather than on paper and that the director is the sole author' (1980: 46). At the same time,

Dunne notes that 'the modern director usually has a hand in all phases of the production' (1980: 42).

Nichols' work is interesting to return to today because of the refusal to engage with siege mentality around the aspirations of the writer or the director. With his eye on the impediments of the factory system, Nichols suggests that there was only one way forward, to become 'a film-maker first, and a writer or director or whatever-you-will afterwards' (1943: xxxi). Nichols' work displays a savvy quality to do with the separation of conception and execution that is lacking in some contemporary discussions of the role of the writer and their relation with the director and the film.

Here, I want to point to a particular rhetorical position that has a long history, but in recent years has gained a louder voice, which has to do with the notion that writers are creative artists and all other film workers are interpretive artists. Linda Seger and Edward Whetmore remark that 'everyone who follows [the script] will be interpreting – for better or worse – this original blueprint' (1994: 11). Dunne broadens this view out beyond film when he suggests that 'in all the performing arts individual interpretation is important but never as important as the basic material' (1980: 99). Reflecting on his career, he conceded he is 'better suited to the interpretive craft of direction than the creative craft of writing' (1980: 336).

While this conceptual distinction allows writers to burst the auteur bubble by reminding us that the director's style is not created out of thin air (Corliss 1974: xxi), it has problems. For example, adaptation (of an existing literary creation) complicates any clear division between creation and interpretation in the space of screenwriting (see Dunne 1980: 43). The distinction seems to deny the idea of writer as interpreter, which is very important to adaptation. Also, it can block a more nuanced understanding of collaboration in which directors and producers are involved in many phases of production. The analogy of the script as blueprint, and the figuring of the writer as author of the blueprint, only goes so far until one must account for the factory system, and the producer as 'master architect' or 'engineer', or the role of the director as key cog in the wheel. As William C. deMille notes: 'the function of the director will be to interpret, not to create … But interpretation is so important that it may immeasurably add to the value of the finished product' (quoted in Blaisdell 1915: 258).

The creative/interpretive conceptual distinction remains a powerful one that requires unpacking. Several examples are worth highlighting. As early as 1913 Esenwein and Leeds ponder a new detailed 'script of the future [that] will be worked out so carefully that the motive for every action of every character will be plainly set forth' (1913: 145). This script form was seen as relieving the producer of a burden of dealing with insufficient information in a scenario. 'Instead, he would become, as he rightly should be, an interpreter' (ibid.; see also Merwin 1912: 806).[72] This idea is grounded in a view of the script as a means of conveying technical information. This focus continues with increasing emphasis placed on the screenplay as primary development object, such that it is 'interpreted by the blueprint reader' (Sternberg 1997: 231).

A version of the creator/interpreter distinction exists in an article by Sidney Sheldon: 'A good director makes a very important contribution to a picture, but he is not basically a creator. In essence, he is an interpreter bringing to the screen what has been created by the writer' (1951: 31). This idea can also be found in the theatre. John Russell Taylor says that 'in the theatre we tend to make a distinction between the "creative" art of the dramatist and the "executive" or "interpretive" arts of the actor and director ... Does this mean, then, that the writer is the real artist of the cinema, and the rest ... only executants of his design?' (1964: 9).[73] Taylor considers this proposition seriously, but also notes it is not a view that has found favour among screen theorists.[74] In the introduction to his collection of interviews with screenwriters, Froug reinterprets the distinction in the space of screenwriting and against the auteur theory: 'But the history of American films is diametrically opposed to the auteur concept. The director was often brought to the production long after the conceptual work had been done. His job was to interpret the work of the writer, just as the actor's job was to interpret the role, the character, that the writer had conceived' (1972: xiii).

Around the same time, the distinction also appears in Corliss's *Talking Pictures*, which continued his work of revaluing screenwriting in the wake of the auteur theory. There, Corliss makes a distinction between 'the creative artist' and 'the interpretive artist' (1974: xix). When Corliss discusses this distinction it is in a section in which he examines the 'critical traps' into which the auteur theory had fallen. More recent activations of the distinction are less reflective. John Truby, adopting a militant stance, states that the emphasis on collaboration confuses a key issue, which is that 'in every "collaborative" medium, the original writer, the architect or the designer is the author, because this person has created the characters, plot, motifs, visual elements and themes which all others interpret' (1994: 86–7). For Ian David, 'film directors are primarily interpretive artists. If a director didn't write the screenplay, how then could he or she have invented the story, the characters, themes, ideas, and emotional rela-tionships? They didn't. The writer nutted them out' (2000: 36).

Informing David's view here is a mode of thinking articulated since at least the 1950s and the work of Clara Beranger. Arguing that screenwriting is essentially a form of literary expression, a view of the function of writer and director emerges: '[The writer's function] ... is to conceive the general progression of the story in terms of character, action, dialogue while the director's function is to translate it to the screen in terms of photography, sound-recording and acting' (1950: 22). Here, a complex distinction between conception and translation is at play, but when it connects with the separation of conception and execution (as we shall see it does) the image of creation and interpretation that emerges seems rigid and inflexible.

In screenwriting discourse, the creation/interpretation distinction is often shad-owed or haunted by the separation of conception and execution. The notion that writers create and all others interpret contains, in its absolutism, an echo of the separation of conception and execution (albeit reinvented for an age in which intellectual property, creative rights and copyright are key concerns). The writer conceives the script; all others execute it. A linear assembly-line logic is evident here (making the question of rewrites and additional writing by others a sensitive issue). There seems to be only one moment of creation – increasingly linked in modern screenwriting discourse to the screenplay – and all the rest is interpretation. This view is expressed clearly by Raymond Chandler:

> If even a quarter of the highly paid screenwriters in Hollywood could produce a completely integrated and photographable screenplay under their own power ... then the producer would assume his proper function of coordinating and conciliating the various crafts which combine to make a picture; and the director – heaven help his strutting soul – would be reduced to the ignominious task of making pictures as they are conceived and written – and not as the director would try to write them, if only he knew how to write. (1945: 53)

Chandler strongly promotes a 'shoot as written' ethos here, but at the same time, ties it to a view that sees the screenplay as a primary creative object from which all else originates: 'Everything derives from the screenplay, and most of that which derives is an applied skill which, however adept, is artistically not in the same class with the creation of the screenplay' (1945: 50). Chandler's innovation here is a kind of creative classism, distinguishing between true creativity and conception, and putting applied skills in a different category. This is also a kind of creative particularism, wrapping creativity around the figure of the screenwriter.

Contrast this view with Nichols' statement that 'a motion picture undergoes a series of creations' (1943: xxxii). Nichols does not deny that the motion picture exists as a conception in the mind of the screenwriter; but what he does resist is a radical separation of conception and execution that reduces the contribution of other film workers to an illustration (to use Truffaut's term),[75] or technical elaboration. Another contrasting case can be found in the writing of William C. deMille, who was well aware of the history of conflict between writers and directors, and also had a strong theatrical and writing background before turning to film directing:

> It is simple enough to say that the writer's function is to conceive, the director's to realise. That is, no doubt, true as far as it goes; but properly to realise a motion-picture manuscript, no matter how well written, the director, too, must conceive in terms of light, sound, motion, and above all, in terms of dramatic values wrought by technical craft ... [The writer and director] are both creating the picture, and I, for one, cannot lay down an exact line of demarcation, or find the spot where the writer ends and the director begins. (1939: 158)

DeMille is an advocate of close collaboration and, as such, he resists a creative particularism that sees conception as exclusive to the screenplay writer.

None of this is to suggest that the visualisation and creative work that the screenwriter does is not important, but rather to question critically the way this work is cast in terms of the separation of conception and execution, or a derivative distinction between creation and interpretation. A final contrast with Chandler's position can be found in Sarris, where he attempts a renegotiation of writing and directing, and the conventional battle lines: 'As a screenplay is less than a blueprint and more than a libretto, so is directing less than creating and more than conducting' (1974: xv). Sarris can be read as defusing the opposition of creation and interpretation when he suggests that 'most movies can be best understood in terms of an aesthetic tending toward the adhesive rather than toward the abstract. In the cinema … players adhere forever to characters, images to words … That I believe in a dramatist's theater at the same time as I believe in a director's cinema is thus, at least in my own mind, not so much an inconsistency as an insight' (ibid.).

The rhetoric associated with the distinction between creation and interpretation leads to the unhelpful distancing of the two, as though conception occurs in a cultural and experiential vacuum. But it can also have adverse effects on how we think about interpretation. 'Interpretation' in this context sometimes gets reduced to a question of fidelity, and of tampering with the work (see Shand & Wellington 1988: 14). Dunne suggests that 'Directing is only interpretation' (in Daniell 1986: 167), but what does the 'only' signify here? The separation of conception and execution can delimit the meaning of 'interpretation' to an extreme point. But interpretation in this context should never simply be treated as 'decoding': it is an act of invention, creation, translation and transfiguration (usually across different media) in its own right. Patterson explores this space in her account of the director as interpreter: she or he is potential audience, furnishes contact between all film workers on the project and anticipates their passions, kindles the spirits of actors and is an interpreter of moods (1928: 113–14).

Of course, it can be questioned whether the notion of interpretation accurately describes what happens in production. 'Interpretation' suggests a deep understanding and a total picture. It implies knowledge of a pre-existent totality – which in the case of film production is rarely available. Production is often portrayed as 'realising' this pre-formed understanding or scheme. There is no doubt that filmmakers work with interpretations; however, they are often suffered under, or worried through, as much as imposed on the material from the outset. The shifting materiality of a project problematises any idea of a single act of interpretation.

The blueprint notion of the script, by fixing 'the idea' into an originary scheme, tends to view production as an act of realisation, closely related to the process of assembly. In contrast to this view I suggest that realisation is not the only way in which to conceptualise production. 'Accretion', that is, a process of gathering, evaluating and piecing together elements, materials, emotions and desires, as a way of giving expression to the world of the story, is another. On this scenario, production occurs through a careful process of crystallisation that involves negotiating uncertainty and ambiguity, and building consensus between collaborators about the shape, character and resonance of the project.

Approaching interpretation merely as a form of execution severely diminishes what is at stake in interpretation, its inventiveness, which in the context of film involves translating and transposing ideas from one medium to another (from word to body, action to sound and image). Reintroducing the separation of conception and execution ultimately restricts the way in which it is possible to think of a film idea, or an idea in film. In making this argument, I am not suggesting that screenwriters should not seek to secure appropriate powers in the creative process. My point is that writers should be wary of the ways in which they do this, and the discourses they draw on: as drawing on the separation of conception and execution can diminish the status and meaning of cinema for everyone, and restricts the terms upon which collaboration can occur. By relying on the notion that the writer creates, and all others interpret, screenwriters take their polemic into a dangerous territory that potentially undermines their own speaking position.

7.

THE FILM SCRIPT
AS BLUEPRINT

In previous chapters I have discussed the idea of the film script as blueprint, noting its function as a management tool, and also issues around reading the script. The idea of the blueprint has a key place in screenwriting discourse. On the one hand the blueprint idea allows screenwriters to gain authority and control in the filmmaking process (they are the authors of the blueprint); on the other this can misrepresent the work of reading and writing involved and lead to a particularist discourse around the script, in which the writer has a unique relationship to the blueprint to the exclusion of others.

The idea of the film script as a 'blueprint' is common in books on filmmaking, and is often used by screenwriters: 'The writer begins with the blank page and must create the story, imagine the characters, and start the long visualisation process that will eventually yield a motion picture. Everyone who follows will be interpreting – for better or for worse – this original blueprint' (Seger & Whetmore 1994: 11). Frances Marion suggests that 'to the director, it [the continuity] is what the blueprint is to the architect; it is the plan from which he builds the picture' (1938a: 219). Philip Dunne takes the idea further: 'The true analogy of script to picture is that of architect's blueprint to finished house. Without the first, the second could not exist' (1980: 43). He elaborates: 'The architect is more important than the contractor' (in Daniell 1986: 166). The 'blueprint' supposedly serves as a plan for the entire production process and for all film workers. However, the writer is very often the special addressee of writing about the blueprint: 'Your screenplay is the intermediary between you and the finished motion picture. Initially it is the means by which you excite and involve producers, directors and actors, and then it becomes a blueprint for each of its production phases' (Mehring 1990: 231).

While the blueprint evokes images of a master architect (often the screenwriter) it also conjures up images of teams of people, engaged in the process of construction, poring over a single set of diagrams and schematics that determine the production. Dudley Nichols alludes to this joint effort when he writes: 'a scenario is the blueprint of a film rather than a written work ... A director comes in like a contractor, takes the blueprints, adds ideas of his own and creates the final job [assisted by the effort of many people]' (1982: 405). At the same time, the notion of the blueprint suggests a fixed master plan. For Janet Staiger (1985) this is the continuity script. But screen-writing discourse uses the idea in much more fluid ways. Lewis Herman, for example, suggests that the treatment, an earlier format in the film development process, is 'a blueprint for the screen play' (1952: 171).

Formulated in a period of centralised 'scientific management' in the studios, the blueprint idea of the script continues to have a key place in narratives about creative control and the organisation of work and materials. It is interesting to consider the discursive conditions necessary for this idea. In one sense, it relies on a conception of the playscript fully describing the drama. James Slevin touches on this idea when he discusses the importance of a 'clear outline ... as necessary to you as a set of plans is to an architect about to put up an important building' (1912: 35). Slevin explains that what he means by outline is derived from the scenario form found in 'regular or legitimate drama':

> In fact, years ago the playwright of the Italian commedia dell'arte depended entirely on such a brief scenario or outline of scenes, leaving it to the actors to fill in the dialogue and action ... This scenario or brief scheme of the coming on and going off of the actors, was used in this way. It was hung up conveniently in the wings where the actors referred to it from time to time to refresh their memories, and then made their entrances accordingly. When on the stage, they talked till they had finished their particular bit or run out of breath, then the next actor or group of actors came on to relieve them... (1912: 36)

For Slevin, the 'more or less complete play' detailing dialogue and action supplanted this form in the theatre. The loose, improvised form of construction was marginalised but curiously found itself drawn on in early picture-play making. He notes, however, 'this order of things must soon give way to the complete and properly constructed picture-play, with detail of dialogue and action as it has in the legitimate theatre' (1912: 37, see also 41–2). The idea of a detailed construction plan for the drama as a whole is an important idea behind the blueprint.

For Staiger the blueprint idea first emerged in a vertically-integrated studio environment in which work was initially centralised around the main producer – a period extending between 1914 and 1931 – and all production departments were subject to a detailed division of labour (see Bordwell *et al*. 1985: 134–5, 322). Throughout the 1930s and 1940s, this system was consolidated. The central producer system was notorious for the lack of incentives given to the writing of 'original screenplays'. Studios preferred to maintain a system in which writers, or teams of writers, had little say in the material they were working on, leaving them vulnerable to directors and production executives who would suggest slight changes and then assume partial screen credits for the script (see Brady 1981: 14). The intensity of the issue of moral rights and creative recognition for screenwriters can in part be traced back to this struggle over material, the fight for proper accreditation of work and the idea of the original screenplay as an object of artistic integrity.

The consolidation of this system of management was concurrent with the introduction of the talking picture. An early reference to the script as blueprint in the post-sound era appears in Tamar Lane's *The New Technique of Cinema Writing*: 'The continuity, naturally, is the last manuscript written in the preparation of a story for the screen; it is the word-for-word, action-for-action plans, specifications, and blueprint, so to speak, from which the director must make the production' (1936: 209). Given its publication date and context, it would be fair to assume Lane's book to be exclusively concerned with questions of dialogue; and he is focused on an 'appeal to the *ear* as well as the *eye*' (1936: 3; emphasis in original). Interestingly, however, Lane's reaction to this change also has to do with overcoming what was perceived to be a greater separation of conception and execution. He explains this via a comparison of scripting before and after the introduction of the talking picture:

> If, after a film had been shot, it was found to be slow, faulty or ineffective in any of its scenes or situations, this could generally be remedied by the writing of new titles ... Once a script has now been completed and turned over to the director for shooting, very few alterations can be made in it. The talking picture, as far as juggling or rearranging the continuity or dialogue are concerned, is practically an inflexible institution ... The producer demands that his shooting scripts be as near perfection as possible before shooting begins. (1936: 4–6)

Lane's comments support Staiger's observation that the continuity script was 'used by the production managers and other technical experts as a blueprint to plan sets, costumes, locations and labour force' (1985: 191). Frank Woods anticipates Lane's comments in 1929: 'a spoken picture must be as completely planned, as carefully thought out a piece of work as a stage play ever was. We shall have no choice but to make talking pictures substantially as they are conceived and written by the author' (1977: 96; see also Patterson 1928: 50).

Lane's thinking about the blueprint provides a useful point of contrast with contemporary articulations of the idea; for Lane does not suggest that the screenwriter is the author of the blueprint. This is a significant point, as contemporary usage of the blueprint idea would suggest that the screenwriter, in preparing the screenplay, is creating the blueprint. However, this formulation masks some key issues, namely the vast 'assembly line' as Dunne calls it (1980: 67), over which producers such as Darryl F. Zanuck presided. In Staiger's research the blueprint refers solely to the continuity script and the system that supports it; the screenplay is largely absent from her account of the development of the script as a blueprint for feature films. Indeed, it is in 1943 that we first find the notion that *screenplays* are 'blueprints of projected films' (Nichols 1943: xxxv). This gesture whereby one format of scripting (the screenplay) is used to qualify the meaning of the blueprint idea is fundamental to the craft politics of the day.

While the production system that first saw the emergence of the blueprint idea is no longer dominant, the appropriation of this term by screenwriters continues, working to resituate contemporary discussion into a particular set of craft politics and debates, and strategically redeploy these debates in new situations. But as conditions change there is a danger that analogies and rhetorical devices that work to improve the position of writers in one system or context, can lock them into that system. An entrenched way of thinking about writing can in this way inadvertently become a drawback. There are also limitations to the blueprint/script analogy itself, and some of these will be considered below.

Virtues

Having traced out the emergence of the blueprint idea of the film script, it will be worthwhile at this point to explore the usefulness of this idea, and also some problems associated with it. The blueprint idea of the script is a powerful construct with at least three main 'positive' aspects. Firstly, the idea connects the script to the process of production of which screenplay writing is a part; secondly, it foregrounds the composition or design dimension of cinema; and thirdly, it highlights the industrial scale of much film production.

Turning to the first point, the blueprint idea resists the tendency to view the screenplay as an autonomous work of art by situating or grounding the script into the production context. Francis Ford Coppola says that 'a screenplay, of course, is not a finished work of art; it's only the blueprint for a film' (quoted in Baker & Firestone 1972: 57). Here, Coppola is building on earlier statements such as those by Clara Beranger, for whom the third and close to final version of the script, 'pretty nearly as you see the picture on the screen', is 'only a blue print and is not a picture. My idea is that a stage play, too, is only a blue print. Until it is acted on the stage, it is not a play' (1977: 142). The blueprint here is purposefully regarded as an incomplete entity. And one frequently finds mention of x being 'only a blueprint' in screenwriting discourse (see also Herman 1952: 171),[76] suggesting further work to come. In this formulation, the blueprint can serve as a counterbalance to the idea that the script is an autonomous entity as well as the idea that the screenplay is a new form of literature. There are, it should be mentioned, legitimate motives for approaching the screenplay artistically: it is a highly effective form for evoking images and sounds, for providing the experience of an 'inner movie'. Nevertheless, there is a risk that the broader collaborative, technical and mechanical aspects of visualisation are placed in a position of secondary importance to a highly individualised act of creative, personal imagination.

The second positive aspect of the blueprint idea is that it goes against the visual bias of film theory and highlights the composition or design dimension of cinema. Since the early psychological film theory of Hugo Münsterberg, attention has fallen on the already realised, finished product as an essentially visual phenomenon (see Azlant 1980: 21). Indeed, William Holden's screenwriter character in *Sunset Blvd* (Dir. Billy Wilder, Writ. Charles Bracket, Billy Wilder, D. M. Marshman, Jr, 1950) could be described as responding to exactly this bias when he says: 'audiences don't know that somebody sits down and writes a picture. They think that the actors make it up as they go along.'

By focusing attention on the technicalities and process of realisation of a film, the blueprint idea draws the overidealised end product into a particular material context. The idea assists in recognising the importance of language (and other elements) to the construction of a film. The multi-material nature of the production process can be complex. Furthermore, production can also involve switching between different models for artistic creation (between creative composition, literary authorship and architectural construction, for instance). As John Ford observes:

> You don't compose a film on the set. You put a pre-designed composition on film. It is wrong to liken a director to an author. He is more like an architect, if he is creative. An architect conceives his plans from given premises – the purpose of the building, its size, its terrain. If he is clever, he can do something within these limitations. (Quoted in Jacobs 1970: 5)

The third positive aspect of the blueprint idea is, as the quote from Ford illustrates, that it highlights the industrial scale of a great deal of film production. The blueprint idea is in this context an extension of a common analogy in writing about the Hollywood studio system: namely, the analogy between making a film and building a house. As Dunne notes: 'If the script is the blueprint for a house and the shooting phase the actual construction, the post-production phase can be likened to the painting and furnishing of the structure' (1980: 67). As Bordwell *et al*. note: 'Part by part, brick by brick: the Hollywood cinema often evokes metaphors from architecture and masonry' (1985: 60).

Not all filmmakers work on an enormous scale, nor see their work in these terms. Others see it in more artisanal terms: as 'not so much an art as fine cabinetmaking' (McGilligan 1986: 166). Others again reject spatial analogies in favour of temporal ones. Questions of 'timing', 'tempo', 'rhythm' and 'duration' are particularly difficult to address when thinking about blueprints, which tend to construct time in terms of Gantt charts or completion dates. Examples from music or painting can provide more fluid analogies for the production process. Andrew Sarris upsets any clear analogy with another medium when he leans towards seeing the screenplay more in terms of conducting a libretto than creating a blueprint (1974: xv). If the blueprint analogy sets up a spatial idea of the script, there are temporal analogies (such as those with music) that compete with it, and which contradict some of the presumptions made about building from a blueprint. Although he is fond of the architectural analogy, Dunne also likens a screenplay to a musical composition:

> In some ways, a screenplay resembles a stage play less than it does a musical composition. A composer will build to a fortissimo ensemble, drop swiftly to a quiet interlude with pizzicato strings or woodwinds, and build once more to an even grander exploitation of the full orchestra's sonorities. A good screenplay will do the same: it will build to its grand climax while giving the audience chances to catch its breath, alternating tempi and moods, above all avoiding monotony. (1980: 243)

Earlier, using the same analogy of conductor and composition, he acknowledges the director is not tied to the notes and orchestration of the composer in the way the conductor is (1980: 42).

While the blueprint idea draws the film object into a material process of construction, there are differing views of how to best imagine this process, and the material can be unruly and resist design (see Millard 2006b). This results in disagreements over the limits and accuracy of the analogy, and questions about the appropriate analogy for the process. For Frances Taylor Patterson, 'the continuity is the foundation on which all production rests' (1928: 35). But this suggests many analogies: blueprint, musical score, bubble blower![77] For Alan Rosenthal, the analogy of an architect's plan 'works only to a certain point':

> A script is a guide or first battle plan, the best device for getting the film under way on the basis of the information known at the time of writing. However, in reality it is only a best-guess guide to uncharted territory. It states where you want to go and suggests what seems, initially, the best route ... The script that looked so appealing on paper may not work out when the material is assembled. (2002: 16).

Problems

Despite its positive features, the blueprint idea can lead to some misconceptions, and three will be outlined here. The first has to do with the blueprint as a means of controlling production, the second with the technical nature of a blueprint and the third with the way the blueprint attempts to have the last word on planning.

The blueprint idea can lead to misconceptions about the nature of control over material. A danger here is the suggestion of a fixed, single moment of control over the filmmaking process – leading to the implication that filmmaking is a mere process of assembly. As a result, the blueprint idea can lead to generalisation of a specific mode of production, often tied to notions of the assembly line and indebted to scientific management (Bordwell *et al.* 1985: 134–5). This mode of production reserves a very particular place for conceptual work, which is regarded as taking place exclusively in the planning phases.

Needless to say, even architectural blueprints are subject to revision. As a way of describing the relationship between scripting and production the blueprint idea can obscure the fact that the 'shape' and 'structure' of the material can be negotiated along the entire length of the production process (a process often involving additional writers and revisions). Scripting and rescripting can happen during rehearsal or work-shops, shooting and in post-production. Indeed, one of the virtues of a complex continuity system is that changes can be made to a project as production proceeds (see Miller 1986: 27). This goes against the notion that a script must be 'shot as written' (Mehring 1990: 232), to the extent that what is written is subject to change.

Indeed, there is a danger that overemphasising the blueprint idea can give a false or limited impression of the roles and functions of the script; Rosenthal details five functions of a script: 1: It is an organising and structural tool. 2: It is central to communicating the idea of the film to everyone. 3: It is essential to director and cameraperson in conveying mood and action. 4: It helps the crew answer a range of questions about technical and logistical requirements. 5: The script guides the editor (2002: 15). The benefits of such a breakdown of functions is that it lays bare the roles and uses of the script. Each function can be performed in a variety of ways. The bundling of many of these functions together into the 'blueprint' is unique, but the analogy itself is not always specific in elaborating how each of these functions are fulfilled.

The second problem with the blueprint idea of scripting is that it suggests a technical idea of precision, embodied in a diagram. Contrary to what the blueprint idea might suggest, a script can be less useful when overprecise or overwritten.[78] No actor, director or cinematographer would like to be faced with the task of shooting image upon image described in terms of mathematical x, y, z co-ordinates (although animators and designers often work in these terms). Weather, lenses, geography, decor, time of day, lighting and performance can all disturb an overdetailed, literal description of an image. In this context, then, a different understanding of the script as a poetic object is useful. A script works as a blueprint not because it is technically precise, but because it is poetic. Poetic writing draws on a different idea of precision that can be described as 'crystalline'. By describing images with poetic clarity and intensity a script can enable other film workers to build on this structure and take the process of crystallisation further.

The blueprint idea of scripting, if misapplied, can work inadvertently against writers by marginalising the writerly, textual dimension of the script. Modern screenplays are both poetic *and* technical documents. The line between the two has become difficult to separate, and by focusing on the technical aspect of the blueprint screenwriters risk failing to educate others on the creative skills required in reading and evaluating a script. With so much emphasis placed on the writing of screenplays, perhaps more thought could be given to the practices of reading required by screenplays, especially in light of the pressure to distil screen narratives into simpler forms (the most reduced form arguably being 'the pitch').

The third problem with the blueprint idea when used by writers is that it can lead to an overidentification of the writer with the script. While the politics behind this gesture are understandable, aligning the work of the writer too closely with the creation of the blueprint can minimise the creative input of other key collaborators and factors in the production process. By binding the process of scripting to a particular format, the blueprint idea can also work to marginalise forms of scripting that seek to deviate from a fixed script format, including the more open-ended or research-orientated approach to scripting found in some documentary production.

Notation: Scriptings Beyond the Blueprint

An important part of the historical baggage associated with the blueprint metaphor is the way the script as blueprint is bound up with a separation of conception and execution in the production process. With echoes of this separation Australian screenwriter Jan Sardi states: 'the process is such that everyone works from the script, and it's what is on the page that everyone attempts to realise'. His colleague Mac Gudgeon adds, 'The pages come first, without them the film would simply not exist. I am the originator. How could I not be the author?' (Australian Writers' Guild 1997).

Both of these statements see scripting as a primarily typographically orientated page-based activity. It is a hallmark of this approach to scriptwriting that the discussion of scripting is tied to the page, and an established format for writing: from 'Blank Page to Blueprint', as the saying goes (see Shand & Wellington 1988: vii). When tied to the page in this way the word 'script' functions as a diminutive of 'manuscript', and relates to the written document supporting the production process. However, not all forms of scripting need to be bound to the page or the format in this way. And binding scripting to the page can downplay the significance of negotiated understandings, meanings and resonances between different creative personnel. It is not as if such a practice, a performative scripting beyond the manuscript, is unknown – especially in other areas of arts practice, and areas that focus on improvisation. The relationship between actor and director, and camera, can often best be described in terms of choreo*graphy*. Constantin Stanislavski speaks of the actor creating a 'score' through physical action (1987: 147). Mike Leigh's method of working with actors, discovering the premise of scenes through rehearsal and improvisation, is of interest here (see 1995). These conceptions of scripting are directed towards the lived body, a 'scripting with the body', as much as towards the page. Rather than monumentalise the script as manuscript, they make use of the script as part of a broader series or circuitry of terms: transcription, description and inscription. The page has many uses from scribbling to sketches, which can be introduced at different points of the production process.

One dynamic idea for thinking about scripting beyond the blueprint is that of notation. Notation is at the heart of scripting because on one level scripting is related to the desire to record affects, images and thoughts. As Ingmar Bergman observes: 'I have often wished for a kind of notation which would enable me to put on paper all the shades and tones of my vision, to record distinctly the inner structure of a film' (1972: 8). In some senses the script is a form of notation; but even when this aspect of scripting is foregrounded some filmmakers have found it to be inadequate. As Wong Kar-wai notes: 'you can't write all your images on paper, and there are so many things – the sound, the music, the ambience, and also the actors – when you're writing all these details in the script, the script has no tempo, it's not readable. It's very boring. So I just thought, it's not a good idea [to write out a complete script beforehand], and I just wrote down the scenes, some essential details, and the dialogue' (in Brunette 2005: 126). Considering that notational forms can be open-ended and unreadable, the balance that a screenplay strikes between recording thoughts, communicating detail, and readability, is unique.

Considering scripting from the point of view of notation may seem unusual, but is not unknown. Ian Macdonald defines the screenplay as a 'record of an idea for a screenwork' (2004a: 89). As Jeff Rush and Cynthia Baughman note, for a blueprint to work as a blueprint some notational system is necessary to provide authoritative identification of the work (see 1997: 28–9). If one looks at the script less in terms of an established form, but more in terms of the functions it performs, it becomes evident that notation plays a significant part in scripting. Building on Rosenthal's account of the prime functions of the script we can say: 1: Notation can serve as an organising and structural tool. 2: It can help communicate the idea of the film (as long as the system of notation is understood, such as LS for Long Shot). 3: It can convey information about mood, and annotations or side markings can be important here. 4: It can help the production team to plan, to the extent that codes such as INT or EXT signify changes in location. 5: Notation can help guide the editor, and assist in decisions about tempo or shot length.

Notational systems are linked to an idea of recording and the record. The application of Taylorist principles of industrial organisation, of breaking down the labour
process into component segments and organising production into functions, could
not have been achieved without the record-keeping. As Janet Staiger notes:

> planning the work and estimating costs through a detailed script became a new,
> extensive and early step in the labour process. This improved regularity and speed
> of production, use of materials, and uniformity and quality of the product. The
> script became a blueprint detailing the shot-by-shot breakdown of the film. Thus, it
> could function as a paper record to coordinate the assembly of the product out of
> order, prepared by a large number of people spread at various places throughout
> the world ... and still achieve a clear, verisimilar and continuous representation of
> causal logic, time and space. (Bordwell *et al*. 1985: 135)

With the development of the continuity system, record-keeping retained its important
role. As Pat P. Miller observes in *Script Supervising and Film Continuity* (1986), the
work of the 'Continuity Supervisor' is indispensable in maintaining the accuracy of this
record. Notations are added to the script to carry over data or details about preceding
or subsequent scenes; script lining systems assist in noting action that has been
covered or not (see Ulmer & Sevilla 1986: 103). Miller's description of procedures for
accommodating revisions to the script are noteworthy in this respect:

> Incorporate all the script revisions into your original script – before and during prin-
> cipal photography. Every revised page is dated and put through in a colour different
> from the previous ones ... When you receive revised pages, heed the following
> procedures:
> - Immediately transfer all your notations from the original pages to the revised
> pages.
> - Revise your Continuity synopsis/One Line (if affected) to conform with the new
> version of the script.
> - Correct your scene and page counts to reflect any deletions or additions.
> - Do not discard previous pages after receiving revised pages. File them numeri-
> cally for reference. There is a good reason for this: occasionally, the director will
> want to see, or will even prefer, an earlier version. As the only person who has a
> complete file of every revision, you will be a heroine or a hero. (1986: 27)

Miller takes the view that the role of the Continuity Supervisor is less about maintaining the record than ensuring that the script remains useful from the point of view
of preserving continuity.

While an examination of the record-keeping practices associated with the script
enables an important assessment of the impact of 'scientific management' on the

division of labour in filmmaking, it can have the effect of leaving discussion of the script in the domain of accounting and management. A more detailed account of the links between practices associated with the script, and more general questions of artistic composition, can put the script and the record back into the domain of aesthetics. Bergman's own discussion of filmmaking provides a useful illustration of some of these issues: 'a film for me begins with something very vague ... split second impressions that disappear as quickly as they come, yet leave behind a mood' (1972: 7). What Bergman describes as this 'brightly coloured thread' is the complete film that has yet to fully emerge. Notation becomes a way to draw out a field of imagination, or idea-formation, in which the mood as 'nucleus' achieves a definite form, a pattern. This involves the 'transformation of rhythms, moods, atmosphere, tensions, sequences, tones and scents into words and sentences, into an understandable screenplay' (1972: 8). Yet, aside from the dialogue, he sees this as an 'almost impossible task'. The detail required would make the script unreadable. Given the industrial aspect of filmmaking, Bergman's desire for a form of notation is not unusual. Such a form would help the artist maintain focus in 'the artistically devastating atmosphere of the studio ... full of all the trivial and irritating details that go with motion-picture production' (ibid.).

Questions concerning notation are not exclusive to film, and are in fact more typical of the other arts, especially music. An interesting facet of John Cage's approach, for example, is his willingness to engage with questions of notation, sometimes turning notation itself into an expressive medium. Cage disturbs the way in which notation is usually subservient to the demands of classical expression, and feels the need to play with notational forms. This experimentation is not simply for its own sake, its purpose is to challenge the way notation stands between music, performers and the musician: music becomes a site for what Cage calls the demilitarisation of language (see 1980: 182–4).

Musical analogies have been prominent in the study of film. The metaphor of composition has served as a crucial counterpoint to an emphasis on the script as written speech, which brings with it the constraint of the sentence form. Scripts are often discussed in terms of narrative and dialogue, and notions of musicality and composition have provided a useful counterpoint to this emphasis on language (see Kahan 1950). Linguistic forms are not in themselves inferior, but their reliance on grammar can suppress a range of non-syntactical, contextual, performative or situational elements crucial to aesthetic existence. John Cage expresses his concern when he writes: 'implicit in the use of words (when messages are put across) are training, government, enforcement, and finally the military' (1980: 183).

Film workers may respond at this point and suggest that film is not a live art, it is already highly collaborative and social, it has too much technological intervention, and is more than usually narrative – all of which would limit the significance of Cage's comments to filmmakers. However, on the level of experimenting with composition and notation, Cage's work has its equivalent in filmmaking, albeit not often within the realm of the Classical Hollywood cinema. Grahame Weinbren, for example, describes a model of composition present to differing degrees in the work of six filmmakers:

> a filmmaker construes a particular idea about cinema in such a way that it contains as a logical consequence a set of procedures which, if followed, yield a complete film. The generating idea is to be cinematic, that is, drawn from cinema's ontology or phenomenology, or from a typical process or stage of its production. A concept found in one of these areas is redefined by the filmmaker so that from it can be inferred a principle of organisation, an algorithm for the construction of a work. The generating idea must be simple, a single, unsegmented fact about film. (1979: 40)

Weinbren's emphasis on procedures and principles of organisation seems to go against Cage's emphasis on openness and indeterminacy. Although it should be noted that given the degree of industrial intervention in filmmaking, one of the first phases of an exploration of composition might be to explore the logic of the machine, apparatus or blueprint, thus opening it up to different perspectives.

Independent and experimental filmmakers have at different times been critical of institutionalised forms of scripting and its impact on film practice, and the incorporation of the script into the business plan. An analysis of the dominant practice of scripting, and an evaluation of other kinds of practice, can be found in a special issue of the *Millennium Film Journal* called 'The Script Issue'. In the case of commercial films, 'scripts and storyboards function not only as patterns to work from: they also form an essential part of the ritual of raising funds' (Pipolo & Weinbren 1991: 5). The editorial in this issue notes that this leads to standardisation of the format of the script. Also, 'it is an unhappy fact that these same documents are later used as blueprints for production, since they result in films that tend to be quite dense in dialogue' (ibid.). As Peter Sainsbury notes:

> When getting a movie financed [it] is always a matter of cracking the market before the film is made, and never the other way around, the script becomes by far the most important consideration in the risk business and its value is increasingly measured by quasi-objective criteria. As such, it has to promise a degree of safety. It has to look and feel familiar. It has to cover all the bases in telling a conventionally intelligible story. It has to comply with certain given rules of the writer's craft. And above all, it has to entirely determine the film that is made from it. (2003)

This practice is not uncontested, however. Different ways of working can lead to dynamic forms of notation. 'Filmmakers still need planning materials from which to work, of course, but these plans take shapes and forms that are as various as the films themselves' (Pipolo & Weinbren 1991: 5). Scott MacDonald's anthology *Screen Writings: Scripts and Texts by Independent Filmmakers* (1995a) forms a significant archive of this work, by presenting a variety of critiques 'of the commercial cinema's dependence on conventional melodramatic scenarios and screenplays. Some of these critiques confront the formal construction of industry screenplays and/or their particular relationships to the films that develop from them' (1995b: 10).

The passages from Bergman quoted earlier signal the exasperation of the film-maker in capturing a fleeting reality on celluloid. An initial impression of this quote is that Bergman is yearning for a personal form of notation, one that would not have a wide readership and would not need to be decoded in his absence. Despite the difficulties of writing the script, Bergman seeks a 'definite contact' with his co-workers, and stresses the need for clear 'marching orders'.

In defence of the page-bound and formatted script, it should be noted that these forms support quantification, evaluation and record-keeping in extremely effective ways, as in the notion that one page of reading time equals a minute of screen time (see Mehring 1990: 233). By linking 'reading' to 'visualisation' page-bound forms offer a relatively low-cost means for pre-imaging a project, and offer one way of placing interpretation in the service of the filmmaking process. These benefits of the page-bound script do not, however, necessarily cancel out the significance of alternative forms of scripting, which invite a broader understanding of the 'creative process', and the multiple forms of scripting (with bodies, improvisations, machines, light, storyboards, notes, scribbles, gestures) that can support production. In other words, alternative forms of scripting can provide different ways of thinking about production, especially collaboration, beyond the blueprint.

8.

WRITING FOR THE SCREEN

Screenwriting today is closely linked to a notion of 'writing for the screen'. Not just a neutral description of what writers do, this refers to a practice of visualising the film via the script, and is the product of discourses about craft, film production, narrative and writing at work from the 1910s to the present. This chapter looks at the historical development of this formation of screenwriting, particularly from the 1910s through to the 1940s, which forms an understudied part of screenwriting discourse sitting between the focus on the story film in early cinema and the later focus on the talking picture. Today, the idea of 'writing for the screen' operates as a virtual shorthand for screenwriting itself, but it has not always been that way, and a complex set of conditions and critical effort has shaped this relationship and furthermore helped institutionalise it. In this chapter I tease out some of the relationships and ideas embodied in this conception of writing. I look at important reference points for the development of writing for the screen such as the art of the photoplay and interest in scenario writing in the 1910s, as well as notions of narrative clarity. Following this I look at the development of writing for the screen in early handbooks, and in particular in the work of key figures such as Epes Winthrop Sargent and Frances Taylor Patterson.

Screenwriting, today, has a specific meaning. When Vachel Lindsay invites the reader to enjoy the hieroglyphic nature of the film, the 'silent language of picture writing' (2000: 32), or when avant-garde filmmakers etch celluloid, they are not dealing in the dominant and most widely accepted definition of screenwriting orientated around the screenplay. Today, writing for the screen represents a profession as well as a set of

well-defined 'craft' problems around adapting novels and plays to celluloid, and identifying what is unique to screen writing. Philip Dunne in his biography speaks proudly
of his profession, 'which was writing for the screen' (1980: 124; see also Nichols
1942: 771) and titles a chapter 'Writing for the Screen' which deals with issues of
transferring 'to celluloid the work of a playwright or a novelist' (see 1980: 236–46).
Writing for the screen relates here to the writing of screenplays and issues to do with
the specificity of the cinematic medium.

This is not to suggest that this notion of screenwriting is uncontested. One of
the points of debate over auteur theory, for instance, is the very construction of the
term 'writing', the relationship between the page and the screen and the separation between 'writing' and 'filming'. Adrian Martin insists that movies are 'written' in
colour, movement and sound (2000: 94). Dunne speaks somewhat negatively of his
experience lecturing to students who 'believe that "films" are written inside a camera'
(1980: 238) – as though that is the dominant formation of writing. Yet filmmakers
outside of the mainstream have often struggled with dominant page-based scripting
practices.

Screenwriting is often simply referred to as 'writing for the screen'. However, it is
only over time that screenwriting developed into the concept of writing for the screen
familiar today, a practice constructed around the screenplay form. Writing for the
screen has not always belonged to the writer; notions of film writing have not always
been so tightly wound around the screenplay.

The story of the formulation and institutionalisation of writing for the screen fills
some important historical gaps in the historiography of screenwriting. Reading some
screenwriting literature it would seem that – aside from the institutionalisation of
continuity – nothing happened in the space of writing until the 'arrival' of the story film
and talking pictures. But this would be a misconception, and a great deal of activity
in the 1910s and 1920s sought to elaborate on technical aspects of the craft of
screenwriting.

A strong tendency exists to draw a rigid line between the talking pictures and
the silent film, as though screenwriting did not exist before 1927. Larry Ceplair and
Steven Englund write:

> the Screenwriter came to Hollywood along with 'mike' booms and the Great
> Depression. The advent of the 'talkie' not only capped an evolution in production
> methods and imposed the need for a producer to standardise moviemaking; it also
> created a permanent need for professional writers who could turn out shootable,
> full length scripts with dialogue. (1980: 2)

The tendency to forget or marginalise the role of screen writers prior to the talkie is
commonplace. Writing in 1935 Ernest Pascal dates screen writing from the talking
picture. His view of the job of screen writing in the silent cinema was that 'stories

were bought, but pictures were not written' (1935: 8); and, as evident in the following passage, even the emphasis on the script as 'blueprint' did not lift the status of writing:

> The result was a 'Script' which was then handed over to the director to use as a sort of guide or blueprint for the real 'creation' of the picture. Being God, he really didn't need this guide at all. He paid no attention to the continuity, because camera angles were his special business; he paid no heed to the titles, because new titles would have to be written to suit what he elected to shoot; in fact, he practically abandoned the script altogether, and 'shot as he went' or, as he himself put it more literally, shot it 'off the cuff'! ... Writing, as writing, had little or nothing to do with picture-making other than what occurred or what was left over from the original material ... Then, suddenly, came talking pictures. *All* the producers prophesied that they were but a passing fancy; none of them believed that picture-making had, overnight, undergone a complete metamorphosis ... From that very instant Screen-Writing took on a wholly different aspect. *It became the same as any other kind of writing. It became – in fact – writing.* (Ibid.; emphasis in original)

But should these developments justify the marginalisation of earlier definitions of writing? Reading these accounts, it is hard to conceive of the fact that serious consideration was given to 'writing for the screen' as early as 1912 (Slevin 1912: 15), and that 'Photoplay Writing was born some time or another in 1909' (Sargent 1914: 199).

The Art of the Photoplay

Janet Staiger argues that central to the early development of scripting practices in the Hollywood mode was a conception of the 'quality' product (1985: 180). This manifests itself in terms of audience expectations of continuity of time and space, verisimilitude and narrative clarity – all of which can be improved through greater script preparation by producers. Central to the circulation of this conception of the product, and the shaping of audience expectations, is the workings of an extended network of screen writers/editors/reviewers/journalists who ran 'Question and Answer' or review columns. For Edward Azlant, this network sought to refine moving pictures 'through intelligent uncompromising criticism' (1980: 111; see also Jacobs 1939: 134). Included here are columns by Epes Winthrop Sargent in *Photoplay* and *Moving Picture World*, which formed the basis of his 1912 handbook, *Technique of the Photoplay*;[79] and articles in the *Daily Mirror* by 'The Spectator', a *nom de plume* of Frank Emerson Woods, who was a collaborator of D. W. Griffiths' (see also Stempel 2000: 19–23), and became the first president of the Photoplay Authors League in 1914 (see Azlant 1980: 91). Staiger draws upon this network extensively and observes that sophisticated continuity arises in part out of meeting the narrative expectations set up by these writers (1985: 179–82; see also Bordwell *et al.* 1985: 106–7).

I shall examine the work of some of these critics in more detail below. For the moment I want to focus on how, in the 1910s and 1920s, general film appreciation and critical discussion, including aspects of the discourse about quality product, were intertwined with the notion of the photoplay. Like the term 'feature', it represented an area of expansion for the industry, and the screen writer in particular. William Lord Wright remarks: 'A new and ever-enlarging field has … opened for the dramatist … and all others eager for a literary career' (1914: 7); 'The photoplaywright is now the hope, and the Fortunatus of a mighty industry' (1914: 6). In order to understand this field of possibilities for screenwriters it will be necessary to understand more about the photoplay.

The notion of the photoplay does not have a significant place in contemporary film studies, except perhaps through mentioning key works such as Hugo Münsterberg's *The Film: A Psychological Study: The Silent Photoplay in 1916* (1916), or Victor O. Freeburg's *The Art of Photoplay Making* (1918). Theorists are more content to use the terms 'movies' or 'motion pictures' than the quaint and archaic 'photoplay', which is seen as a transitional or passing term, introduced in the early teens and later followed with calls to replace it with 'film' (see Bush 1915). William Paul has examined how the photoplay represents an alignment of film with traditional theatre (1997: 327); but while this view provides insights on the level of exhibition and inter-media relations, it does not allow us to explore the significance of the photoplay in screenwriting terms.

Terry Ramsaye reports that in 1910, against the background of discontent with the term 'movie', 'the Essanay Company with an eye on advertising opportunity, offered a handsome prize of twenty five dollars for a new name for the motion picture' (1926: 551).[80] The winner was the term 'photoplay', suggested by Edgar Strakosch, an exhibitor from Sacramento, California (see Paul 1997: 323; Slide 1994: 221). As Kenneth Macgowan notes: 'So great was the desire of the movie-makers – and the movie critics – for dignity, that everyone decided to accept the winning word, and to produce, advertise, and discuss the "photoplay"' (1965: 185).

The notion of the photoplay is closely intertwined with the rise of the feature, initially referring to films of greater than one reel, or forming the greater portion of a 1,000ft. split reel. For Staiger the term 'feature' was at first 'a marketing judgment that a film merited special billing and advertising (1985: 185–6), or as a 1904 Kleine catalogue puts it, 'long films' admitting of 'special advertising' (see Pratt 1973: 36). For Jesse L. Lasky, the feature was part of a strategy to 'elevate the industry': 'Features are nightly offerings' drawing on 'the finest class of patrons' (1914: 214). Features saw exhibitors adopting theatrical methods of promotion, and 'compelled recognition from the daily press' (see Higashi 1994: 26). Elaborating on the notion of the feature, Peter Decherney sees 'photoplay' mainly as a term 'used to distinguish a "high class" feature film from a "movie"' (2005: 43). The term held special meaning, assisting in attracting audiences, and differentiating the product to give, as one *Moving Picture World* editorial from 1913 puts it, 'emphasis that the photoplay is not the cheap and nasty thing it [once] was' (quoted in Slide 1994: 222). The slang 'movies' was held not to 'advance the cause of photoplay', the latter seen as more 'dignified'.

Defining the photoplay in great detail is not an easy task because of the varied forces in screen culture that it is attached to. It is linked to forces of uplift surrounding the 'photodrama': 'photoplay writing is a new profession, for the simple reason that the photodrama is a new form of dramatic expression' (Phillips 1914: xxi). For Howard T. Dimick 'photoplay' is a term linked to 'individual ART – related to the drama in structure but unique upon its pictorial side' (1922: 11). It is also a story-film. At the start of their handbook, *Writing the Photoplay*, J. Berg Esenwein and Arthur Leeds address the question, 'What is a photoplay?': *'A photoplay is a story told largely in pantomime by players, whose words are suggested by their actions, assisted by certain descriptive words thrown on the screen, and the whole produced by a moving picture machine'* (1913: 1; emphasis in original). They go on to explain that not all moving-picture subjects are photoplays, citing scenic, educational and topical subjects as examples. If a moving picture programme is like a magazine, the photoplay is like a short story. In these terms, any fictional motion picture qualifies as a photoplay.

The photoplay is bound up with the challenge of holding audience attention for longer than one or two – and eventually up to five – reels of film.[81] 'Most men in the industry were firmly committed to the belief that anything longer than a dozen minutes on the screen would throw such a burden on the mental capacity of audiences that many patrons ... would cease to visit the theatres' (Hampton 1970: 93–4). The idea of a one-reel limit was institutionalised in the distribution regime dictated by the monopolistic Motion Picture Patents Company (MPPC), or more specifically through the General Film Company. Films were billed in a standardised one reel/1,000ft. length (which could be between 700 and 1050ft. and last from 'fifteen to twenty minutes at its slowest speed') or a shorter 500ft. split reel length (see Bowser 1990: 191). As a multiple-reel picture the photoplay is thus linked to efforts to break the restrictive business culture of the MPPC: not just the one-reel distribution standard, but also the short run of films and the principle of 'no publicity and no exploitation of stars' (Woods 1977: 44). Frank Woods speaks of a group of producers such as William Fox, Carl Laemmle and Thomas Ince as engaging in showmanship and theatrical methods. Producers such as Adolph Zukor, Samuel Goldwyn and Jesse L. Lasky, and directors such as Cecil B. DeMille, broke with the established distributors of the day and turned to the idea of the photoplay to give new legitimacy to the motion picture form, to the 'story' and also to differentiate their products from other cheaper products. The photoplay became a unique object around which different ideas of 'quality', and visions for the future of cinema, were expressed – embodied in Zukor's slogan 'Famous Players in Famous Plays'.[82] As Lasky points out in a 1914 profile article, however, not all producers sought to use 'famous plays': 'Eventually we will have stories by authors of recognised standing and written especially for the screen' (in Blaisdell 1914: 35). Here, an early use of the idea of writing for the screen opens up a different conception of authorship, albeit one still circumscribed around the author of 'recognised standing'.

One way of dating the photoplay is from Adolph Zukor's purchasing of the US distribution and exhibition rights for the multiple-reel feature *Les amours de la reine Élisabeth* (Dirs Henri Desfontaines, Louis Mercanton, Writ. Émile Moreau, 1912), also known as *Queen Elizabeth*. The appearance of Sarah Bernhardt in this production convinced other famous players to appear in photoplays. This is not the only marker possible, however, and in 1912 Sargent writes that 'the history of the photoplay dates back less than five years' (1912: 3). This puts the start of the photoplay earlier than Zukor's efforts. Coming into active use in the early 1910s, the notion of the photoplay continued to play a central role in screen culture right up to the late 1920s and beyond. Tamar Lane used the term in his 1936 handbook and, but perhaps in a different manner, it persisted in the title of the monthly fan magazine, *Photoplay*, which ceased production in 1980 (see Slide 1994: 221).

The significance of the photoplay is that it becomes an arena of development for screen writing; and it can often be found at the centre of competing arguments about craft, and specifically writing. On one hand, some critics suggest the photoplay has little to do with the craft of writing, and is simply another object of manufacture that requires 'story' as its raw material; according to this view the photoplay is a somewhat high-minded feature. On the other hand, however, the photoplay is important to the elaboration of the craft of writing for the screen.

The most vigorous proponent of the first view is Benjamin B. Hampton, in *History of the American Film Industry: From its Beginnings to 1931* (first published in 1931 as *A History of the Movies*). Hampton argues that the 'movies' could not be contained within conventional business practices (1970: 170). His is a tale of responsible and prudent managers, investors and companies versus radicals, 'showmen' who understood what the public wanted. By meeting the demands of the consumers, these radicals continually changed the goal posts for the industry in terms of how much could be paid to see a movie, how much an actor could be paid and how far the public was willing to absorb the costs of large-scale, star-orientated filmmaking. For Hampton, the motion picture is a 'revolutionary' form, moulded not by the elite but by the public; from this point of view, the photoplay is an alien idea strongly associated with high culture, literacy, the elites, Europe (see 1970: 103). The 'making of photoplays for the classes instead of the masses' is a development that 'has been wholly different from the course of the American movie' (1970: 63). In Hampton's account the photoplay is an emblem for the sad attempt of theatre actors, dramatists and intellectuals to keep themselves in a game that they do not understand. The reality as Hampton saw it was that writers, whose 'craft had not yet acquired standing in the studios ... were regarded as hacks whose business it was to shape and distort feeble stories to fit the limitations of stars' (1970: 193).

In contrast to this argument, however, there is another that regards the photoplay as intrinsic to the elaboration of the craft of writing for the screen, which is exemplified in Lewis Jacobs' *The Rise of the American Film: A Critical History* (first published in 1939). While Hampton takes the view that even around 1915–1917 the writer's craft had not yet acquired standing in the studios, Jacobs sees the same period as one in which efforts 'were focused on the task of raising the standards of moviecraft: every element of movie making was improved and new elements were added. Direction, photography, acting, writing, and criticism, no longer professions of low reputation, were now rationally adapted to the possibilities of the medium' (1939: 120). For Jacobs, the fact that the movies could be designated a medium represents a qualitative shift from mere pictures.

Against Hampton's criticism that intellectuals were hopelessly tied to an older dramaturgy associated with the stage, Jacobs gives credit to a range of works, by Sargent and others, examining the specificities of the new medium and responding to it: 'Thus by 1914 screen writing was established as a distinct and individual craft, a branch of literature and drama' (1939: 131). Ramsaye offers some support to Jacobs' argument here: 'The mere ability to crank a camera and develop films was no longer sufficient. Now the motion picture had to reach out for players and stories and directors. A whole creative craftsmanship had to be evolved' (1926: 440). *Contra* Hampton, Jacobs seems to suggest that the notion of the photoplay was not so 'European' and had roots in the screen culture of the US.[83] Furthermore, the development of the photoplay is intertwined strongly with the craft of writing. As Bannister Merwin notes in a piece entitled the 'Future of the Photoplay', 'the real future of the business absolutely depends upon the development of the art of writing photoplays. Without this art the business, as a provider of entertainment for the people, will vanish into shadow' (1912: 805).

This affirmation of the photoplay points to the way the term can be utilised to raise the profile of screen writing. While there is a strong tendency in the literature to engage with the photoplay as the procession of photographic images that constitute a film (see Ball 1917: 5; Freeburg 1918), the term also carries with it expectations to do with the nature of scripting. It is significant that, as Azlant points out, 'photoplay' can denote both the 'written script' and the 'completed fictional narrative film', and draws on a strong theatrical tradition (1980: 212).[84] These two senses of the term echo throughout many accounts of the craft, such as when John Emerson and Anita Loos define the continuity as 'the technical form of the photoplay' (1920: 15). While Emerson and Loos usually refer to the photoplay in terms of viewing, and the script as 'the typewritten copy of the photoplay' (1920: 19), a construct like 'photoplaywriting' draws the photoplay into a page existence (see 1920: 2–3). Such a construct suggests that photoplays can be written by 'the photoplay writer' as much as produced in the usual sense of the word. Sargent refers to the 'writing of photo-plays' (1912: 3); Leslie T. Peacocke refers to the 'writer of photoplays' (1916: 28) and 'photoplay writing' (1916: 32). Peacocke describes the 'scenario of a photoplay, which practically means the photoplay itself' (1916: 27). Perhaps the most explicit usage of photoplay to apply to the written script is to be found in Catherine Carr's work. In a section on 'photoplay form' she explains the intricacies of the written manuscript, and gives advice on technical terms (1914: 24). Esenwein and Leeds push the photoplay back into a visual medium when they deploy the term 'photoplay script' (1913: 26).

From a writing point of view, the photoplay serves as a unique crossover term between ideas of the filmed object and ideas of the written object, and often relates to an awareness of what works 'before the camera-eye' (Ball 1917: 5; see also Patterson 1921: 3; Emerson & Loos 1920: 53–6). The idea of the photoplay facili-tates an emphasis on technique, as in the title of Sargent's *Technique of the Photo-play*, a phrase that recurs often (see Carr 1914: 5; Patterson 1921: 3). The photo-play solidifies expectations to do with dramatic value and action, and is put forward as a movement beyond early films in which 'novelty held the interest' and spectacles in which 'no story was needed' (Emerson & Loos 1920: 12). 'Today an audience fed up on scenic effects demands nothing more – and will take nothing less – than the story with the dramatic quality' (ibid.). Eustace Hale Ball is at pains to stress that at that time (that is, in 1917), 'the play's the thing' (1917: xi, 43), and goes so far as to suggest that 'the greatest future in this industry is for the film playwright, without whom nothing else matters' (1917: 58). In another version of his text he notes that the photoplay form of entertainment has brought forth new sentiment in audiences, and the deeper significance of this movement opens real opportunities for the writer (see 1915: 165; 1917: 127).

Scenario Fever

A second key reference point for discussion of the early development of writing for the screen is what has been termed 'scenario fever', an intense public interest in screen-writing. The space of scenario fever is important for the codification and formalisa-tion of ideas about writing. Even if viewed conservatively as a promotional campaign largely conducted by production companies, it still forms a context for various kinds of statements (especially in handbooks that capitalise on it and seek to either nurture or dampen it) about who can write, and what writing is like for the public.

To set the scene for scenario fever: while the story film had established its impor-tance in the early 1900s – especially *Jack and the Beanstalk* (Dirs George S. Fleming, Edwin S. Porter, 1902), *Life of an American Fireman* (Dirs George S. Fleming, Edwin S. Porter, Writ. Edwin S. Porter, 1903) and *The Great Train Robbery* (Dir. Edwin S. Porter, Writ. Scott Marble, Edwin S. Porter, 1903)[85] – a 1911 Supreme Court copyright ruling (prompted by Gene Gauntier's ultimately copyright breaching adaptation of *Ben Hur* as a subject for the Kalem company in 1907) restricted the free use of theatrical and literary source materials and led to the purchase of literary properties as well as increased demand for original stories. An industrial struggle between independent producers and the Motion Picture Patents Company further contributed to a volatile screen culture, with producers entering the uncharted waters of the multiple-reel film (see Azlant 1980: 122). Popular fascination with the motion pictures, the amount paid for screen writing and corporate demand for photoplay stories and writers, combined to produce an extraordinary interest in the technicalities of screen writing. Manufacturers advertised for superior photoplay ideas and offered good prices, as well as the possibility of training (see Jacobs 1939: 130). Studios also communicated the types of stories required, according to their particular resources or strengths (see Stempel 2000: 13). As Calder Johnstone, Scenario Editor for Universal, remarked, 'when it is realised that over one hundred stories are purchased every week of the year by the several motion picture companies in the business, the lay mind can begin to appreciate the difficulty of originating new thoughts and themes' (1914: 108). He goes on to explain that the Universal Company receives 'on the average of 1,200 scripts a week' (ibid.). Louella O. Parsons reports that the Essanay Film Company 'receives approximately six hundred scenarios a week' (in Carr 1914: 116). Peacocke tells his readers that 'the average scenario department receives 100 to 150 scripts daily' (1916: 126). Famous Players reports 'some days we receive as high as three and four hundred scripts, and many times not one is found acceptable' (in Peacocke 1916: 112).

Encouraging submission of story material was seen as a way for the industry to address a perceived shortage of appropriate story ideas, and the payment given for scripts was attractive. Disseminating information about screen writing helped studios to ensure a steady and rapid supply of stories. As Jacobs notes, a 'growing awareness of the necessity for skill in story writing for the screen was evident' (1939: 131). For Ramsaye, writing of the period around 1909, 'the demand for screen stories was growing with the industry and rumours of easy money "writing for the pictures" went through the gossip channels of the actor tribes, reaching picture patrons as well. The beginning of the motion picture craze was in sight' (1926: 512). Some trade magazines responded to this reader interest by establishing departments dedicated to teaching the craft of writing. Sargent's columns informed *Technique of the Photoplay*, which went through three editions between 1912 and 1916. A specific emphasis on technique, due in part to the increased complexity of the scripts and the terminology of filmmaking, gave impetus to the formalisation of writing for the screen.

Azlant characterises this period in the history of screen writing as one of 'scenario fever', using the term to describe an extensive public promotion of scenario writing and the figures involved. The encouragement of public submission of story material and ideas was an effective means of promotion of the movies, and numerous magazines and newspapers ran scenario contests (see Azlant 1980: 128; Ramsaye 1926: 667) – with some of the magazines themselves set up by studios to support the star system (see Azlant 1980: 132). The combination of lucrative payment, and a perception that little talent was required to submit stories, led to problems for handbook writers. Carr notes in the introduction to her text: 'Anyone can write a scenario – the very advertisements say it needs neither brains nor literary ability' (1914: 5). She implies such a view comes from ignorance. Esenwein and Leeds pour cold water on the alluring promises of 'ten to one hundred dollars a month' with 'no previous literary training required' (1913: 15).[86]

There has been some confusion about the dating of scenario fever. While most critics treat it as one period, scenario fever occurred in at least three discernable waves, with different critics focusing on different periods. While Decherney focuses on the post-1911 period, Staiger identifies an increase in output after 1907, when writers had been hired to provide plots and 'firms increasingly sought freelance contributions' (see Bordwell *et al*. 1985: 131). By 1908, 'studio personnel increasingly failed to supply enough material as production was rapidly expanding. As a result, film companies began advertising in trade papers for ideas from outsiders' (Staiger 1983: 34). A 1909 report in *The Nickelodeon* states: 'Until a year ago, persons who aspired to write moving picture plays and submitted them to manufacturers of motion pictures usually received them back with the reply, "We are not buying moving picture plays"' (McMackin 1909: 171). But then a shift occurs because 'the well went dry and the producer found he must have aid from outside sources' (ibid.). According to Staiger, by 1910 this wave of scenario fever was in full swing, and Wright confirms that Lubin, Essanay and other companies advertised in magazines around 1910 (1914: 10; see also Sargent 1914). This interest was brought to a close by the 1911 Supreme Court copyright ruling, which had a two-pronged effect: it institutionalised the use of 'ironclad' release forms for freelance material, and also hastened the turn towards purchasing the rights of already published and popular theatre plays and novels (see Bordwell *et al*. 1985: 132; see also Azlant 1980: 122–5).[87] Staiger sees the judicial decision on copyright as a factor as 'reliance on freelance submissions decreased after 1912 as the regularised, institutionalised sources of stories … became standard' (1985: 190).

Azlant takes a different view of this development. He argues that in the wake of the KALEM CO. v. HARPER BROS. ruling 'the already intense demand for original stories exploded' (1980: 104). Partly as a means of avoiding the purchase of expensive rights, and partly as a way of searching for talent, the public submission of original story material that had begun earlier was further encouraged: 'Many producers began using the burgeoning fan and trade magazines to inform the public of this exotic new opportunity, and most gave out instructions or "form sheets" on scenario formats' (1980: 104–5). For Azlant, the Kalem suit triggers a mass publication of handbooks between 1912 and 1920.

If Azlant is more upbeat than Staiger on the post-Kalem law suit period, it is because he links scenario fever to the anti-Trust activities of the independent exhibitors, now turning producers: 'By 1912 the film industry was pulsing with phenomenal growth and the lively operations of a flourishing group of independent producers, who were shaking off the restraints of the Trust and attempting every conceivable experiment to capture the public's fancy' (1980: 122). This period of growth coincides with the scenario fever of 1912 to 1915, as demand continued to outstrip supply for films, the amounts paid for film rights to literary and dramatic material increased and escalating star salaries spurred popular interest. For Ball, the sheer scale of film manufacture meant that the 'field of novels and stage plays for picturisation' has been exhausted (1915: xii). This provides a real opportunity for writers of scenarios. Peacocke reports that 'the need for good photoplays is growing stronger every day' (1916: 115).

> Original stories! Original photoplays especially written for the screen by competent scenario writers! That is the urgent need of the film manufacturing companies. It had to come, as we all knew it would. Nearly all the stage plays and published books that lent themselves to film adaptation have been produced or are in the course of production. (1916: 11)

Here, Peacocke articulates a position to do with both original writing and writing for the screen that anticipates many of the arguments of Dudley Nichols and Sidney Howard in the late 1930s and early 1940s (see also Blaisdell 1914).

By the mid-teens, however, the industry shows signs of earlier behaviour. In his discussion of the period 1914–1918, Jacobs notes that studios were no longer seeking freelance work, 'having often become involved in suits for plagiarism, companies were wary of accepting stories from unknown sources' (1939: 218). There were also signs that the flood of material received by the studios did not guarantee a sufficient supply of stories, and that in 1919 'submissions had grown so heavy that no quality control could be maintained' (Koszarski 1990: 108).

Another wave of scenario fever arguably took hold from the end of World War One to 1921, when studios were caught short of material other than war films. Koszarski cites figures that up to $20,000 could be obtained as an average price of a successful play (ibid.). 'By 1920, it was open season for scenarios. Everyone was writing for the movies; studios were overwhelmed by scripts and stories from amateurs all over the world' (Brownlow 1968: 277). This period was to end when the acceptance of outside submissions again produced litigation problems for the studios (see Patterson 1928: 160–1; Hampton 1970: 206–8). As concern over thinly disguised plagiarism grew – along with suits against the studios for allegedly stealing the ideas of the volunteer scenario writers – the studios reassessed their relation to scenario fever. 'Finally, in self-protection, the studios built a stone wall between themselves and the amateur writing tribe' (Hampton 1970: 209), with a 'virtual elimination of the free-lance market' being an aspect of the postwar era (Koszarski 1990: 108). Frances Marion saw this as an act of 'sheer necessity' (1938a: 186), but interestingly starts her 1938 handbook declaring a 'new and great opportunity for the amateur writer' willing to submit original motion picture fictions (1938a: 14).

It is fair to say that a cumulative effect of these waves of interest is that a gold-rush mentality developed in relation to the photoplay, an interest that handbook writers and, more importantly, scenario writing correspondence schools capitalised on and exploited (to the chagrin of photoplay authors who would mount concerted campaigns against them). Azlant observes that 'an industry directory published in 1915 listed sixty-one ... scenario or photoplay schools scattered throughout the country' (1980: 131; see also Sargent 1913: 10; Morey 1997).

Narrative Coherence and Forces of Standardisation

A third key reference point for the development of writing for the screen should be considered, namely the focus on narrative coherence and clarity that has been analysed by Staiger. A major concern of early handbooks has to do with precepts of dramatic art and proper construction, such as when Sargent insists on the importance of a basic inciting incident (1912: 17–19), or when James Slevin writes that 'the dramatic crisis deals in emotions, and the more emotion and greater variety you can get out of a situation, the nearer you are to the dramatic' (1912: 24). In an early example of the emphasis on 'central conflict' in screenwriting, Slevin asserts that 'Dramatic action is made up chiefly of contrast and conflict' (1912: 89). In one sense, these aesthetic arguments are legacies from other areas such as the 'legitimate' theatre, and will not be of major interest in our discussion of writing for the screen. But Staiger has shown how such arguments have played a key role in the development of film, through increased expectations of narrative quality and the well-made product. Staiger characterises this in terms of a film 'in which an initial cause produced a chain of effects which ended in a "satisfactory" resolution'; a 'clear, logical – and realistic – story was desired' (1985: 175). For Staiger, 'continuous action' became an important criteria:

> The goal of continuous action (pertinent events only, linked causally through time and space) derived from a belief in perceptual continuity as the basis for causal logic in the physical world. Narrative continuity, verisimilitude, dominance, and clarity (visibility – and later audibility) became primary standards of the well-made product. (Ibid.)

For Staiger, this conception of quality runs parallel to a limitation in the reel length of films, and this was seen as 'one of the major causes of inadequate narratives ... as filmmakers tried to fit the story into the thousand-foot limit, there seemed to be abrupt connections and sudden conclusions' (1985: 175; see also Esenwein & Leeds 1913: 91). The problem for producers, as Staiger sees it, was 'to ensure complete narrative continuity and clarity despite the footage limitation' (1985: 176). The double focus around what is acceptable material for studios, and the focus on adequate and inadequate narratives, frames the need for screenwriting advice. The narrative expectations identified by Staiger are readily evident in screenwriting discourse.[88] Handbook writers are very prepared to say 'What you cannot write', 'What you should not write' and 'What you should write' (see Esenwein & Leeds 1913: 221–73). This discourse once focused on what satisfies and registers with the audience (see Esenwein & Leeds 1913: 124), but arguably continues today in an emphasis on stories which are 'lost in the telling' or have structural flaws (see Aronson 2000: 237).

Staiger's work shows how careful attention to preparing a script helped film producers meet these narrative expectations, and crucially work within footage limitations. But, while Staiger mentions and cites numerous screenwriting handbooks to support her thesis, her work operates on a broader level than just screenwriting, and her main focus is conditions of manufacture. In relation to screenwriting, however, I want to suggest the terms of discourse change and that within the space opened up by Staiger's approach there is more to be investigated, particularly in the way these conceptions of quality were internalised and incorporated into screenwriting discourse. Methodologically speaking, there is a risk of turning Staiger's important work on the blueprint into an account of total codification, in which all developments are explained through 'the film industry's adoption of the script as a precise blueprint for the final film' (Decherney 2005: 43). It may be that 'efficient production (shooting out of order) and a standard of clear, continuous action governed the preparation of the script' in 1909 (Staiger 1985: 176), but other layers of discourse open up different possibilities, revealing rhetorical strategies around an emerging discourse of writing for the screen and not just standardised script style.

Of course, there are limitations to any study of standardisation. Staiger herself notes variations in the modes of film practice (see 1985: 177), and mentions that individual personnel could, depending on marketability, tailor working conditions to some extent (Bordwell *et al.* 1985: 137).[89] Interestingly, even within a text that Staiger takes as exemplary in its description of the standard scenario script (see McMackin 1909: 173), there is a reference to 'chapters' that she does not mention and which does not fit her account (see Staiger 1985: 177) – a term that indicates a lack of autonomy of this form, or rather strong links to prose forms. Also against the norm, during the period that Staiger describes in terms of a 'shift from the scenario script [1904–1908] to the continuity script [circa 1908–1914]' (1985: 177),[90] Esenwein and Leeds focus on what they call the 'photoplay script' (1913: 26).

Furthermore, drawing on an issue discussed in chapter five, the use of the term scenario is varied. Staiger asserts that 'The detailed continuity script was standard practice by 1914' (1985: 189), and although she acknowledges that 'uneven devel-opment occurred' around representational styles (1985: 178) this caveat does not fully account for variations in the way the term scenario was employed.[91] My reason for drawing out the link between expectations of narrative quality, processes of standardisation and screenwriting discourse is to suggest that some writers respond to expectations of the quality product not simply by policing conventions, but by creating a fuller vision of writing practice. This is part of a neglected aspect of screenwriting discourse in which the notion of writing for the screen plays a key role. This can be seen in two examples, one from 1917 and the other from 1929, that demonstrate the way that writing for the screen was formalised within screenwriting discourse.

The first example is a chapter written by Maibelle Heikes Justice, on the 'Photo-drama', in the 1917 edition of a handbook by Parsons, 'probably the best known freelance scenario writer in America' (Justice 1917: 237). Justice praises Parson's handbook for its excellent handling of 'the technique of writing for the screen' (1917: 251). But, more significantly, Justice is one of the first authors to fuse together a notion of the 'screen writer' and the task of writing for the screen. This idea, still formative in her eyes, is closely linked to a conception of the 'photodramatist', 'this is the author-dramatist, he who can conceive his original story, put it into synopsis form, then writes his own dramatic action' (1917: 242–3). Justice identifies a new 'game of screen writing' (1917: 245). 'Moving pictures are advancing with rapid strides – the possibilities for fresh, original treatment are untold and producers are on the alert for writers who can visualise in a new way. We *must* develop the new school to get out of the old ruts' (246–7; emphasis in original). One of these ruts is the way the work of the screen writer is spliced with that of the staff writer, and subjected to directorial interference.[92] Justice wishes for an arrangement where author, director and actor work in collaboration, 'but the day when all others work to the exclusion of the writer is gone' (1917: 243).[93]

The second example is a 1929 text from screenwriter Clara Beranger, which demonstrates how this idea of writing for the screen became fully associated with screen-writing. Beranger's talk is to students from the University of Southern Cali-fornia enrolled in a course 'Introduction to the Photoplay'. Her aim is 'to help you to understand what writing for the screen means' (1977: 136). She explains this idea of writing: 'The working out of a story in pictorial dramatic form is the job we writers of the screen have had to learn' (1977: 137). The role of 'screen writer' is linked to the rise in story expectations discussed by Staiger: 'When action changed to dramatic action, there began to be the need for screen writers; and a scenario became more than a mere blocking off of scenes' (Beranger 1977: 136). But Beranger also develops this idea through certain 'requirements': the need to 'think up all kinds of ways of showing in action what other people can say in words'; the power of visualisation; a knowledge of 'technique of the screen'; a 'sense of dramatic values' (1977: 140).

This conception of screen writing has a progeny: 'the step child of screen writing – the original story' (1977: 137). Writing for the screen is thus linked to stories 'written for the screen'.

The Picture Eye and Writing for the Camera

In order to probe more deeply into the elaboration of the idea of writing for the screen in early American screen culture, it is necessary to pay some attention to the handbooks of the day, many of which sought to explore the art and technique of the photoplay. Azlant observes that 'over *ninety* books in English on the silent scenario, many by accomplished scenarists or studio scenario editors, were published from 1910 through 1920' (1980: 134; emphasis in original).[94] Before 1910 suggestion sheets and small booklets served a similar purpose (see Sargent 1913: 9; Sargent 1914; McMackin 1909). A comprehensive account of this output is beyond the range of this study, but it remains of special interest because it is a key place in which screen writing, and its industrial context, is explained to the wider public.

There is a set of handbooks, or mode of handbook writing, that will not be addressed in great depth here. This set or sub-set relates primarily to the accumulation and marketing of story material, and handling by the studios. They have titles such as *The Photoplay: How to Write, How to Sell* (by John Arthur Nelson 1913), *How to Write for the 'Movies'* (by Louella O. Parsons 1915) and *Cinema Plays: How to Write Them, How to Sell Them* (by Eustace Hale Ball 1917). Sometimes the information is found in chapters such as 'manuscript preparation' (Peacocke 1916: 84). This mode guides writers in appropriate subject matter at a time when story content was subject to various kinds of criteria and assessment.[95]

Of more interest to us are examples in which writing for the screen is articulated in terms of techniques of visualisation and notions of the 'picture eye': 'Try and look at things with a "camera eye"' (Peacocke 1916: 13, 40). Parsons states: 'the art of visualisation is necessary to the art of your photoplay' (1915: 44). 'Cultivate the picturing eye' Esenwein and Leeds suggest, 'so that by being able to visualise each scene as you plan it in your mind you cannot fail to produce in your scenario a series of scenes whose action is logically connected and essentially natural and unforced' (1913: 118). Photoplay action plays a key part in Esenwein and Leeds' theory, as one would expect from Staiger's perspective, but they also attach it to the need to 'visualise your story *as you write it* – yes, even *before* you write it' (1913: 112; emphasis in original). In an early anticipation of 'the read' they ask of the novice writer, 'how can you expect the editor, the producer, the spectator to "see" your plot understandingly unless you yourself are able to visualise every scene' (1913: 113).

These are admittedly nascent attempts to develop writing for the screen in relation to expectations of continuous action. But the notion undergoes further development, and one of the ways this happens is in terms of writing for the camera, a notion closely related to writing for the screen. Patterson suggests that 'the photoplay has a language of its own – the language of the camera' (1921: 3; see also Peacocke 1916: 40). 'Hence situation and character must undergo selection. Only those which have pre-eminent cinematic qualities should be chosen' (Patterson 1921: 68). This concern for the camera enters into the space of writing for the screen when it becomes aligned with notions of visual content and visual writing, and the visual operations of the screen (see Patterson 1921: 66). In this context writing for the camera finds a connection with the elaboration of plot. In 1929 Patterson suggests that 'unless he knows the camera, unless he plots out his ideas in action, which is camera language, he is apt to write a story which is not photographic. His synopsis will have greater pantomimic quality and be the more vivid for a knowledge of continuity' (1929b: viii).

Towards Photoplay Form: Epes Winthrop Sargent

Beranger insists that 'there is a distinction in writing for the screen and writing for the camera. Certain people who can visualise how a thing will look on the screen, cannot put it into scenario form' (1977: 141). This observation is relevant in the context of Sargent's screenwriting, which focuses on the issue of writing in photoplay form.

Sargent's work offers an interesting archive for developments in photoplay form. Take, for example, the first edition of his *Technique of the Photoplay*. There, 'the writing of photoplays is at once the most simple and the most difficult form of dramatic construction' (1912: 3). By the second edition, 'the art of writing photoplays has become possessed of a technique that is applicable only to the writing of picture plays and to no other form' (1913: 7). A distinct and separate domain of technique opens up, beyond the normal sphere of dramatic construction.

Format considerations are common in the most basic modes of handbook writing, as rules for presentation are often laid down. In the first edition of Sargent's handbook this is called 'scenario form', and it relates to issues primarily to do with the presentation of the 'perfect' manuscript. Format is here very much an end in itself (getting your manuscript accepted). But Sargent goes beyond this, and in his hands issues of presentation give way to a new form of writing: the format becomes a condition of the writing and a new emphasis on expression as intrinsically bound to 'photoplay form': 'Photoplay form is not a printed blank form on which plays should be written' (1913: 31), it is 'merely the form in which the photoplay should be written' (ibid.). 'Form' here refers both to 'sheet form' and a form of expression, and combines written presentation with issues of construction and creation (1913: 143). Sargent is here creating a space to do not just with the written manuscript but the writing of a visual entity as well. In other words, this is a space of writing for the screen (even if that phrase is not exactly applied to it). For Sargent, 'photoplay form' is certainly about presentation, but the matter goes beyond presentation on the page: 'form is the flesh, the idea is the spirit; the soul that vivifies and gives life to the flesh' (1913: 66). Photoplay form is a mode of expression impacted (or vivified) by what a photoplay is, 'a story told in action'. Beyond questions of format, then, there exists a transfigurational dynamic (between flesh and spirit or soul); an interaction between written form and photoplay as projected entity in a unique relationship of expression.

The third edition of Sargent's handbook shows that developing an idea of photoplay form is not achieved in one stroke. And in that edition, although he promotes a position similar to that found in his earlier volumes, he renovates his argument to focus on plotting. He once again insists that form is 'more than the mere setting down of idea in words of action, in leaders and in inserts' (1916: 2). He argues against forming a product by following a model script, instead linking writing to the writing of action: 'Technique, then, is the combination of an idea and the expression of that idea, in competent and adequate action' (ibid.). Creation and expression are linked through action. He insists on the link when he suggests: 'technique is complex and many sided ... The technique of form alone is but the means of expressing the idea – of creation' (ibid.).

Central to Sargent's view of creation is plotting. This term is at work in the second edition and is central to Sargent's idea of photoplay as a 'story told in action' (1913: 66), as well as the idea that 'photoplay form is merely the means to an end and not the end itself' (ibid.). In the third edition, he elaborates this position. Plotting incorporates 'the imaginative and creative part of photoplay writing' (1916: 18). Consistent with Staiger's emphasis on narrative coherence, Sargent warns the reader that incidence is not plot but 'Plot is that which makes these connected incidents a story by giving those incidents some reason for being shown' (1913: 66). In the third handbook he reiterates the distinction between plot and incident, and goes further to say 'on plot rests the entire structure of photoplay' (1916: 25). Reworking his previous formulation, 'Plot is to photoplay at once the skeleton upon which the flesh of incident is hung and the spirit that animates that flesh' (ibid.). In this sense, plotting has taken a far more prominent position in photoplay form.

In these passages, Sargent seems to downplay the importance of photoplay form in relation to the technique of creation and development of plotting. But the structure of the book shows a different emphasis, with Part III devoted to 'Photoplay Form', and Part IV 'Writing in Form'. In Part III Sargent connects plot to form: 'The plot finds its most complete exposition in photoplay form' (1916: 99). At the same time, he once again confronts those who make a 'fetich [sic]' of form (ibid.), who do not see it as a 'means to an end' (1916: 100), who see form as a thing on which photoplays are expressed rather than in which they are expressed. Sargent is adamant that 'photoplay form is the form *in* (not *on*) which photoplays are best ... expressed' (1916: 99; emphasis in original). He suggests: 'learn thoroughly the language of photoplay form and then you can write with vigor and conviction' (1916: 100). His comments suggest a preoccupation with writing in format, using appropriate jargon: form consists of *'title*, a *synopsis*, a *cast of characters*, a *scene plot* and the *plot of action'* (1916: 101; emphasis in original). But the aim of writing in form for Sargent is the ability 'to give the plot the finest and best exemplification in dramatic or comedy action' (1916: 213), which involves a consideration of premises and development, a diagramming of plot action (see 1916: 217). He looks at continuity, establishment and preparation for events. This is a paradigm that is shared by many contemporary screenwriting manuals interested in story and structure.

What does writing in photoplay form mean for Sargent? On a surface level, it is writing a plot of action. In the second edition of his handbook, the plot of action is what most commentators would know as a scenario, although Sargent is adamant that in its proper sense, 'a scenario is a brief sketch of the plot of a story. A few years ago scenario was used to apply to all photoplay scripts, but the use of that word is incorrect. It is one of the misnomers brought into the business by the stage managers and players' (1913: 28).[96] The synopsis is a place where fine writing or literary skill is desirable, in order to impress the story editor with something 'that is almost like a prose poem' (1913: 61). The plot of action, on the other hand, is characterised by 'brevity with clearness' (1913: 62). All punctuation is dispensed with except for dashes bridging condensed descriptions of action. For example: 'Street. Jack and Tom meet – greetings – Tom speaks – Jack assents – they exit' (1913: 65). 'The simple direction is less confusing to the director and at the same time gives point to the action and throws it into relief' (1913: 62). On the question of literary style, Sargent is consistent in stating that the photoplay writer is 'not required to possess literary style beyond that which will enable him to write with correctness and intelligence' (1916: 23). This is in accordance with a view at the time that the photoplaywright must 'hide the light of his diction under a bushel of business' (Phillips 1914: 32). However, Sargent goes on to make the apparently opposite point:

> It has been repeatedly stated that literary style is not required in writing photoplays. This is true. The most fluently written script would be worthless if it did not sell a story, but there is a style in photoplay, though as yet not one person in a thousand realises it. As the matter stands producers are but dimly realising that they can get more help from the author than the bare plot. They do not want to realise it, for this makes them less vitally necessary to the studio than they were when the director was the sole arbiter and made a script well or badly as he chose. Style in photoplay is not the literary grace with which your explanations are phrased. It is the completeness with which you convey to the director the little touches that give individuality to the expression of your story. (1916: 89)

The plot of action is purpose-made for use by the director, reducing the drama down to the bare business that should appear in the photoplay.

The plot of action demands a specific style of writing, one that demands a specific kind of visualisation. Sargent calls this 'the picture eye ... the ability to visualise words or thoughts into actions. Unless you can see the action with your mental vision you cannot write it and your picture will be flat and unconvincing' (1913: 81). Visualisation is today popularly associated with imagining in one's own mind's eye. But Sargent's practice requires a further step of writing 'only the action that helps tell the story' (1913: 82). The aim is to give the director 'only the really important business' (ibid.); 'keep your eyes open for striking situations and effective bits of business' (1913: 83).

Literary style and the picture eye come together in Sargent's discussion of 'values and emphasis'. The equivalent to italicisation in a book, or special emphasis in the theatre, through 'the handling of the action of the story, the situation or through the individual acting, it is possible to produce precisely the same effect' (1913: 98). When dealing with the assignment of values, Sargent advises the reader that it is appropriate to offer greater detail despite his earlier emphasis on brevity, 'because we are gaining our emphasis through the action' (ibid.). His overall view of 'writing photoplays' is that while 'the mastery of phrase and literary style that are demanded of the other forms' is not required, it is 'offset by the need for being able to write in action so clearly that this action is as plain and understandable as the written word' (1913: 144). The fiction writer can hide the poverty of an idea behind beautiful expression, but 'the ability to direct imagination are [sic] even more essential to the photoplay writer' (ibid.). In the third edition of the handbook he discusses holding or slowing down action 'until the spectator has a chance to grasp the idea and then we go on to the next development' (1916: 233). Noteworthy here is the closeness to a concept of the read; here is a prototypical moment of the writer directing the reader/spectator on the page.

As Azlant has noted in his discussion of Sargent, the three editions of Sargent's *Technique of the Photoplay* form a significant archive, representing a 'distillation and ongoing revision of public instruction' (1980: 211). While he does not literally refer to 'writing for the screen' – his preferred phrase is 'writing photoplay' or 'writing for photoplay' – his emphasis on writing in photoplay form underpins some now common aspects of writing for the screen. Indeed, without a strong sense of photoplay form, writing for the screen would lose much of its meaning. Over time, the notion of photoplay form is framed in terms of the scenario or the continuity. The 'art of the photoplay' as such becomes less central, and notions like the picture eye merge with other concepts such as writing for the camera and eventually writing for the screen. The form will become naturalised or normalised until a change in institutional and discursive conditions requires the formation of a new one; and it is thus perhaps not a coincidence that in the 1940s Nichols returns to the theme of writing as a camera (see 1942: 773), and suggests that 'there are certain prescribed forms, but the forms are not final' (1943: xl).

Cinematic Plot: Frances Taylor Patterson

There is much in common between the handbooks of the 1910s and the 1920s, and in many respects they operate in similar courses of development, often sharing terminology and truisms. However, shifts can be identified in relation to the institutionalisation of writing for the screen, especially in the work of Frances Taylor Patterson, an instructor of 'Photoplay Composition' at Columbia University. Like Sargent, Patterson makes a unique contribution to screenwriting discourse, especially through her attempt at photoplay criticism. At the same time, in her writing on photoplay composition she fuses professionalism and writing for the screen. In two works, *Cinema Craftsmanship: A Book for Photoplaywrights* (1921) and *Scenario and Screen* (1928), as editor of the early anthology of scripts, *Motion Picture Continuities* (1929a), and through her extension teaching, Patterson takes up the task of formalising the idea of 'writing for the screen' as a particular craft activity, along with the notion of being trained for this activity. At a time when she declares there to be 'no screen authors' (1928: 125), Patterson strikes a common cause with 'young photoplaywrights', as it is 'they who will write directly for the screen in the tomorrow of the movies' (1928: ix).[97]

Sargent's work foregrounds the importance of photoplay form and writing in form through plotting. In Patterson's writings there is a similar concern at work – although she does not draw explicitly on Sargent's handbooks – in the sense that her main focus is cinematic plot: 'Concomitant with the youth of the photoplay is the lack of analysis of cinematic plot' (1921: 7). The student, according to Patterson, should become familiar with dramatic criticism, but then 'carefully translate his findings from stage craft into screen craft, eliminating all principles not applicable to the development of plot through action … He should be in mind that the cinematic plot evinces itself in action presentation rather than word presentation' (1921: 7–8).

In *Cinema Craftsmanship*, Patterson includes a long chapter on scenario technique in which a straightforward account of writing continuity emerges, placing fundamental emphasis on action and a kind of writing 'capable of being captured by the camera', that has 'screen value' (1921: 116). While Patterson's focus is not specifically writing in photoplay form, a similar interest in issues of values and emphasis to that of Sargent's is apparent when she advises 'let the scenario reader play the part of the ideal spectator obtaining the facts in the development of the plot no sooner and no later than the audience would' (1921: 128). Evident here is an emphasis on 'the read' of the script, functioning as a movie before the mind's eye. This emphasis is more evident in her later work: 'a knack for choosing "action words" … a facility for emphasising important points and subordinating minor plot details … may earn many a check' (1928: 9). Looking at 'picture words' and 'action words', 'the scenario editor ought to see pictures' (1928: 15).

In his account of film study at Columbia University in the 1910s, Decherney views Patterson's contribution as primarily to do with maintaining industry sponsorship as well as the vision of other key Columbia figures, such as Victor Oscar Freeburg (see Decherney 2005: 44). Her investment in screenwriting, and 'celebration of the screenwriter as auteur' is seen in the context of wider industry and educational forces at Columbia University. Dana Polan offers a different assessment of Patterson's work, insisting she was 'in no way a mere acolyte of Freeburg' (2007: 58). Polan presents a portrait of Patterson as a diligent figure knowledgeable in film business, involved in the general cinema culture of the time. He notes that it may not be productive to try to distil a general aesthetics or philosophy of film from Patterson's work, but what he does show is a dual commitment in her work to a fusion of practical orientation and aesthetic matters. Her extension teaching is seen as practically orientated, but permeated with an interest in cinematic ideals and critical intelligence (see 2007: 67).

Through her ideal of praxis one can say that Patterson carves out a niche in film education at Columbia University. But I also want to suggest that Patterson's practical orientation can be explored further in relation to screenwriting discourse, and it is significant that many of the books she presents as a bibliography in her work *Cinema Craftsmanship* relate to screenwriting. Polan begins to examine this aspect when he notes Patterson's discussion of the relationship between professionals and amateurs, and the fact that the latter can more easily learn to 'write directly for the screen' (2007: 72).

It was noted earlier that one characteristic of the age of the photoplay was that, as Azlant writes, the photoplay could be understood in two senses (either the written script or the completed fictional narrative film). Patterson's work also situates itself under the banner of the 'photoplay', but the dual sense of the term recedes. In its place is a view that the writing of scenarios is not the same as the creation of photoplays.[98] She unravels what is termed the 'paradox of "*writing* a picture"' (Eve Unsell, quoted in Patterson 1921: 90; emphasis in original). For her, 'the photoplay has no objective reality until it reaches the screen' (1921: 2). Here, Patterson internalises the screen-based existence of the photoplay. Building on a distinction between writing and composing, between scenario and screen (to borrow the title of her book), she suggests that 'there may come a day in the development of the moving picture when the scenario is dispensed with and the picture is composed directly by the camera' (1929b: v). At the same time, reflecting a development beyond photoplay form *per se*, the script is identified much more strongly with 'the continuity', which Patterson defines as 'an approximation of a finished photoplay' (ibid.).[99] She defines the continuity as the 'professional script', arranged 'in a series of scenes for the guidance of a director' (1928: 212). She still refers to the 'writer of motion pictures' (1921: 3), the 'photoplay writer' (1921: 4) and the 'writing of photoplays' (1928: 7), but the main emphasis now falls on the figure of the 'successful scenarioist' (1921: 3; see also 1921: 126, 172) who knows the 'stages of development through which the photoplay has passed', and also the 'technique of the photoplay' (1921: 3).

Three aspects of Patterson's work are particularly relevant to understanding her contribution to the development of writing for the screen. Firstly, while she continues the emphasis on expression found in Sargent's writing, she focuses strongly on the uniqueness of the screen medium. Because the photoplay does not exist until it exists on film, a notion of 'the cinematic' becomes crucial to Patterson's work. Here, in confirmation of Decherney's argument, she can be seen as echoing Victor O. Freeburg's concern for differentiating between the arts, and realising the potential of the photoplay. Freeburg makes reference to the need for the 'cinema composer' to become master of the medium (1918: 28) and also to emphasise specifically 'cinematic' composition (1918: 69). For Patterson, the stage drama and photodrama are linked, but she sees them as 'two widely diverging media' (1921: 6–7). The photoplay is not 'step-sister to the stage', a 'lowly handmaid', but a cinematic narrative (1921: 7). Patterson demonstrates a highly evolved sense of the medium specificity of the photoplay, to the extent of entertaining the possibility (in the quote above) of a day 'when the scenario is dispensed with'.

Secondly, she ties an interest in cinematic composition to a vocational ideal. The vocational dimension of her work appears when she writes: 'to the person who has trained himself to think in terms of pictures the cinematic is easily distinguishable from the uncinematic … Plot is visualised. It is worked out as it were in charades. It could be acted for the camera, and is therefore cinematic' (1921: 8). She adds:

It has been consistently maintained that photoplays should be composed directly for the screen with screen possibilities and screen needs in mind. The story, from its primal inception, should be thought out in terms of pictures and not words. Material that has been written to be read rather than acted is usually far from fitted to cinematic presentation. (1921: 67)

Patterson's work can be read as an attempt to construct writing as a vocation for the writer or scenarioist, which extends to having scientific aspirations for the field, such as when Patterson declares that 'writing for the screen is an art but it is also a science' (1921: 2). This impacts on her advice to frustrated novices: 'If they [aspirant writers] would learn the art and craft of motion picture writing … if they would write directly for the screen … their wails of lamentation would be heard no longer. For then and only then would the material be suited to the medium of pictures and merely the lightest changes would have to be made by the continuity writer' (1921: 172).

The third aspect of Patterson's work of interest in terms of the institutionalisation of writing for the screen is the emphasis she places on the writing of original material, or writers who 'compose directly in picture form' (1928: 154). Other figures such as Lasky, Peacocke, Justice and Beranger, raise the issue of original material, and link it to writing for the screen. The early push to take the photoplay beyond the one-reel standard relied in part on the use of already successful novels and plays. Patterson, however, sees herself as writing in the 'final segment of the cycle of evolution, the return to original stories written directly for the screen' (1921: 65): 'The ideal photoplay must be of the screen, by the screen and for the screen' (1928: 157).

Institutionalising Writing for the Screen

By the late 1930s and early 1940s, the 'art of writing for the screen' was being discussed in numerous contexts (see Keisling 1937: 71; Nichols 1942: 770, 774; Nichols 1943: xxxii, xxxvi). Two brief examples show how writing for the screen was increasingly being linked to the work and aspirations of screenwriters. In 1937 Sidney Howard writes: 'The screen will presently have to revise its method of dealing with its writers, just as writers will have to revalue their attitude toward the screen' (1995: 215). Howard emphasises a need for original screenplays and for those writers capable of it to cease rewriting and write 'on their own account' (1995: 216). He promotes an emphasis on original writing, although 'the unknown work written directly for the screen is a mystery to the public except as a vehicle for a popular star' (ibid.). But he held out hope for the day 'when our O'Neills and Kaufmans will be writing for the screen as independently as they now write for the stage' (ibid.).[100] I have already examined Nichols' work, and his attempts to reintegrate the work of screen writing around the screenplay. Nichols' contribution to the formation of writing for the screen is to further anchor his work in a notion of writing as a camera: 'Does one write for the camera? Of course. One is not a screenwriter until one writes "as a camera". You key your visualising faculties to all the possibilities – and limitations – of the camera' (1942: 773; emphasis in original). He also extends Patterson's emphasis on the idea of writing *directly* for the screen. He acknowledges the necessity of adaptation, but privileges the 'originative faculties of screenwriters' (1942: 774). 'But the time is coming when dramas will be written directly for the screen and there can be slight doubt that these will be the superior films of the future' (ibid.). Later he writes: 'Hollywood is used to taking works of fiction in other forms and translating them into film; and for this and other reasons the talented writer does not feel encouraged to write for the screen' (1943: xxxii).

In 1950, the publication of Clara Beranger's handbook *Writing for the Screen*, demonstrates how central the term has become to screenwriting. In 1957, writing for the screen appears in the Academy Awards for the first time in the form of the categories of 'Best Screenplay – based on material from another medium', and 'Best Story and Screenplay – written directly for the screen' (the older category of Best Screenplay (original) is replaced by it). Today, writing for the screen is virtually a synonym for screenwriting. I have stressed that this notion is not simply a neutral description of what people do, but embodies assumptions about the nature of screen writing. But there is another dimension to this term that should be noted, namely the way it is caught up in a discursive struggle between craft groups and between different kinds of writers. Intertwined with this idea of screenwriting is a view that writing for the screen is the work of professionals rather than amateurs, insiders rather than outsiders. These assumptions form the basis of our discussion in the next chapter.

9.

THE RULES OF THE GAME

In this chapter, extending the discussion of the history of writing for the screen in the previous chapter, I look at the socio-politics behind attempts to define the 'rules of the game' of screenwriting. I identify gestures of gatekeeping and particularism in which writing for the screen (and sometimes 'story' itself) seems to belong to the screenwriter.

In the previous chapter Maibelle Heikes Justice identified a new 'game of screen writing' (1917: 245), played by those who belong to the 'new school', the 'trained and experienced screen writer' (1917: 246). Of course, contemporary film discourse is no stranger to the idea of screenwriting as a game played by 'players'. The scene from *The Player* (Dir. Robert Altman, Writ. Michael Tolkin, 1992) comes to mind, where studio executive Larry Levy (Peter Gallagher) dreams of eliminating the writer from the artistic process: 'We need to give them [the mass public] the kind of pictures they want ... not the kind writers want to give them.'

For those hoping for success in the industry, especially writers working on a free-lance basis or trying to write 'on spec', the 'rules of the game' take on a particular significance because they define the 'playing field'. This is not to suggest that the rules of the game are always articulated clearly or in a consistent manner, however. In an article entitled 'Rules of the Game', Jack Mathews focuses on the game of yes/no, or green-light/red-light in Hollywood. A reader of this article might expect a clear list of rules articulated across the industry, but what Mathews finds is that 'while everyone says there are rules, no two people named the same ones' (1990: 32). Once the content of the rules is put to one side, what is left is what I have been calling a gesture of particularism, a process where discourse is wrapped around a particular industrial grouping or formation, with group interests embodied in a particular aesthetic orientation or preference.

Perhaps because of the codified nature of scriptwriting, writers keenly feel the stress of rules; as Justice confesses, 'whenever anyone began to set up rules and regulations for me to do things by – it was always hopeless' (1917: 237). I want to suggest, however, that beyond the craft maxim that one should master rules before breaking them, a different critical or socio-political understanding of the rules of the game is warranted. Drawing on the work of French sociologist Pierre Bourdieu, Ian Macdonald suggests that an analysis of the practice of screenwriting should be accompanied by an analysis of 'the field':

> The field of film and TV drama, like other fields, is effectively a way of thinking which requires attitudes and competences, with behaviour determined not by overt and 'universal' rules or principles, but by judgements and distinctions based on a covert set of social relationships which are adhered to even if not referred to directly. (2004b: 267)

For Macdonald, informing these judgements and distinctions are norms and values that are held to be natural, but are in fact positions inscribed in discourse. A field of practice connects to a field of power with an internal logic, guiding judgements to do with originality, and what is a 'good' piece of work or a 'bad' one.

An important aspect of the critical analysis of the rules of the game is how rules operate over time to function as a received tradition. David Bordwell has explored the notion of tradition in a two-fold sense: as part of a set of group norms central to the Hollywood style and also as part of a tradition of 'continuity and innovation' (2006: 27). His analysis has special relevance to screenwriters, as from the 1960s the contract system of employment declines, and story departments begin to shrink, leaving a void or gap in the communication of tradition. Bordwell provides an account of what happened next, and what he finds is that both the game, and the rules, became harder for moviemakers to access, and the legendary storytelling principles established in the studio era became part of a legacy that was difficult to get practical experience in. As Bordwell notes, in the studio era, a young director could find out 'through routine assignments, what genres he had a flair for' (2006: 22), but in the 1970s this became difficult.

Screenwriting occupies a unique and complex place in the 'great tradition' (Bordwell 2006: 23). Bordwell suggests that contemporary screenwriting handbooks represent a 'consolidation of studio-era principles' (2006: 27), operating as a form of quasi-tribute. In combination with new modes of story development in the age of package production, the scene was set for a 'flood of manuals' (ibid.) – a screenplay fever to match the scenario fever of the past. 'Thousands of aspiring writers faced a decentralised market and lacked common training. They needed advice on format, plotting, and what the producers wanted. Above all the script had to win the support of gatekeepers, the development staff known as readers or "story analysts"' (Bordwell 2006: 28).

Bordwell's evaluation of contemporary screenwriting handbooks, while a noteworthy development in the encounter between film studies and screenwriting, is quite specific. His emphasis is to show that the Hollywood tradition remains vigorous by exposing 'some central constructional principles of contemporary moviemaking' (2006: 17). He is interested in the persistence of the Hollywood tradition through 'crucial practices of storytelling ... despite the demise of the studio system, the emergence of conglomerate control, and new methods of marketing and distribution' (ibid.). Bordwell is not interested in an in-depth analysis of screenwriting discourse (although in places his discussion of figures such as Joseph Campbell and Lajos Egri has the appearance of one), and he is surprisingly quiet on the wider politico-aesthetic implications of this new phase of laying down the rules of the game. He seems to see the handbooks almost as part of a self-help literature, 'guiding hopefuls to write scripts that would galvanise the frontline reader' (2006: 28); although he does acknowledge the area has become an 'academic enterprise' (2006: 34). Beyond this, his focus is on 'structural templates', and while he suggests that 'few screenplay manuals inspire confidence', what he does have confidence in is the narrative architecture that supports both Classical Hollywood style and the handbooks. And from this perspective the manuals 'remain a fruitful point of departure' (2006: 35). His discussion of the handbooks becomes a reflection on structure, on the details of three-act structure, its source (as 'trade secret') and institutionalisation.

> Once the three-act template became public knowledge, development executives embraced it as a way to make script acquisition routine. The page-count formulas became yardsticks for story analysts and studio staff. Today, most screenwriters acknowledge the three-act structure, and around the world it is taught as the optimal design for a mass-market movie. (2006: 29)

Bordwell does not explore the implications of this on screenwriting discourse *per se* . His focus is on the continuing tradition of Hollywood story, a fine-tuning of Hollywood dramaturgy. As a result, it is difficult to know how to read this last passage: in terms of a 'consolidation of studio-era principles', a 'long conga line of sales people from west coast [sic] United States ... selling craft' (Castrique 1997: 106) or, as Raúl Ruiz puts it, 'a system of ideas which devours and enslaves any other ideas that might restrain its activity' (1995: 14).

In response to this seemingly de-politicised account of screenwriting norms, I want to foreground some gestures of particularism in screenwriting: moments when writing is wrapped around a particular group who in turn have a key role to play in defining the rules of the game. Such gestures frequently arise in moments of tension or struggle. As media scholar Michael Schudson notes in a study of journalism:

> Cultural contact and conflict can provoke the articulation of norms inside the group. Here, the prescription that 'the way we do' things is 'the way one should do' things is a function of a kind of group egoism, a way of defining the group in relation to other groups. This may lead groups to claim independence or separation from other groups, but equally it may prod them to claim affiliation with other groups. (2001: 152).

Particularism is a broad social phenomenon. Screenwriting is not immune to forms of particularism organised around gender – and the plethora of early women screenwriters compared to their scarcity in the 1930s and 1940s should be noted (see Francke 1994; McCreadie 1994; Beauchamp 1997). Nor is particularism limited or specific to screenwriters, and it could be argued that screenwriters themselves suffer from other particularist games (such as those played by producers or funding bodies). However, thinking about particularism and screen writing (as a form of writing) allows us to understand how the shape or definition of writing can change through social and cultural group dynamics.

This chapter identifies several forms of particularism, and different games. In one sense the big 'game' is literary authorship; the default idea being that the writer is the natural author, the custodian of literary expression. This default position has historically opened up difficulties for screen writers because of their working with a filmic medium, but also because of their complex industrial and institutional conditions. There are also smaller 'games', which are like skirmishes between groups. Clara Beranger's conception of writing for the screen, for example, puts in place a clear distinction of roles between writer and director: 'it is the writer's function to create and develop the story. The director's function is to bring it to life' (1977: 143). But the primary form of particularism I am interested in is the melding of an idea of writing for the screen with the figure of the screenwriter.

Particularism and Writing for the Screen

While discussing the handbooks of the 1910s and 1920s, and also scenario fever, it is worth noting that the rules were not simply standing in the wings waiting to be employed. Initially, the provision of photoplay writing advice required breaking down boundaries between the practices of different studios, so that the 'fixed rule' related to more than 'but a single Editorial office' (Sargent 1916: 100). Providing clear advice to 'impossible amateurs' on the 'rules of the photoplay writing game' was an essential pragmatic response to scenario fever (Esenwein & Leeds 1913: 39–41).

Writing for the screen did not simply develop as a benign clarification or expression of craft, it was also defined in adversity as screen writers and editors struggled to explain their work to others and, in some cases, draw borders around their craft. With the development of writing as a craft area, tensions emerged between craft departments, with different roles or functions receiving special comment from screen writers (especially the director and producer). For Leslie T. Peacocke, there are too many companies 'in which the directors have it all their own way' (1916: 116), writing stories themselves or getting unqualified intimates to do it. He complains of the 'authority-drunk director' (1916: 117), but also adds that there are very few producers encouraging a 'new school of authors' (ibid.): 'The scenario editors and staff writers cannot raise their voices in protest, because they have to kow-tow to the directors' (ibid.).

These statements, while about the producer or director, are also expressions of an emerging (and usually elite) group identity in which scenario editors and staff scenarists lay claim to their craft. As Epes Winthrop Sargent notes: 'the mystery thrown about studio methods and a lack of established working rules has operated to keep this number small' (1912: 3). 'Only a few of the elect have the entree [sic] to the studio and editorial office where a knowledge of the possibilities and limitations of the camera may be obtained. The rest write blindly in the hope of achieving result [sic]' (1912: 5). Within this grouping, writing about the work of different writers sometimes has the feel of a 'who's in' and 'who's out' narrative (see Sargent 1914). In keeping with the professionalisation of US society that was occurring throughout the late 1800s and early 1900s this group identity is linked to a sense of professional uplift. Even in those handbooks that work against an elitist idea of screenwriting by encouraging novices, there is a rider that the chance comes only to those who have ideas, and who vow they will 'soon cease to be a mere amateur' (Esenwein & Leeds 1913: 12). Eustace Hale Ball, for example, notes how excellence in manuscript preparation affects purchasing agents so that they 'show a partiality to the scripts which possess less originality and dramatic value, when properly prepared, rather than "wading through" the amateurish offerings of less skilled writers whose work may have more intrinsic worth' (1915: 16).

A tension is evident in the handbooks between a closed idea of screen writing open to few, and an open one accessible to many. This leads to differing views on the appropriate form that submissions should take. For example, Ball advises readers to submit complete scenarios, arguing that the submission of 'ideas' and 'crude plots' is out of favour. This seemingly suggests that screen writing is open to all, but on closer examination Ball's advice is about exploiting a gap in the market related to 'experts' in a 'special class of writing' being overworked (1917: xiii–xiv). At the same time, he makes a wider point about the need for original stories in an exhausted field (1915: 176; 1917: 136). Peacocke supports the submission of synopses only: 'it is good general advice to beginners to submit nothing but two synopses, one very brief, the other extended to cover the story in its important details, instead of attempting the creation of a professional scenario script. Many producers so prefer. Of course if you feel competent – go ahead' (1916: 7).[101] He presents the views of one editor who favours the submission of a 'detailed synopsis, two or three thousand words in length, outlining the story' (1916: 108). This focus on the synopsis rather than a full plot of action supports Kevin Brownlow's observation that by the mid-1920s 'the motion picture business was now the exclusive domain of professionals' (1968: 278). John Emerson and Anita Loos write that 'producers would rather have your story in synopsis form, and let a trained writer put it into continuity' (1920: 3; see also 1920: 32). Frances Taylor Patterson also discourages submission of continuity, but stresses that studios will employ the ability to write continuity (1928: 39).[102] She recommends the form of the extended synopsis (frequently drawing on a knowledge of continuity), 'a narrative which conjures up a story in terms of scenes', a 'summary of pictured action' (1928: 14). Beranger explains to students in 1929 that the studios 'never buy an original continuity' (1977: 145). Discussing the importance of training in the technique of pictures 'they may buy synopses from an outsider' (ibid.).

Esenwein and Leeds' 1913 text is an interesting handbook in this context, as it responds to and seeks to redefine scenario fever – and as authors they are aware of doors closing. They speak of a 'weeding out' process carried out by studios, aimed at identifying writers from whom good material can be expected (1913: 16). They openly discuss the question of the field becoming overcrowded. They compare the chances of the established fiction writer and the novice (1913: 42), and highlight the need for competency and preparation: 'the proper preparation of the photoplay script has almost as much to do with its being accepted as has the fact that it tells a good story' (1913: 39). They also point out that 'Only those who are thoroughly equipped will be able to remain in the ranks of photoplaywrights when once the various manufacturers have drawn out enough competent writers ...: There will always be room for the competent writer, but a competent writer he must be' (1913: 62).

Esenwein and Leeds' awareness of the opportunities for different kinds of writers is tied to an important concern of the day, which has to do with the relative standing of the freelance or independent writer and staff writer. As C. B. Hoadley of the Biograph Company explains, commenting from the other side of the fence to Esenwein and Leeds, 'with the demand for the finished script, with strong plots carefully worked out, came the staff writer, the man on salary, which has mitigated in a measure against the freelance writer. The staff man has an advantage over the outsider, for he is in constant touch with the producer and has a first-hand knowledge of the requirements of the firm' (in Carr 1914: 106). For Ball, however, there are some advantages to freelancing. The independent writer is able to evade the deadening and narrow environment of the studios (see 1917: 131); 'the independent writer can read more ... and mingle more with the people who are interested, as laymen, in picture production. The professional never forgets his position, seldom ever understands the attitude of the outsider' (1915: 171). Howard T. Dimick suggests that 'few authors care to be staff continuity writers – a position that tends to submerge and strangle all originality and idealism' (1922: 330). Peacocke suggests that because of the desire to protect turf, 'Staff writers should not be allowed to read scripts submitted by freelance writers' (1916: 123). He sees a definite role for the staff writer as they whip original ideas into shape for directors, but they 'cannot be expected to supply all the original stories required' (1916: 128). There is a role for the freelance writer, but 'their stories have been wilfully kept back through the selfish motives of others in salaried positions, until hundreds of these writers – many of them with big plots and ideas ... – have grown discouraged and have discontinued their worthy efforts in disgust' (1916: 129).

A remarkable aspect of early screen writing handbooks is that, confronted with tremendous popular interest in the motion pictures, writers found themselves in a position to have to popularise the principles of drama to a wide audience. The handbook writers of the day thus found themselves drawing – with differing degrees of success and rigour – on classical notions of drama and rearticulating them in the context of the motion picture for an audience that may never have encountered them before. As a result, writers such as Sargent, and also Frederick Palmer (see 1924a: 144), became arbiters of aesthetic norms. What is especially noteworthy, however, is that this popularisation of principles of drama is not presented as part of a general course of instruction in drama. It is presented as a guide for the successful writing and selling of photoplay scenarios, and as such is frequently grounded in the point of view of the scenario editor. Sargent's work is particularly important in this respect, since he regularly refers to industry practices and figures, giving the impression of an extended 'club'.[103] He presents his work as setting forth 'rules for the guidance of the author ... with the full knowledge of the needs of the studio gained through service as an editor of scenarios' (1912: 3). Catherine Carr (1914) includes the contributions of a number of editors in her handbook, and presents her work very much as a glimpse behind the scenes of the profession of scenario writing and writing 'acceptable' scenarios. This aspect of the handbooks sets up a pattern that will be ongoing, namely the way in which aesthetic norms are institutionalised through attachment to the desires of specific individuals or groups. Thus even though rules may be explained as having their origins in supposedly unchanging and universal principles, they also have a link to a particular social or cultural context.[104]

When thinking about particularism, various interactions and relationships should be kept in mind, namely those between screen writer and other authors, screen writers and the general public and screen writers and other craft workers. But there are also interactions within the craft of writing between writers with different roles. A curious facet of the handbooks caught up in scenario fever – which makes them different to today's handbooks – is that the screenwriter was rarely the master of every aspect of screenplay format. Instead, they seek to reconcile the input of different writers and editors. While submissions from novices were more than encouraged, the technical dimensions of scripting became increasingly identified with the work of professionals in the field, particularly the continuity writer as craftsperson. James Slevin promotes the idea that while a picture play can be regarded as a piece of writing, and the work of the author, this is distinct from the 'art of the picture playwright or scenario editor', which deals with situations 'properly arranged for representation on the screen' (1912: 9). For Janet Staiger, around 1913 'a separate set of technical experts began rewriting all the stories ... material was handed over to these technicians who put it into continuity format' (1985: 190). Emerson and Loos go further and reserve some screen writing techniques for staff or trained writers, not to be attempted by novices (1920: 3, 34, 59). After surveying the varied production methods employed in the studios Jeanie Macpherson explains 'to all outsiders just why producers do not want stories submitted in continuity form' (1922: 29).

The status of the continuity writer was acknowledged as an issue for debate. Macpherson, a champion of the well-trained continuity writer, wonders 'perhaps there is some foundation for this widespread misconception as to the importance of the continuity writer's work, in the fact that there are still a few studios where it is considered mere hack work' (1922: 27). According to one view, the continuity writer is a mere technician, who simply works in format or works out the plot line (see Dunne 1980: 44; Staiger 1983: 35). For Emerson and Loos, however, the continuity writer at first appears as a format worker, but becomes the 'dramatist of the photoplay', or 'the craftsman of this trade' (1920: 34). For Patterson, the continuity writer is an 'original writer ... The continuity writer was long looked upon as a mere hack. This attitude is now taking its place among other vanished illusions' (1921: 67). In Macpherson's view, the continuity writer is the 'architect' and the director the 'master builder' (1922: 25, 26). Alongside the tendency to regulate the nature of material submitted to the studio, and codify scripting practice at ever-earlier stages, this development is about organising the 'real' work of scripting around a particular figure.

But the continuity writer is not always the sole focus. For Justice it is the figure of the screen writer who writes for the screen, and certainly not the 'scenario writer': she clarifies 'the title scenario-writer should never be applied to anyone but a staff writer or one who is content to do "continuity" alone' (1917: 242; see also Dunne 1980: 44). The 'true photodramatist' by contrast 'does all the work' (ibid.): conceive the story, put it into synopsis form, write dramatic action (ibid.). They are the only 'atom' of screen production (1917: 243). This is a rare person: 'one in a hundred among fictionists and stage dramatists can grasp this vitally necessary scheme of screen action' (1917: 240). Justice draws on a collective 'we' to enthuse about what the 'trained and experienced screenwriter' can bring to the screen. Justice's writing is a gesture of particularism, but one that resists the organisation of screenwriting around the staff writer. She writes:

> One cannot blame the human tendencies of regular staff writers for trying to hold down their position, but it is a bad place for the young writer with new ideas to be consigned. Far too many scripts are turned over to staff writers 'to see if there is anything in them'. If there is anything new, the scripts are likely to be thrown out as quickly as if perfectly hopeless. (1917: 247)

Here, Justice perfectly articulates how an established social grouping (often contrasted with new arrivals) can dominate a process and engage in gatekeeping. A similar gesture operates around the Eminent Authors scheme, discussed below.

Particularist gestures have a strong influence on the development of the notion of writing for the screen. They emerge at times when the position of a social or professional grouping is under threat or needs redefinition. Technique frequently becomes an important site of definition and contestation. For Emerson and Loos, success in the industry 'in every case came through technical mastery of the art of photoplaywrighting' (1920: 2). At the beginning of *The Art of Photoplay Writing*, Carr affirms the notion that 'anyone can write a scenario', but she hastens to add that the 'gulf' between watching and understanding 'can only be safely crossed by the study of technique' (1914: 5). For Henry A. Phillips it is technique that distinguishes the superior writer from the method of the 'poor plotter' and 'shallow artificer'. As he makes clear, in a chapter called 'The Rules of the Game':

> In no literary effort is technique more important or essential than in the construc-
> tion of the photoplay. There are arbitrary rules that must be followed and conven-
> tions that cannot be ignored. We must cater to the manufacturer's possibili-
> ties; we must conform to fixed mechanical limitations; we must interpret our
> art thru [sic] 'business' ... And, greatest obstacle of all – our photoplaywright
> must accomplish his eloquent task by remaining technically silent! We come to
> the conclusion that construction and technique are equal in importance – if not
> superior – to idea or conception of the writer. (1914: 97–8)

Here, technique becomes a site of negotiation or compromise between a range of interests in the field of screen writing. But note how the form of this compromise is couched in the pronoun 'we'.

Here, as in many other handbooks, the study of technique becomes a key marker of the difference between the aspirant or amateur writer, and the successful scenario writer. The ability to write in continuity form draws special attention. As Emerson and Loos put it, 'If your story is accepted the editor will have it written into continuity form by a staff man. Learn continuity, but don't attempt to sell stories in that form until you have thoroughly mastered it' (1920: 32). Technique is a key term when various authorities advise the new writer not to submit full scenarios, but to only submit detailed synopses: 'for some years continuity has been written only by those on the inside, who were trained to write it – and the outsider can't do it. It is virtually impossible for the plot builder unacquainted with the inner rules and regulations of a motion picture studio to prepare a motion picture continuity' (Wright 1922: 9). Beranger, commenting on the importance of studying drama, remarks, 'But the technique you cannot get anywhere but in the studio' (1977: 148).

The focus on technique can be seen in terms of a broader emphasis on craftspersonship that Dana Polan suggests is a key aspect of the American tradition (see 2007: 26). It is not necessarily particularist in that it is based on the assumption that 'you make yourself by making things'. Crafting, as Polan suggests, need not necessarily lead to a career, and can be based on the intrinsic value of workmanship. While this may be true, the particularist impulse informing the handbook genre gives it a pedagogic quality, separating players from non-players in a broader game of industry, in which industrial knowledge belongs to a social minority. Indeed, Peacocke distances himself from an orthodoxy based on technique, when he writes:

> What is the 'technique' of a photoplay? I'm sugared if I know! All the wiseacres who are writing on the art of photoplay writing keep continually harping on that word, as if it were a mythical something that we grasp from nowhere, but which must be vitally essential to insure success. Bosh! To the Devil with technique! We want to be photoplay-writers, not technologists. (1916: 37).

Here, Peacocke is sensitising his reader to a particularism specific to the 'wiseacres'. While technique was initially an important term in the development of screen writing, at a certain point it came to represent a blockage to that development. In 1914, while William Lord Wright insisted that 'photoplay writing is a profession, and a difficult one' (1914: 224), he also expressed concern that 'many writers pay too much attention to technique, and not enough attention to the story' (1914: 62). He quotes Benjamin P. Schulberg, a photoplay editor, saying that '"The greatest difficulty in the path of the scenario writer today is – too much expert advice"' (1914: 63).

Eminent Authors, Inc.

Placing the emphasis on the study of technique bears within it a dilemma, in so far as it relies on a decision about the kind of technique. The 'study of technique' can be used to discern between proven scenario writers and unpublished aspirants or novices without great difficulty. It is harder, however, to distinguish between authors from other literary disciplines and scenario writers. This dilemma is highlighted in the controversy over the so-called Eminent Authors, Inc. established by Samuel Goldwyn in 1919, which sought to import successful authors into Hollywood to work on motion pictures, and promised greater involvement and control in the treatment of their work.

All the works of the authors involved were under exclusive control for film adaptation, and the corporation held production rights for future works (see Kemm 1997: 95). As Terry Ramsaye writes:

> The Goldwyn concern experimented with a drive aimed at creating in the author a new order of stardom. 'Eminent Authors' were imported by the Hollywood studio in quantity lots. They included Rex Beach, Rupert Hughes, Mary Roberts Rinehart, Sir Gilbert Parker, Eleanor Glyn, and others of magazine glory. No new stardom resulted. The authors proved to be writers still, not picture makers. (1926: 753)

Staiger has noted that Goldwyn's scheme was not the first of its kind (1983: 34),[105] although it was perhaps unique in the formality of its structure and promises to authors. Its significance is its part in formalising the notion of writing for the screen, and the way the scheme highlighted the failure of authors to adjust to film writing.

One reading of the Eminent Authors scheme focuses on the efforts of established authors from the East Coast of America being blocked by veteran writers of the screen (see Fine 1993: 56), resulting in a tension between the serious writer and studio writer that dominates accounts of the fate of East Coast novelists in Hollywood. But this venture can also, thanks in large part to Tom Stempel, be read in relation to the defence of writing for the screen as a particular formation of writing. It was through conflict with authors imported into Hollywood that continuity writers already in Hollywood refined their notion of writing for the screen. Particularism is frequently established or founded, and reinforced, through interaction between different groupings. Behind scenario fever is contact between the general public and the scenario editor or continuity writer. But the Eminent Authors scheme represents a different kind of interaction between studio and company writers and celebrity writers.

The Eminent Authors scheme was a way to capitalise on the involvement of fiction writers and playwrights in the filmmaking process – remembering that the use of novels, short stories and plays as source material was widespread, and rights to literary properties were expensive. It was also designed to 'put the emphasis on stories rather than stars' (Stempel 2000: 52). Eminent authors were selected to write stories for the Goldwyn films, but met with resistance from screen writers established in the studios: 'There was a resentment against the Eminent Authors [sic] from the writers who had learned the craft of screenwriting' (Stempel 2000: 53). Stempel sees the main consequence of this episode being 'the growing intellectual putdown by the New York literary establishment not only of the movies, but particularly of screenwriters' (ibid.). He quotes Goldwyn: 'The great trouble with the usual author is that he approaches the camera with some fixed literary ideal and he cannot compromise with the motion picture viewpoint' (ibid.). Elmer Rice recounts:

I had accepted Goldwyn's offer largely on the strength of his promise of free creative scope. But he had reckoned without the scenario department's entrenched
bureaucracy. The practitioners of the established patterns of picture making saw in
the invasion from the East a threat to their security. (1963: 179)

Rice adds, however, that 'the proposed revolution in writing came to nothing. All story
material was channelled through [John] Hawks [the head of the story department],
who vetoed every innovation with the comment that it was "not pictures"' (ibid.; see
also Stempel 2000: 54). In his narration of these events, Stempel stresses the fric-
tion between the East and West Coast of America, the resentment of the scenario
department and the eminent authors. Clearly, ignorance of 'studio methods' underpins hostility between the eminent author and the continuity writer (see Patterson
1921: 87–9).

Stempel highlights Mary Roberts Rinehart's observation that:

The stubborn resistance ... he [Goldwyn] met was not in the authors, most of them
humble in their ignorance of the new art, but in his own organisation. If authors
could arrange in what sequences their stories were to be developed, leaving to mere
technicians the details of that development, the high-salaried scenario department
would become superfluous. (2000: 53; see also Rinehart 1931: 292)

Stempel may be correct in observing that 'Rinehart obviously had very little sense of
what was required to translate a prose story into a script and a film' (2000: 53). Rinehart also fails to consider the issues surrounding the status of writers in the studio
system, as evidenced in her reference to 'mere technicians'. Yet she is also making
an assessment of the particularism of the day.

While agreeing with Stempel's argument, I want to suggest that the terms upon
which the disagreement between writers and screenwriters took place had much
to do with writing for the screen as a discipline of writing and as an invented craft.
Support for the view that the controversy surrounding the Eminent Authors scheme
was about writing for the screen can be found in a passage from Beranger:

When the producers realised that there had to be stories written for the screen,
they did not use writers trained in screen technique, but brought out a perfect
avalanche of writers from New York – novelists, playwrights, short story writers.
When the producers said, 'Go West, young man', the writers went – in special
trains and deluxe compartments. The companies treated them well on the way out;
the return trip was less deluxe ... The reason these writers did not succeed was
because they maintained an attitude of superiority and looked down on pictures.
They had absolutely no humility, and made no effort to study the technique of
writing for the screen. (1977: 138)

Whereas the eminent authors found the bureaucracy of the scenario department a disabling entity, this structure was highly invested in the notion of writing for the screen. Frances Marion writes:

> All of us who had been schooled in writing directly for the screen grew a little fearful of being undermined by so much talent, yet we knew that sooner or later these authors would find out that the screen was not an easy medium to write for. It entailed many special aspects of which they would have had no previous knowledge, such as the importance of camera angles, the ability to make stories come to life without the power of speech to explain their actions, and the measuring of scenes which, if permitted to run too long, would make the theatre audiences restless. (1972: 83)

Brownlow describes the situation in the following terms:

> Regular continuity writers, despised as hacks, were called in to rescue many an Eminent Author from many an elementary muddle ... Some of the scenarios written by the Eminent Authors have remained in Hollywood legend as Awful Examples. 'Edward Knoblock wrote a scenario for my father', said Agnes de Mille, 'but like most ... he couldn't think visually. One line in the scenario came up as: "Words fail to describe the scene that follows"'. (1968: 276).

What this passage from Brownlow suggests is a set of expectations about how writing for the screen should work; expectations that already function as a normative conception of screen writing (or were set up as norms prior to and in the wake of schemes such as the Eminent Authors).

The Eminent Authors scheme constitutes a key instance in which writing for the screen is elevated to the status of a normative practice in order to police the boundaries of screen writing practice. These boundaries are not simply boundaries between forms of writing, but between media. Frances Taylor Patterson draws out this point in her assessment of the Eminent Authors: 'Yet, because of their very excellence in using the medium of prose fiction or dramaturgy, because they have been trained by years of finished artistry to express themselves in words rather than in pictures, some of these writers are predestined never to become great writers of the screen. True though it is that they have a marvellously developed sense of plot ... they still must learn to develop plot in terms of action, and delineate character through the medium of pictures' (1921: 66).

Making Sense of the Division of Writing

With the detailed division of labour in the studios, the early practice of writers helping out with editing, lighting and acting became less common. But alongside the greater separation of different crafts the space of writing itself becomes more divided. Underlying tensions between staff and freelance writers and eminent authors, is a rapidly developing studio context. Staiger has explored the conditions leading to the need for story departments, and also a distinction between 'the "caged" writer, who wrote original plots, and the continuity writer (often seen as a mere technician), who transformed these plots or other media into script blueprints for use by shooting units' (1983: 35). Staiger notes that these two functions might be 'combined into a single individual but more often were split among several employees' (ibid.).

While one way of thinking about these studio divisions is through the idea of the 'corporate laboratory', another possible perspective is to think about how screenwriters sought to process these divisions of writing, internalise them into craft or professional identities, shape their own discourse and make claims to original writing for the screen. I have already noted how the process of writing continuity was linked to the art of the photoplay, rather than to hack work. Another example here is Dimick's book, *Modern Photoplay Writing: Its Craftsmanship*, which is addressed to the aspirant 'screen author', the 'authors for the screen'. He provides an account of screen writing that fuses the screen author to writing for the screen, but also maintains a close eye on changes in screenwriting discourse:

> From the point of view of the screen author the change in attitude of those who control the industry toward the contributor of screenable stories has undergone a complete cycle, ranging from the day of borrowed literature, rehashed from standard literature by some studio hireling, to the day of the original photoplay written directly for the screen by an author whose importance is recognised. (1922: 11)

Dimick heralds the 'era of the screen author, whose profession is the creation of stories in dramatic form for the camera' (1922: 12). For him, adaptations are still important, but their preparation is 'the recognised work of still another class of recognised screen authors – the continuity writers or dramaturgists proper, who correspond to the adapting dramatists of the stage' (ibid.).

For Dimick, the emphasis on the continuity as blueprint did not always work in favour of screen authorship:

> The era of 'ideas' was succeeded by the era in which the producers demanded the 'scenario' or continuity; and this era may be called the era of smug incompetence, for the selection of scenarios fell into the hands of people as little fitted by educa-

tion (if they could claim any!) and ability to judge the merits of proffered plays as well could be imagined. And in practically no instance was any chosen scenario produced as written by its author. (1922: 12–13)

He goes on to mock attempts to improve this situation through the publication of handbooks purporting to 'unfold the art and business of scenario writing'. This passage provides a context for his account of strained continuity writer/independent author relations. It is a background marked by grievance and political struggle with a kind of particularism that looked to limit the art of the photoplay to the few. Dimick's view is that it is a misconception to locate the problem in a lack of gifted scenarists. He suggests that the 'so-called "gift" of the scenarist, tightly clutched to the breasts of the fifth grade morons who formerly presided over authorial destinies in the industry, is not confined to the few' (1922: 14–15). If Dimick sees new hope for screen authorship it is because of a new avenue of submission via a detailed synopsis rather than continuity: 'a synopsis amounting in length to a short story, cast in the dramatic form, establishing the events, developing the characters, introducing the atmosphere, but minus all dialogue and moralising not pertinent to the pictorial demands of the MECHANISM it is intended for, the CAMERA' (1922: 14). Between the story idea and the continuity sits the detailed synopsis 'based upon and intended for continuity' (1922: 26). Dimick seemingly sets the screen author and continuity writer up as part of the same brotherhood. An accord of sorts seems to have been worked out between the 'independent author' and the continuity writer. 'In the modern photoplay world, then, playwriting may be divided into two branches or variations: synopses or continuities' (1922: 15). But he adds quickly, 'It can not be too strongly asserted, however, that the author of the plot is the playwright in the true sense' (ibid.). Here Dimick reveals his own investment in a different game, that of playwriting.

Dimick's work is an example of the changing dynamics of the industry in the 1920s. With talking pictures, the dynamics behind the divisions of writing change again, and different couplings of writers appear. As Larry Ceplair notes:

The advent of sound in the late 1920s altered the scenario-writing constituency. Dialogue writing became the rage, and production heads stripped their payrolls of gag and title writers, retaining only the most-trusted constructionists and pairing them with imports from the theatre – anyone with a track record of writing 'lines'. From this mating of constructionist and dialoguer emerged the screenwriter of the studio era. (1996: 38)[106]

But this 'mating' was not straightforward. By the 1930s, the work of the continuity writer seems to be once again transformed, linked to the breaking down of the script in financial, administrative terms (in Howard 1995: 214). With the greater influx of writers from the East Coast in the sound period, the division between literary types and continuity writers shifts. Howard describes the resentment towards continuity writers:

> A continuity writer is a gentleman who shakes his head gravely over any idea the screenwriter may have to offer and remarks: 'That may be all right but it isn't pictures'. His function is to relieve the writer of the obligation to learn his job and to complicate the already complex collaboration with the director. (Ibid.)

Note the echoes of the declaration 'not pictures' from the Eminent Authors period.

It is easy to overstate the antagonism between the author and the continuity writer.[107] Newly arrived authors tended to see Hollywood as a virgin field, and failed to credit writers already working there. Discussion of the fate of 'authors' in Hollywood also tends to view the continuity writers of Hollywood in a negative light, turning 'technician', yet again, into a pejorative, and delegating 'the staff writer to anonymity' (Staiger 1983: 41). However, as Staiger notes: 'These tame writers' contributions to the final film's form and style undoubtedly was more significant than the label technician implies. Furthermore the term suggests an implicit devaluing of that essential part of the work process' (ibid.). In many cases the efforts of these continuity writers were crucial to the gains of screenwriters in the 1940s.

In the 1940s, a new stridency in screenwriting discourse around the notion of writing for the screen emerged, once again tinged with particularism. Raymond Chandler puts it in aspirational terms:

> And there is an intense and beautiful hope that the Hollywood writers themselves … will recognise that writing for the screen is no job for amateurs and half-writers whose problems are always solved by somebody else. It is the writers' own weakness as craftsmen that permits the superior egos to bleed them white of initiative, imagination, and integrity. (1945: 53)

In this passage, writing for the screen is again linked to laying conditions on access to the craft. It is no job for amateurs. A series of 'proper' functions are assumed for production personnel: producers will produce, directors will direct. Writing for the screen becomes a term linked to a particular space of screenwriting, reserved primarily for screenwriters.

10.

CONCLUSION:
A PLURALISTIC APPROACH
TO SCREENWRITING

A key problem in screenwriting discourse has to do with thinking about a variety of approaches to screenwriting and scripting. A pluralistic approach to screenwriting, one that recognises different styles of scripting, can be difficult to imagine when the dominant focus is on rules for storytelling, proper construction and norms for writing. In this concluding chapter, as well as revisiting some key points about improvisation, notation, creation and interpretation, structure and production, I focus on the issue of pluralism and some obstacles to it. From this point of view I look at the seminal work of Ken Dancyger and Jeff Rush in Alternative Scriptwriting, and suggest that there is a tension in their work between the concept of 'the Alternative' and pluralism. Building on the work of Kathryn Millard, I argue for a more historical approach to writing for the screen. I then return to the argument that our understanding of screenwriting is shaped by the idea of a separation of conception and execution. Increasingly, the separation of conception and execution is being challenged in practice, especially from new ways of working linked to digital filmmaking techniques. I want to suggest that with this challenge to the logic of separating conception and execution comes the need to reconsider, on a conceptual level, our notions of screenwriting beyond ideas of the blueprint and the screenplay.

Beyond 'the Alternative'

There are many ways of making films and 'doing' screenwriting. Obstacles exist, however, in embracing pluralism in filmmaking and screenwriting. There are numerous attitudes and biases one can point to here: the focus on box-office success, purist approaches to genre and formula, or the belief that the rules of screenwriting are timeless, and that what held for Aristotle, for example, holds today. One obstacle to a pluralistic approach to screenwriting is a tendency to define a particularly dominant model of industry practice as a normative form of practice that others must either follow or situate themselves against. Thus, exciting possibilities in the realm of screenwriting practice are pre-positioned in the space of 'the alternative'.[108] In their important work *Alternative Scriptwriting: Writing Beyond the Rules*, Ken Dancyger and Jeff Rush seek an 'inclusive' approach to narrative options. They indicate an interest in the plurality of forms of writing when they seek to celebrate 'a multitude of approaches to screenwriting and filmmaking' (1995: ix). They go beyond the imperative to write a structurally sound screenplay and reconnect scriptwriting to a broader storytelling tradition. Rather than rest their work on undeclared rules and principles, they 'outline conventions and then suggest practical ways to undermine or alter those conventions' (1995: 1). Reacting to the restrictions of conventional structure, Dancyger and Rush encourage the reader to 'develop alternative narrative strategies that prompt you to write the best screenplay you can write' (ibid.). The topics at issue include form, content, character and language.

Dancyger and Rush respond to the norms and attitudes explored in chapter nine by encouraging authors to go 'beyond the rules'. But while their work is at the vanguard of thinking about different approaches, it also operates within a particular space of screenwriting. Ultimately their goal is to help the reader develop and write better screenplays. Their vision of pluralism is linked to a space of 'the alternative', which is marked out from 'mainstream forms' and a 'strictly formulaic approach to scriptwriting' (1995: x). It is a space that seeks to go beyond 'restorative three-act structure' (1995: 21). Dancyger and Rush's work provides a shake-up of screenwriting, but from the perspective of pluralism there is a tension between their emphasis on multiple approaches and an idea of 'the alternative' residing 'beyond' the mainstream. The task of finding a 'counter-structure', and of detailing 'alternative structures' (1995: 31), can take over from the task of thinking pluralistically about screenwriting.

This point returns us to the distinction introduced at the start of this book, between screenwriting as a primarily page-based form of writing for the screen, focused on the script as a manuscript, and an extended idea of screen writing not necessarily limited to the page or a page-based format for script writing. Screen writing in this latter sense can utilise the page in unorthodox ways. Also, it is not limited to writing for the screen but extends to writing on or with the screen. To distinguish this extended space of screen writing from solely writing for the screen, I have used the term 'scripting', by which I refer to practices of 'writing' understood very broadly, encompassing writing with bodies, with the camera, with light, and so on. Even when page-orientated the focus is on movement, rhythm and physicality (see Kahan 1950).

Viewed in these terms, Dancyger and Rush's understanding of alternative screenwriting, as valuable as it is, does not necessarily challenge the conventional relationship between screenwriting and scriptwriting as it is received through ideas like writing for the screen. Scriptwriting for them is the writing of screenplays. As such, their vision of 'the alternative' is not boundless; it is an alternative approach to the writing of screenplays. It is not a notion of the alternative that automatically extends to radically different visions of screen writing and modes of working. They come closest to this when they discuss what they call 'personal scriptwriting' (1995: 276) towards the end of their book, but ominously the subtitle to this chapter is called 'beyond the edge' (ibid.). Here, they admit candidly that 'up to this point, we have been discussing scripts for feature length, theatrical films written in standard screenplay form so that others might direct them' (ibid.). This section of the book responds to 'growth in alternative sources of funding and low-tech production opportunities' (ibid.). These new approaches to production raise questions about screenwriting technique, and also issues to do with giving underrepresented groups or individuals a voice. While Dancyger and Rush can be considered brave in ending their book by looking at a 'different notion of writing' – those 'not written in standard screenplay form', and 'usually designed to be directed only by the writer, and ... not feature length' (1995: 284) – they tend to treat this style of filmmaking through the lens of 'personal scriptwriting' and experience which in a sense narrows the implications of these forms of scripting for the mainstream.[109]

I want to suggest that this focus on 'the alternative' needs to be supplemented with a broader analysis of the rules of the game of screenwriting. As an example of this, take Mike Leigh's approach to filmmaking, which has a very limited reliance on scriptwriting *per se*. For him, a range of other 'scriptings' take precedence, many of them taking place in the space of rehearsal.[110]

> The rehearsals consist of an accumulation of experienced events; there's a lot of discussion, research and, above all, improvisation. But there are no scenes as such until much later on: they're what I'm concerned with when I come to shooting the film itself. First, there is a journey that leads to the film, involving elaborate improvisations that create the premises for scenes. I create scenes distilled from improvisations. But I don't go away and sit in a room and write a script. We do it by going through it and building it up so that it is being written by actually rehearsing it. (In Fuller 1995: xv)

I want to draw three points from this quote. The first is that the conception of writing that Leigh draws on in this passage is different to the conception of writing underlying the notion of writing for the screen. It is not fully page-based and rehearsal is treated as a practice of writing. Indeed, when Leigh is questioned regarding how the script literally gets written down, he downplays the importance of this step: 'In the strict sense, it doesn't [get written down] because it doesn't need to be, provided the actors know what to say. In other words, we could rehearse this conversation without anyone writing anything down' (ibid.).

The second point that can be made relates to improvisation. This way of working often suffers from being understood in terms of the real or perceived 'absence' of the script. Screenwriter Terry Southern describes improvisation as 'a last resort to save an obviously sinking ship' (in Baker & Firestone 1972: 77). However, improvisation can also be considered in less negative terms, and as George Kouvaros notes of John Cassavetes' approach, improvisation 'reveals itself as a deliberate attempt to open the performance of character up to resonances, questions and points of view which cannot be answered or contained by the narrative' (1998: 251). Rather than be seen in terms of a reinterpretation and refining of the script (see Crimmings & Graham 2004: 247), improvisation can be viewed as a scripting in its own right. In Leigh's account, the discussion of improvisation is not limited by the question of the presence or absence of the script, but is linked directly to the process of scripting and creation.

The third point that can be made in relation to this passage is that there is more at stake here than just a question of alternative screenwriting. Because Leigh's approach is different, it runs the risk of being misunderstood by a funding/theory nexus whereby funding bodies draw on particular interpretations and understandings of narrative structure – such as the three-act formula (see Thompson 1999: 339) – to make their decisions. As Peter Sainsbury notes:

> the films emerging from a given funding system largely reflect the values and proc-
> esses at the heart of their funding organisations, whatever they may be, and that
> films produced in any given cultural zone in any given period reflect the diversity of
> the funding systems that existed then and there, or a lack of diversity as the case
> may be. (2003)

Sainsbury's point about diversity goes to the issue of pluralism. A particular funding/ theory nexus can either nurture plurality or exclude particular approaches to film-making. In Raúl Ruiz's case, diversity is limited by central conflict theory: 'To say that a story can only take place if it is connected to a central conflict forces us to elimi-nate all stories which do not include confrontation and to leave aside all those events which require only indifference or detached curiosity' (1995: 11). Ruiz suggests that the central conflict theory is 'a predatory theory' that preys on other approaches to narrative and story ... fictions which do not comply with these rules have been consid-ered unacceptable' (1995: 14–15). In Mike Leigh's case, the issue is not limited to central conflict theory, but a failure to recognise and accommodate a different way of working. 'I'm the man who doesn't have a script, won't say what it is going to be about, and doesn't want to discuss casting – not by any standards a viable commercial proposition!' (1995: xvii).

Diversity in itself may not lead to commercial box-office success. Intertwined with this emphasis on diversity, however, is the idea that screenwriting, to remain invigorated, needs to explore and evaluate different forms of scripting and approaches to filmmaking. But to do that, it also needs to cast off limiting frames of 'the alternative' and explore what a fully pluralistic understanding of screen writing might look like.

The Gospel of Story

Alongside normative conceptions of screenwriting there is another potential obstacle to pluralism, which has to do with a lack of historical perspective on screenwriting, and ideas such as writing for the screen. One area in particular relates to a closer historical understanding of the role of the 'gospel of story' in screenwriting.

Given its place in film culture, it is natural that writing for the screen is a resilient idea. A 2006 journal issue on 'cinematic screenwriting' is an example of how the notion of writing for the screen persists as a stepping off point for discussions of screen writing, as well as attempts to create a more pluralistic space of screenwriting. The editor Kathryn Millard writes:

> This special issue … explores cinematic approaches to writing for film and television and explores the place of 'story' in the movies. Are 'story' and structure everything? How can the unique qualities of cinema as a medium be brought more into the writing and filmmaking processes? What does it mean to write for the screen? After all, not only is cinema currently going through an era of substantial and far-reaching transformation, but in our digital era the very notion of writing itself is shifting. (2006a)

This description of screenwriting highlights several points of anxiety over writing for the screen. There is a concern over how story and structure have become an orthodoxy in screenwriting – the primacy of story is questioned. The unique qualities of cinema are posited as somehow being undervalued. The reliance on an idea of the cinematic is linked to changes in the digital era. There is a sense that the tensions articulated in this passage are familiar (see Kahan 1950). Historical antecedents to Millard's critique include Victor O. Freeburg's and Frances Taylor Patterson's focus on the cinematic aspect of the photoplay in the 1910s and 1920s. Placing cinematic approaches in a tension with story and structure can operate as a gesture of rejuvenation and experimentation, but can also work to reinscribe the debate in well-worn dichotomies of the cinematic and the narrative. But, as Millard notes, the very notion of writing itself is shifting. While in agreement I would, however, want to recognise 'writing for the screen' itself as a significant 'shifting' of writing that has been under-analysed.

I have argued that screenwriting discourse is today framed by terms such as the screenplay, the blueprint and writing for the screen, but within this frame certain key concepts such as story and structure can dominate discussion and also work to limit pluralism in the space of screenwriting. At a time when understandings of screenwriting are being contested, it is worthwhile to reflect on the terms or terrain of contestation. Millard asks, 'Are "story" and structure everything?' In asking this question, she is attempting to engage with a key set of terms in screenwriting discourse. These terms have been dominant since early screenwriting: addressing the problem of putting stories into structure Francis Marion suggests that 'the successful writer knows that the story must have a particular structure and that no amount of polish will conceal structural defects' (1938a: 21). Furthermore, for Marion, what makes a good story and structure is not just dependent on satisfying an audience, but related to what the studio wants. More recently, the problem of story and structure has taken on new dimensions; because, as William Goldman puts it, 'if screenplays are structure, and they are, then movies are story' (2000: ix).

In themselves, the concepts of 'story' and 'structure', and their relationship, are open to a range of interpretations.[111] But what does Millard mean by the question 'Are "story" and structure everything?' Another question she poses points us to an answer: 'Why do so many screenwriting theorists and industry personnel insistent [sic] on the primary importance of Story in cinema?' (Millard 2006b). Millard is responding here to a particular nexus of interests around script development and screenwriting knowledge. Adrian Martin takes on the same nexus in this passage: 'According to relentlessly established current convention, a film story is a good story, well-told and well-constructed, if it flows, if it makes sense … if it moves towards the fulfilment of a goal or the resolution of a struggle' (2004: 84).

This particular focus on story has gained a key place in the dominant mode of film practice. As Staiger (1985) has shown, it dates back at least to discussions of the quality product in the early 1910s. Staiger suggests that, from 1955, what she refers to as the package model of production has become dominant (see Bordwell et al. 1985: 330). This system has placed increased focus on the script as a means of securing the right 'package' (the right actor, director, concept). While it has given rise in some cases to innovation and differentiation, it has also been accompanied by a set of orthodoxies about story. For some critics, including Millard and Robert McKee, something is not right in that so much money is spent 'for options on films and rewrites on films that will never be made' (McKee 1997: 13; see also Millard 2006b). These projects enter what has been dubbed 'the Black Hole of Development' (Stempel 2000: 185). Millard does not share the solution put forward by McKee, however, which is to focus on story: 'Wistfully he looks back to a golden era of Hollywood where seasoned story editors oversaw the training of their apprentices, insisting always on the pre-eminence of story. The flood of screenwriting texts and How-To-Write-A-Screenplay manuals crowding bookshelves today share McKee's emphasis on story' (2006b). Sharing concerns voiced by filmmakers such as Raúl Ruiz and Wim Wenders, and theorists such as Jean-Pierre Geuens, Millard questions the over-arching emphasis on story.[112]

Millard's essay goes on to explore other approaches to writing based on her own practice, and the practice of others (such as Wenders and Atom Egoyan). Working from images, photographs, maps, places and people, are set in opposition to the gospel of story. Working from unique rules for story design, of structure and selection (Ruiz), or linking through 'rhythms of movement and colour as [much as] by theme and motif' (Wong Kar-wai) are described approvingly. She celebrates 'improvising with the camera'. She also sees a link between digital technologies and these 'less prescriptive methods of scripting and filmmaking'. Digital cinema has allowed 'more fluid relationships between the stages of planning, shooting, editing and post-production'.

Millard's work opens up a crucial question: 'what does it mean to write for the cinema?' (2006b). In answering this question she draws inspiration from 'the inventiveness of early cinema', from 'a time before the screenwriting manuals were written, before the rules of cinema were seen as fixed'. She finds the 'more fluid relationships between writing, performance and shooting … commonplace in the [early cinema era] of particular interest'. But reading Millard, there is a sense that her account of the gospel of story lacks a detailed historical dimension; for, as I have argued, early cinema (by which she means circa 1914) was not a screenwriting manual-free zone. Indeed there were many manuals, actively articulating the rules of the cinema, and working out what it means to write for the camera. This is not to downplay the significance of the pluralistic approaches to writing she explores (comedy writing in early cinema was particularly unique), or to argue against her suggestion that the film industry adopts particular ideas about screenwriting as a norm or gospel,[113] but rather to make a case for the need to engage with the history, theory and practice of screenwriting in greater depth.

As part of making this case, I suggest that there are at least four layers to the problem of 'story' as Millard articulates it, each with their own particular historical dimension.

On the first layer there is the rise of film as a self-sufficient product, distinct from the contexts of presentation of early cinema. Charles Musser argues that the work of story presentation in early cinema has particular qualities: 'its representational system could *not* present a complex, unfamiliar narrative capable of being understood irrespective of exhibition circumstances or the spectators' specific cultural knowledge' (1990: 2; emphasis in original). In the presentational mode 'many narratives were highly conventionalised and operated within genres far narrower than those found in later cinema' (1990: 4). This system depends on familiarity with the story and intertextual references. 'The filmmakers assembled spectacular images that evoked the story rather than telling the story in and of itself' (1990: 5). In this period the issue of story and structure was not contained in the space of the self-sufficient film. However, as films become stand-alone products, their intelligibility becomes a key focus. 'Continuous action' becomes an important desideratum (see Pratt 1973: 37; Staiger 1985: 175). Joseph Medill Patterson provides an account of narrative expectations in 1907:

> Today, a consistent plot is demanded. There must be, as in the drama, exposition, development, climax and dénouement. The most popular films run from fifteen to twenty minutes and are from five hundred to eight hundred feet long. One studio manager said: 'The people want a story ... When we started we used to give just flashes – an engine chasing a fire, a base-runner sliding home, a charge of cavalry. Now, for instance, if we want to work in a horse race it has to be as a scene in the life of the jockey, who is the hero of the piece – we've got to give them a story; they won't take anything else. A story with plenty of action. You can't show large conversation, you know, on the screen. More story, larger story, better story with plenty of action – that is our tendency.' (In Pratt 1973: 50)

This passage illustrates that the focus on story is long-standing, but also that there were clear determining factors behind it.[114]

A second layer of the problem of story has to do with issues of dramatic construction. With the emergence of film as a self-sufficient product, and increasing demands for story as a means of narrative clarity, one area of concern for critics was 'action for action's sake', a problem William Morgan Hannon identifies with 'plot-ridden' chase films. Relying on a distinction between plot and incident, Hannon opens up the issue of construction. He insists that 'plot is not a hazy, haphazard affair but a structure that possesses an "architecture" of its own' (1915: 36). This architectural issue is central to the problem of structure. Different critics will favour different theorists – from Aristotle to Gustav Freytag to Georges Polti – but the impulse will be similar. While the problem of structure today seems to be dealt with in terms of where to place a turning point in the screenplay, it is important to recognise the different ways different critics have approached it.[115] For example, for Tamar Lane the introduction of dialogue into film, the standardisation of projection speeds, the loss of intertitles, all contributed to a transformation in structure. He advises readers that stories may now be episodic and need not strictly follow the 'rising-scale type of dramatic construction ... [that] builds steadily without a letup to the climax' (1936: 18). Indeed, he declares that through speeding up the film and in the use of shorter sequences, along with process or composite shots, the Aristotelian unities of time, action and place are being left by the wayside (1936: 14–15).

On the third layer of the problem of story – in addition to film as a self-sufficient product and dramatic construction – exists the contemporary focus on screenplays and screenplay form, which itself dates back to the 1940s. Contrast, for example, Hannon's discussion of construction and architecture above, with the contemporary view that 'screenplays are structure' (1984: 195), or Syd Field's attempts to represent the screenplay in diagram form (1994). In what is a relatively recent development, the problem of structure has become compressed, and as a result, the 'essential opening labour' has become 'deciding what the proper structure should be for the particular screenplay you are writing' (Goldman 1984: 196).

The fourth and final layer I wish to highlight has to do with Staiger's conception of the 'package-unit' mode of film practice after 1955. This mode saw the end of the 'self-contained studio'. As Staiger explains:

> Rather than an individual company containing the source of the labour and materials, the entire industry became the pool for these. A producer organised a film product: he or she secured financing and combined the necessary laborers … and the means of production (the narrative 'property', the equipment, and the physical sites of production). (Bordwell et al. 1985: 330)

Staiger's focus on narrative property has significant implications for screenwriters who found themselves as 'players' in the package. Stempel describes this period as one of 'projects' and describes the exemplary case of William Goldman selling his original screenplay for *Butch Cassidy and the Sundance Kid* (Dir. George Roy Hill, 1969) for $400,000 in 1967: 'the money that went to Goldman for this script said that an original screenplay, which had very little status previously, could be a major element in a project' (2000: 181). The salient issue for us here is the way this context becomes the 'Church' in which the gospel of story is told, with the 'sermon' taking the form of a properly constructed 'spec' screenplay.

Taken together, these four layers give a sense of the discursive and institutional context in which story and structure has become a particular kind of problem in screenwriting. Millard's question 'what does it mean to write for the cinema?' is indeed worth engaging with. It has historical and current relevance not only for our understanding of screenwriting, but of the production process and the nature of expression in cinema in the past and in the future. But this case also demonstrates how an understanding of screenwriting discourse can contribute to our understanding of practice, and how it is shaped in particular ways – an understanding that has consequences for our appreciation of different forms of scripting.

Digital Scriptings: Challenging the Separation of Conception and Execution

Screenwriting has always been impacted on by technological and industrial developments. Digital filmmaking and scripting techniques represent a new area of development. While screenwriters use software to write and format their scripts, the very nature of the screen is transforming. 'Scripting' today can be easily extended into the domain of computer programming, motion-capture, algorithmic decision-making, interactivity, dynamic media,[116] and avatars, visualised across a range of screens (from mobile phones to iPods to *Second Life*). According to Andrew Bonime and Ken C. Pohlman, writers today are expected 'to exercise an understanding of the syntax and grammar of these new media that are as unique as those needed by screenwriters to successfully write for film' (1998: 2–3).

One of the key arguments of this book is that our understanding of screenwriting (along with other aspects of film production) has been shaped by the idea of a separation of conception and execution. Different forms of filmmaking practice can work against this separation (improvisation for instance); and in the late twentieth and early twenty-first century digital filmmaking has been linked to a challenge to this separation. With any challenge to the logic of the separation of conception and execution comes the need to reconsider, on a more conceptual level, our notions of screenwriting beyond ideas of the blueprint, the screenplay and writing for the screen. However, screenwriting is awkwardly placed for this task: a great deal of screenwriting discourse can be seen as a response to the separation of conception and execution, but at the same time screenwriting is today moulded by the separation.

Considering the expense of much large-scale film production, and the requirement for more thoroughly prepared material, it is doubtful that the page-based script will disappear from the scene of production in the near future. What has, and will, come under greater scrutiny, however, is the idea of a sovereign script arising, presiding over the production process – the product of a single gesture of conception or pre-planning. What will be challenged are the terms on which the separation of conception and execution and division of labour were achieved in the 'blueprint' era of production.

Digital filmmaking techniques have long been recognised as a challenge to the 'assembly line'. For Scott McQuire, in an early study of the impact of digital techniques on filmmaking, one of the hallmarks of crossing the digital threshold is that the sharp distinction between pre-production and post-production, conception and execution, is being challenged: 'Such a neat separation between different stages no longer seems so certain or desirable' (1997: 36). According to McQuire, digitally-orientated film production work that may traditionally have been seen as 'post-production' can happen now during the shooting phase. 'Film post-production processes are increasingly running parallel to each other. Post-production will now often begin during the shooting of a film. An increasing role is played by computer pre-visualisation in production planning' (1997: 3). Pre-visualisation, which refers to the practice of using computers to do rough planning or versions of scenes before shooting, has become especially important in relation to very expensive effects, where thanks to computer modelling a sequence can be previewed and perfected as the production goes (see McQuire 1997: 36). As David Dozoretz describes it: 'Pre-visualisation ... means to use all of the computer technology that is normally associated with the end of the filmmaking process – post-production – and bring all of that technology and technique into the earlier part of the process, into pre-production' (2004).

This development can have a direct effect on screenwriters who can benefit from the 'liberation of imagination' of digital technology, but must at the same time 'be aware of the consequences of certain script choices' (Greg Smith in McQuire 1997: 38). One view of a solution is for producers to involve 'post-production' houses at earlier stages, once the 'heart and soul is there', but before the budgets are finalised. Another implication is that visualisation happens not only in the writer's imagination but on the screen.

As the arrangement between conception and execution is modified, especially in the context of digital filmmaking techniques, the relationship between words and images also changes. Scripting is not simply a word-based activity, but happens with visual aids, sketches, models. This has historically been the case to some extent, with sketches and storyboards forming an important aspect of production – Alfred Hitchcock is a popular case here.[117] But I would suggest some digital techniques impact on the relationship between words and images in new ways.

Exploring the case of 'pre-visualisation' in greater depth, it is usually imagined within an art direction framework with the main focus placed on design and planning: the focus is on realising vision, or getting the vision out. When constructed as a form of 'pre-'visualisation – the prefix is contested by Francis Ford Coppola, who sees it simply as a form of visualisation (see Ferster 1998) – it is difficult to imagine a relation between screenwriting and pre-visualisation except through the written page, and a kind of factory-line of visualisation: from page ... to drawing ... to animatic ... to actual scene. It will be worthwhile unpacking this relation, however.

Pre-visualisation overlaps with the space of screenwriting to the extent that both pre-visualisations and scripts are about the communication of ideas. In the case of pre-visualisations, the communication is often about particular issues: set design, texture, blur, detail – although screenplays can suggest ideas here as well. Bill Ferster suggests that 'pre-visualisation is the process where scenes in a film are rendered beyond the simple descriptions on a script or storyboards' (1998). Here pre-visualisation is being framed, I would argue, as more or less a kind of visual and communicative aid. As a form for the communication of ideas, pre-visualisation can be studied in its own terms or, following Ferster, put in a subordinate position to the script. Through this frame, the space of screenwriting is not massively disturbed by pre-visualisation. But there are other ways of looking at the relationship. An overlap (and perhaps merging) of pre-visualisation and the space of screenwriting becomes greater in relation to storytelling. As Dozoretz suggests: 'when you are doing pre-visualisation, you're not worried about final effects, final quality, or how wonderful it looks or how perfectly it moves. What you are worried about is storytelling, you're in the same mind set that a director is. You're worried about blocking, timing, pacing and most of all readability' (2004). Readability brings pre-visualisation into the space of 'the read' in screenwriting, although by the term Dozoretz means discerning what is happening in very brief (sometimes less than a second) amounts of time.

Screenwriters might be quick to make the point that this idea of readability is about the *telling* side of the story, not the *story* itself; that it is on the 'realisation' or 'execu-tiuon' side of the vision (if one chooses to invest in that term). And in this sense the relationship between screenwriting and pre-visualisation can be characterised along the lines of the split between creation and interpretation. But there are other possible narrative models to work with here, and if one adopts the view that story arises out of the telling, that performances can create the story, then it is possible to say that the sequence is being 'written' or 'visualised' in pre-visualisation to some extent – an arrangement that threatens the stability of the prefix. Motion-capture technology and 'on-set' pre-visualisation technologies are interesting examples to consider here, as they can allow the scene to be created in the acting-out, and viewed immediately. It is perhaps not a coincidence that many motion-capture artists come from the areas of dance, acting and pantomime (see Taylor & Hsu 2003: 102) – areas that under-stand writing with the body and forms of choreography. This example suggests that digital technology can bring these 'storyboarding' techniques into the realm of crea-tion, rather than 'interpretation' of some already existing text.[118] For Thom Taylor and Melinda Hsu, pre-visualisation is an 'integral step of art department pre-production' (2003: 101), but this technique has the potential to break away from a supporting role for the written screenplay, and become a form of scripting in its own right.

As I am interested in a range of forms of scripting, it is worth noting that a heavy reliance on animated scenes or 'animatics', can lead to constraints on the actor's scriptings whereby the actor needs to match, or at least work with, a pre-existing animatic performance. Increasingly software can help 'create a set and experiment with the position of actors and cameras prior to shooting ... Blocking and camera placement/setup can be visualised using video representations of the actual actors and sets' (Higgins 1995).

While a full account of how digital production techniques are transforming audio-visual creation is beyond the scope of this book, digital filmmaking is of interest to us because it is an important area in which screenwriting is being reworked (see for example Munt 2006, 2008). For George Lucas, digital filmmaking prompts a chal-lenge to the separation of conception and execution in film production. In what he calls 3-D filmmaking the traditional separation between conception as an act of pre-production and execution or assembly as a sequential unilinear process is disturbed.

In this mode of working, conception is more closely linked to practice. 'You work on it for a bit, then you stand back and look at it and add some more onto it ... You basically end up layering the whole thing' (in Kelly & Parisi 1997: 163–5). Against the separation of functions typical of the centralised studio system, Lucas's system attempts to reunify these functions, and restore them to a craft context: 'Filmmaking by layering means you write, and direct, and edit all at once' (in Kelly & Parisi 1997: 163).

This conception of filmmaking by layering forces a rethink of the place given to writing in filmmaking, and the separation of labour around it. For Lucas, 'the film business is designed in a kind of industrial way ... The architect does the blueprint and hands it over to the contractor' (in Kelly & Parisi 1997: 165). Lucas envisages a mode of filmmaking where the divisions of labour around writing are not so rigid, but also where writing is less structured by the separation of conception and execution. He states: 'It is very hard to have planned out at the beginning what is going to happen at the very end' (in ibid.).

Whereas the classical Hollywood mode of film practice privileges the sovereign script or blueprint over other forms of scripting (exploration through rehearsal, writing with the camera), Lucas's approach is attuned to multiple scriptings: small video cameras allow for visual forms of notation. Storyboarding, writing, shooting and editing occur at the same time: 'whether I am doing notes on paper or doing notes electronically it all comes down to the same thing ... It's like a painting. You rough it in ... You can see it evolve; you can sort of be with the work, rather than draw' (in Kelly & Parisi 1997: 165). In this way, Lucas reconnects the script to a range of scripting practices: 'Instead of making film into a sequential assembly-line process where one person does one thing, takes it, and turns it over to the next person, I'm turning it more into the process of a painter or sculptor' (in Kelly & Parisi 1997: 162). What is significant here, however, is that Lucas's disturbance of conception and execution opens up the 'process' of writing to include a range of scripting processes in production.

At times, these comments from Lucas have a speculative dimension to them; but a similar approach is evident in the work of other filmmakers. In his account of making the Australian low-budget film *Blacktown* (Dir. & Writ. Kriv Stenders, 2005), Kriv Stenders refers to what he terms 'live filmmaking': 'This method attempts to create a more organic and fluid atmosphere on the set and is opposed to the traditional approach, where you film a story and then cut it. I'm more interested in filming, writing and shooting concurrently, in a similar way to documentaries' (in Phillips 2007). In relation to story, this leaves room for improvisation and interpretation: 'although the story is already pre-determined, it's not written in the traditional script format, but more like a story outline. Everybody knows where the story is going – the beginning, the middle and the end – and who the characters are. What is left open to interpretation and for the actors to play with is how the scenes are articulated and how the characters present themselves' (in ibid.). Drawing on a range of influences, from documentary, Dogme and music video, Stenders develops a disciplined approach to story and scripting that does not privilege screenplay-script form (see Munt 2008). The director develops this approach for his next film, *Boxing Day* (Dir. Kriv Stenders, Writ. Richard Green, Kriv Stenders, 2007). As Sandy Cameron notes: 'The writing process for *Boxing Day* never advanced to a full draft screenplay, but what Stenders calls a "scriptment", which had precisely laid out story beats and sample dialogue, but with enormous scope for flexibility and improvisation' (2007). Noting that Stenders borrows the term 'scriptment' from James Cameron, Alex Munt highlights the hybrid nature of this form, 'half-Script and half-Treatment':

> Some scenes are fully written, some scenes are not. What it is, primarily, is a script in terms that you have each scene numbered (a scene breakdown) but it's written in a Treatment style. The story is very precisely mapped out from scene to scene. You can schedule it: you could basically shoot it. It's not like a Treatment, where what becomes is a scene, or a new scene, is left open-ended [sic]. (2008)

Munt also notes that the 'scriptment was not written with a view to progression to a standard script – but as a lean document activated for (micro-budget digital) production' (ibid.). Implicit in this form are broader conceptual issues to do with the relationship between treatment and script, and treatment writing as a form of scripting in its own right rather than an 'unedited' first pass.

Returning to Lucas's remarks about 3-D filmmaking, these can be seen as a direct response to the traditional separation of conception and execution in the Hollywood model. This is not to suggest that the separation of conception and execution disappears altogether. Indeed, the boredom of computer rendering takes 'execution' to another level (interestingly, mini pieces of code called 'scripts' often handle these operations). Computer effects work often relies on an extremely detailed division of labour organised around the pixel and every frame, and McQuire notes the emergence of a 'new Fordism predicated on extreme specialisation of tasks' (1997: 45).

New forms of digital cinema can have an ambiguous relationship to the logic behind the separation of conception and execution. On the one hand, the separation is maintained: Taylor and Hsu, in their writing about digital cinema and the script, work very much in the Hollywood 'paradigm' of screenwriting and of the commodity. Cast, personnel, target audience, niche markets and return on investment are all key considerations of the package (see 2003: 35–7). A separation of conception and execution is evident in their advice to 'make sure your script is ready before going out to shoot it' (2003: 40). Staged readings, videotaped rehearsals and pre-visualisation are all linked to helping 'pre-edit' the script. This approach maintains an idea of the script as blueprint, and a more or less traditional view of the development process leading to a shooting script (see 2003: 66). With the script in place, digital cinema opens up a range of tools offering different forms of execution and ways of telling the story. It offers 'independence in shooting and finishing' (2003: 25). Interestingly, however, their work also gestures towards a different understanding (see 2003: 54), in which access to a digital video or DV camera can translate into improvisation over time, incorporating shoots and reshoots (a layered approach in Lucas's terms). In this mode, the smaller scale of DV production allows a mode of scripting that supports rehearsal and improvisation. It also leads to less disruption of these script-ings/performances through the use of smaller crews, and more intimate relations on the set, especially between cameraperson and actor. Taking stills of actor perform-ances with the video camera allows one to create storyboards that maintain the visual integrity of these performances (see 2003: 68). Actors can feed directly in to the visualisation/scripting process and make discoveries of their own rather than simply interpret the script (see 2003: 73).

There is a need to resist hyperbole about the digital revolution in filmmaking. But some reflection on how older ideas of screenwriting get imported into the space of 'new media' would also be useful. In other words, there is a need to reflect carefully on how the separation of conception and execution is being transformed, but also persists.

For example, the separation of conception and execution can persist *organisa-tionally* in digital filmmaking, with the director and pre-visualisation team working out scenes in advance. The film script still plays a key role in project development. Mean-while, on the level of *context*, the nature of the separation of conception and execu-tion is changing. Whereas once the separation was an organisational principle for the entire studio, today what once required many workers can be achieved on a desktop or the 'digital backlot' (McQuire 1997: 4). So digital filmmaking transforms the studio in this sense, allowing for new possibilities in DIY filmmaking, and a new age of the 'studio without walls' where technology and effects that were once the province of the studios become available on the desktop (see O'Regan 2000: 64–7).[119]

On the level of *concept*, the kinds of stories told are impacted on by the crea-tive possibilities and financial economies of scale of digital techniques, including the inter-relationships between forms of 'screen media' (movies, games, subscriber and mobile television) (see O'Regan 2000: 62). Screenwriters are being reinvented as 'content creators'.[120] While on the level of *execution*, the nature of how things are done can be transformed. In a process that began with video, digital technologies allow for the simultaneous viewing/recording of images, as well as editing on set or the editing of 'digital dailies' (Thomas & Hsu 2003: 68). It can thus change the way one reflects on a scene or an edit.

On the level of *communication*, whereas once the script as blueprint was the primary form for intercommunication between producers and departments, today that role is being replaced by animations, mock-ups and so forth, although it is important to note that the script is not entirely supplanted. Working on *King Kong* (Dir. Peter Jackson, Writ. Fran Walsh & Philippa Boyens, 2005), cinematographer Peter Lesnie notes: 'The script makes great use of what I'd describe as "fragile" times of day – pre-dawn, dawn, dusk, twilight – to represent certain emotional states, not as short, transitional scenes, but as extended sequences that were very complex to achieve. This dictated all sorts of scheduling, design and lighting approaches so that we could allow Peter [Jackson] the maximum flexibility to find the dramatic truth of each scene in an organic manner' (in Gray 2005). This passage demonstrates that the script can retain an important role in the visualisation process. With changes on the levels of execution and communication, new modes of collaboration and cooperation are being explored. Ed Jones notes: 'there is a great potential for significantly altering the collaborative process. Instead of the cinematographer trying to interpret the vision of the producer and director ... they can now preview and tweak the images together, and maybe make subtle changes in an interactive environment. This can make a big difference in the dramatic content of the film' (in McQuire 1997: 34).

Digital technology can assist in reconnecting conception and execution, of introducing more acts of conceptualisation alongside the execution (as with Lucas's concept of layered production), or of increasing the number and forms of execution – as with setting up 3-D camera locations, positions, and lighting them, in a software package. These set-ups compete with the script as blueprint, having the additional benefit of being visual, having motion and open to live updating and editing. The emergence of 'concept rooms' filled with visual references and 'concept artists' (Gray 2005) are indicators that the separation of conception and execution has not magically disappeared from the space of production, but also point to the way that the circuitry between two aspects is changing, with the script becoming one of a number of elements.

This book has sought to address what it terms the 'object problem' in screenwriting – by which I am referring to the difficulty of defining screenwriting as an object, and identifying an object for screenwriting – by opening up a multi-pronged analysis of screenwriting. It has proposed history, theory and practice (and the interconnection between them) as important terms for reflecting on screenwriting. At the same time, through concepts such as scripting, discourse and the separation of conception and execution, I have sought to clarify and critically examine the nature of theory and practice. While my primary focus has been on the feature film, I have sought to contrast practices in this area with other approaches to scripting. Space has prohibited a detailed discussion of documentary scripting, which is intersecting dynamically with digital filmmaking, and raising important questions to do with the appropriateness of 'feature' or fiction-based notions of structure (see Wingate & Fischer 2001), the dominance of observational 'scriptless' documentary (see Delofski 2006; Hampe 1995), and the view that 'everyone knows the [cinéma vérité] film is made in the cutting room' (Rosenthal 2002: 266). An interest in the discursive underpinnings of practice has led me to examine the way the script is situated in production, the literary status of the script, the question of reading in relation to screenplays, and debates to do with auteur theory. I have suggested that three issues in particular help shape a modern or contemporary understanding of screenwriting: these include the idea of the script as blueprint, the idea of the screenplay and the notion of writing for the screen. While this book does not provide a total history of screenwriting from its origins up to the present it has sought to articulate and address some key issues in the historiography of screenwriting, fill some neglected areas and tease out the way screenwriting has become intertwined with norms that mould practice in particular ways. It has been a concern of this book to highlight the dynamism of screenwriting, and give a sense of the energy with which history, theory and practice interconnect and inform our sense of writing for the screen. Today, screenwriting seems on the brink of a significant transformation. While digital technology and changes in film-making techniques may prompt reflection about what writing for the screen means, established ways of thinking about screenwriting continue to structure or 'haunt' debates about screenwriting, and perhaps limit a more pluralistic understanding of writing. A challenge in this context is to comprehend how past understandings of craft and practice mould not only screenwriting as a practice, but ways of talking and thinking about screenwriting as well.

NOTES

1   Several works have attempted to expand out the film/writing connection in film in unorthodox ways, including Ropars (1981), Ropars-Wuilleumier (1985), Hansen (1985: 339), Brunette & Wills (1989) and Conley (1991). But this work has rarely broached the space of screenwriting in the mainstream sense.

2   Although I cannot offer a complete survey of screenwriting in other contexts, studies of early screenwriting in the UK (Macdonald 2007), France (Raynauld 1997) and Australia (Cunningham 1987), are a useful starting point.

3   The work of teasing out the theoretical aspects of screenwriting has also been developed by a number of works that are clearly the product of university degree programmes in screenwriting and film studies. A text such as Ken Dancyger and Jeff Rush's *Alternative Screenwriting* (1995) can be seen as a response to the orthodoxies that have built-up around the packaging of 'high concept' projects in the new Hollywood (see Wyatt 1994). Margaret Mehring's *The Screenplay: A Blend of Film Form and Content* (1990), seeks to draw attention to a wider concept of 'filmic writing'. Finally, Kristin Thompson's *Storytelling in the New Hollywood: Understanding Classical Narrative Technique* (1999) draws on screenwriting handbooks as part of its analysis of classical narrative technique.

4   The number of special issues on screenwriting in scholarly journals is a good indicator of interest here. Since the 1970s there have been special issues in *Film Comment* (6, 4, 1970/71); the *Journal of Film and Video* (36, 3, Summer 1984 and 42, 3, Fall 1990); *Millennium Film Journal* (25, Summer 1991); *Film History* (9, 3, 1997); *Cinema Journal* (45, 2, Winter 2006), as well as Australian journals *Media International Australia* (85, November 1997) and *Scan: Journal of Media Arts Culture* (3, 2, October 2006), not to mention projects such as *Creative Screenwriting*, which in its early editions sought to bridge academic and professional perspectives. The

Journal of Media Practice in the UK has also actively published work on screenwriting (see Macdonald 2003, 2004a, 2007; Nelmes 2007), and reported on events (see Dunnigan 2004). A proposed Journal of Screenwriting should further crystallise academic activity in the area.

5   Take, as an example, David Bordwell's study On the History of Film Style (1997). While mentioning the script in passing (see 1997: 166, 199), it does not engage with the attempt to rethink screenwriting history, or with the issue of screenwriting and style that is central to, say, Richard Corliss's book Talking Pictures (1974).

6   By way of illustration, whereas Terry Ramsaye's 1926 seminar on the history of cinema is seen as 'the first college course devoted to cinema' (Polan 2007: 94), this ignores earlier efforts to study photoplay composition. Dana Polan notes how historical accounts of the discipline acknowledge Vachel Lindsay's The Art of the Photoplay (first published in 1916, with a revised edition in 1922), but ignore other figures such as Victor O. Freeburg or Frances Taylor Patterson (see 2007: 19). Epes Winthrop Sargent could be included in this list.

7   Kristin Thompson's Storytelling in the New Hollywood is a possible exception here, as it specifically tries to interest screenwriters by offering 'a more fine-grained account of how actual films work than do screenplay manuals' (1999: ix). Her work can be seen as an attempt to bridge film studies and the analysis of storytelling as screen-writers might understand it.

8   Ian W. Macdonald has proposed an approach to the analysis of the field of practice of screenwriting, based on the work of Bourdiueu, which allows for a more 'critical position in relation to the rhetorical approach of the ubiquitous manuals' (2004b: 270).

9   I do not provide an in-depth analysis of three-act models for example. This is partly because an analysis is already well underway (see Coleman 1995; Thompson 1999: 11–36; Bordwell 2006: 29), but also because I want to focus on less well under-stood aspects of screenwriting discourse.

10 The production schedule of this project did not allow me to include content from Marc Norman's book, What Happens Next: A History of American Screenwriting (2007) in my argument.

11 In the following I engage with Azlant's thesis in some depth, and it is unfortunate that Azlant did not/has not published this work more widely (the exception is Azlant 1997). Other figures such as Stempel have made extensive use of Azlant's work, and in this sense I feel justified to focus on a dissertation as though it was a published book.

12 Corliss's works, while utilising history, could be more productively considered as an attempt to develop a mode of criticism that revalues the work of screenwriters in the context of auteur theory.

13 Richard Fine's West of Eden: Writers in Hollywood, 1928–1940 (1993), first published in 1985, shares links with these works, but also sits awkwardly with them,s

somewhere between a historiography of screenwriting and revisionist film history. His study is not a response to auteur theory or related to contemporary politics around screenwriting but is a study in the profession of authorship and literary culture. It has a very specific focus in that it seeks to put the 'Hollywood as Destroyer' of New York writers myth in historical and cultural context by re-examining it in light of concerns of professional authorship in the 1930s.

14   While it is not our key focus, it is appropriate to refer here to a developing litera-ture on screenwriting by women. Eileen Bowser makes the point that evident in the serials of the 1910s that starred brave women is the emergence of the New Woman: 'She wore less restrictive clothes, she was active, she went everywhere she wanted, and she was capable of resolving mysteries, solving problems, and escaping from danger. In the movie industry the New Woman was not only adored as a star, but also pioneered a new profession known as the "script girl" (keeping track of every detail during the shooting of a script) ...' (1990: 186; see also Singer 2001: 221–62). She also wrote screenplays. As Cari Beauchamp notes: 'half of all the films copyrighted between 1911 and 1925 were written by women' (1997: 11). The figure of the New Woman is uniquely intertwined with women screenwriters in early cinema, with figures such as Frances Marion, Anita Loos and Gene Gauntier, gaining a public profile in popular magazines. Scenario writing was 'touted as "a new profession for women"' (Beauchamp 1997: 42).

15   In case my comments on history writing could be taken as setting up an opposition between 'systemic' and 'life and times' approaches, I should stress that statements and recollections by individuals can form useful glimpses into discursive conditions at a particular time (see deMille 1939; Powdermaker 1950; Brownlow 1968; and Goldman 1984). Any analysis of the situation of the screenwriter in the Hollywood system eventually merges with an account of the studio system. Formal works on the history of the film industry and studios are useful here. Several works have been especially influential on the historiography of screenwriting including Ramsaye (1926), Hampton (1931), Jacobs (1939) and MacGowan (1965) (see Azlant 1980: 114). My own work is indebted to volumes in *The History of American Cinema* series by Charles Musser, Eileen Bowser and Richard Koszarski.

16   Kristin Thompson contributes to the discussion of structure/turning points in film and screenwriting circles, and goes head-to-head with Syd Field's theories (1999: 27–31). As such, hers is a contribution to screenwriting analysis, building on the insights of screenwriters which she cites (see 1999: 43).

17   Although related, Cecil B. DeMille and Agnes de Mille chose to use variants of deMille, the family name that William retained.

18   One way of approaching this issue has been to look at the emergence of writing departments. Agnes de Mille's assertion that the first time the words 'Scenario Department' appeared in Hollywood was in 1916, when William C. deMille arrived at Famous Players Lasky (see Brownlow 1968: 275; de Mille 1952: 12) could be

taken to imply that this was the first department. For Janet Staiger, however, 'By at least 1911, all the licensed and the major independent firms had a writing department turning out original material as well as a scenario editor and staff to read and select free-lance submissions' (1985: 190; also Bordwell *et al*. 1985: 146). Staiger and Patrick Loughney both cite Benjamin Hampton when he suggests that the organisation of scenario writing as a separate branch of production took place at the Biograph Company in 1900 (Loughney 1990: 212; Staiger 1983: 34; Hampton 1970: 30; also Stempel 2000: 5). Frank Woods credits Clifford Howard (circa 1908) with writing the first picture stories in continuity form at the Vitagraph Company (see 1977: 44), and Tibbetts credits Griffith's Fine Arts Studio for Triangle with developing the story conference for writers: 'The writing of films was no longer simply the results of one mind, barnstorming its way through a scenario' (1977: 41).

19   This amnesia unfortunately works against recognition of the role of women screenwriters in early Hollywood especially.

20   A note accompanying the list is instructive: 'A Suggestion: The above list, while far from complete, is the best obtainable of the work of scenario writers in productions released during the past year. This is primarily due to the fact that very often producers fail to give credit to the scenario writer. Very often investigations to determine the name of the scenario writer are blocked for reasons best known to the producer' (Dannenberg 1923: 123).

21   Loughney posits that the desire to draw on pre-existing written compositions in the making of movies is as old as commercial cinema production in the US itself. Rather than search for scripts *per se*, he looks at film-related production texts. He identifies some early playscripts as contenders. He is interested in the way these written compositions seem to be part of a development where pre-existing narrative texts are acting more 'screenplay'-like in terms of their role in the production process and shaping the film.

22   Any analysis of early screenwriting is faced with a problem that i) the underdeveloped division of labour often meant that film-workers performed multiple functions and had concurrent responsibilities; ii) processes of scripting are variable, some formal and others informal, some discursive (word based) and others non-discursive (staging) and were not always attached to a particular figure or department; iii) any idea of scripting should encompass the forms of scripting carried out as part of exhibition (including editing and rearranging of subjects, and lectures), and look at the pressures towards producing self-sufficient works with narrative clarity.

23   While Vertov maintains an anti-scenario position, it is interesting to note that he reserves a place for what he called the 'small scenario' or 'micro scenario' in documentary. This is a situated form of scenario writing done for a particular subject by camera people or their assistants (see Vertov 1967: 104–5).

24 Azlant is aware of the piece by Eisenstein that is relevant here (see Azlant 1980: 47), but refers to it as 'A Russian View of Scenarios' (*New York Times*, 30 March, 1930, X3).

25 Azlant refers to it as a 'kino-novel' that has similarities to the modern treatment form (1980: 47).

26 As each of the parts of *The Classical Hollywood Cinema* are identified with a particular author, when I refer to separate parts I will refer solely to the author/s of that part.

27 Peter Decherney, for example, has used Staiger's work on expectations of quality in the studio and the role of the blueprint (2005: 43). As I argue in chapter eight, there is a risk of turning Staiger's work on the blueprint into an account of total codification, in which all developments are explained through the adoption of the blueprint. Some variations to Staiger's scheme have been put forward. Musser suggests that while the cameraman system was used for actualities, a collaborative system of production was in effect around 1905–1907 (1991: 325), and that it might be more accurate to speak of a shift from a collaborative system to director-unit system rather than from cameraman system to director system (1991: 449). Richard Koszarski ponders if the central producer system is sometimes confused with an extended factory arrangement around one key figure, such as Thomas Ince (1990: 109). In terms of the development of the continuity system there is evidence that it was in use in the early teens (see Lonergan 1997: 275).

28 In *The Classical Hollywood Cinema*, Staiger's account of the script is circumscribed by her definition of Hollywood's modes of film practice. This framework alleviates the need for a broader theory of the script and scripting in her work. However, once she steps out of this framework an account of different understandings of the script and scripting becomes important. Staiger perhaps recognises this by the simultaneous publication of an article entitled 'Blueprints for Feature Films: Hollywood's Continuity Scripts' (1985) that cites *The Classical Hollywood Cinema* at one point. This article, which operates in a slightly different conceptual framework to that of *The Classical Hollywood Cinema*, follows up many of the questions raised by her other work, and raises others such as the relations between the blueprint and the screenplay, and the relations between the continuity script and other forms (such as the scenario) which do not disappear with the arrival of the blueprint, but persist in modified form.

29 Ian W. Macdonald (2004a) draws on the concept of the 'screen idea', the germ of anything destined to be a screen work, to approach the production and development process – especially the collaborative aspect of it – through a different lens.

30 The desire to have scripts shot as written is part of the emergence of the script as blueprint, but it was also used rhetorically as a signifier of professionalism and a strategy to counterbalance tampering by directors and editors (see Carr 1914: 8, 118).

30   Some writers shy away from the possibility of the screen drama as a form of litera-
      ture. Sidney Howard suggests in the late 1930s that the 'screen drama will not be
      literature but something else, something new' (1995: 217).

31   Nichols refused the Academy Award for his work on *The Informer* in 1936 on the
      basis of his work with the Guild, and became President of the Guild in 1937 (see
      Schwartz 1982: 51).

32   John Howard Lawson draws on Gassner and Nichols' work in his 1949 text, *Theory
      and Technique of Playwriting and Screenwriting*. Pieces by Carl Foreman and Sidney
      Howard share many of the preoccupations of Gassner and Nichols' programme (see
      Foreman 1972: 29–36; Howard 1995). Larry Ceplair and Steven Englund cite these
      anthologies in terms of an attempt to address the anonymity of screenwriters (1980:
      12–13).

33   Gassner and Nichols' collection was not the first anthology of screenplays published.
      An earlier collection is Frances Taylor Patterson's *Motion Picture Continuities*
      published in 1929. Béla Balázs suggests that scripts first began to be published in
      the 1920s in Germany (1970: 247). For a more detailed discussion of the history
      of such publishing see Morsberger & Morsberger (1975).

34   Richard Fine confirms but also questions some aspects of this view, arguing work
      practices included short contracts and working from home, and did not always fit the
      chained to the desk image (1993: 91–3).

35   A 1906 article provides an interesting counterpoint here because of the emphasis it
      places on writing: 'The stories are written, just as other stories are, with not so much
      care as to diction and detail, perhaps, but written with close enough coherences for
      the man that makes up the pictures therefrom to understand every movement and
      situation' (Anon. 1906).

36   Some critics refuse the category of literature. Lawrence J. Tretler suggests that 'as
      English teachers we must realise that when we teach drama, we step quite out of
      the realm of literature' (1981: 45).

37   Although Gassner notes that there are more than twenty screenplays in the collec-
      tion, and another 'Twenty Best Film Plays' is already in preparation (1943: vii).

38   Interestingly, since the 1940s the relationship between literature and the literary
      has been challenged from the point of view of popular versus high culture, the
      performing arts and the institution of English itself. Our distance from Gassner can
      be measured in part by the emergence of performance studies as a discipline critical
      of literary approaches to the theatre, and the analysis of performance via literature
      (see Styan 1984: 1–22; Phelan 1997).

39   Gassner's emphasis on gratification and pleasure can be read as a response to the
      argument of Henry Arthur Jones that 'the film cannot afford the quality and kind of
      pleasure that spoken drama can give – the pleasure of literature' (see Jones 1977:
      53). In a later collection of screenplays Sam Thomas also emphasises reading with
      enjoyment and satisfaction (1986: 1).

40 Novelisation of entire photoplays was practiced by fan magazines of the mid-1910s (see Higashi 1990: 193).

41 Indeed, the specific problem faced by Gassner endures today. Sam Thomas notes concerns voiced by readers of the *Best American Screenplays* series that screenplays were not being published in their original manuscript form (1990: 3). He addresses concerns regarding the dual column format used in that book (similar to Gassner's), which does not respect the original presentation. In one of many echoes of Gassner the subtitle of Thomas's anthology is 'complete screenplays'.

42 Another example from Shakespeare comes from David Bradley, who looks at the status of prompt books and the work of the 'plotter' in Shakespearean theatre, and their involvement in casting, props and utilising the stage. Bradley focuses on these, rather than the play-script manuscripts, in order to revitalise interest in the protocols of performance in the theatre which have been written out of the play scripts (1992: 4). It should be kept in mind that actors in this period would generally not have access to the entire manuscript of a play-script for study.

43 Adaptation theory has continued to develop and has found stronger theoretical foundations (see McFarlane 1996). Intriguingly, while adaptation theory does not always analyse the textuality of the script in detail the figure of the screenwriter as author is gaining greater attention, as (in the case of the screenwriter characters of the film *Adaptation*) an agent caught in a 'struggle to produce a screenplay that satisfies his ultimate personal convictions as a unique and creative writer (to remain true to the thematic concerns of the book) and the need to conform to the accepted Hollywood ideal of a high-budget feature film' (see McMerrin 2007). Sergio Rizzo observes that 'Oddly, for a self-reflexive movie about the creative process, it [*Adaptation*] has little to say about the "environmental pressure" of the studio system and its toll on the artist' (2007).

44 Screenplay length in handbooks is very often 120 minutes, despite the fact that it is sometimes hard to pick up a standard duration from what is shown in the movie theatre. William Goldman says the ideal length for a screenplay is 130–135 pages, which allows 15 pages to be cut, leaving the writer with around 115 pages (in Brady 1981: 89).

45 Although not all screenwriters, present and past, subscribe to this view. William Goldman states: 'I use tons of camera directions, all for rhythm. It often upsets the directors, who shoot the scenes the way they want them anyway. But it *looks* like a screenplay, and yet it is *readable*. The standard form cannot be read by man or beast' (1983: 56; emphasis in original). William Lord Wright advised photoplay writers to add a section, 'Suggestions to the Director' at the end of the scenario (see 1914: 191; see also 1914: 177).

46 For an application of Iser's theories to the film *Adaptation* (which in a sense represents/embodies a dilemma of how to properly activate a scheme that is difficult to pin down), see Bartlett (2007).

47   I have not fully investigated the origins of this correlation. It is not treated as universal to all forms of filmmaking, and seems to primarily apply to the writing of 'Spec' screenplays, or what Lewis Herman calls 'master-scene' screen plays (1952: 169), rather than shooting scripts. Intriguingly, Herman does not mention the rule in an otherwise detailed chapter on 'Writing the Screen Play', which includes sections on timing action and dialogue. A 1982 handbook by Eugene Vale, similarly does not mention the rule, yet develops an expansive theory of the exposition of time. At the same time, Vale sees the shooting script at sitting around 130–150 pages, longer than the 120 pages recommended by screenplay theorists. Yet Syd Field treats the rule as a given when he writes that 'One written page of screenplay equals one minute of screen time' (1984: 27). James T. Boyle focuses on the idea as a pacing principle (expand or contract the written scene depending on screen time). A weakness of the principle is the specification of the length of the page. To address this, and to avoid the misinterpretation that each page should take a minute to read he presents the fuller equation of A script page (11 inches) = Reading time (Approx 25secs) = Projection time (one minute) = Fictional time (variable) (in Cole and Haag 1983: v). The origins of the principle could of course be much earlier, based on studio lore and practice, and only required to be explained to the public when a new kind of spec scriptwriter emerged in the post-1970s period.

48   Thanks to Alex Proyas for this point.

49   In tune with Thompson's observation, one 'further constraint' elsewhere in the production process is in the form of script supervision and continuity. The 'Master Scene Page Count' sees each page of a script divided into eight-eighths (8/8). As Miller explains, 'every master scene is measured by the number of eighths it contains. A master scene may add up to only one eighth (1/8) of a page, and if there are several master scenes on that page, each master will score its own page count; for example 3/8 and 4/8 – the sum total of the page being 8/8' (1986: 26–7). This system, designed to calculate shooting time, developed as an alternative way of measuring scene length by pages when shooting out of sequence on a particular location. While it does not rely on a strict page/minute equation (although the system can give an indication if a film is running fast or slow) the master scene page count gives some indication of the mechanisms for script supervision in the studio system, which include practices such as timing both rehearsals and performances (see Miller 1986: 56). Through careful shot/scene timings, and calculation of screen time/film footage ratios, progress and efficiency can be gauged during production. Estimates of running time may identify overruns, which can lead to rewriting (see Vale 1982: 273). Miller signals the importance of this work when she notes that 'daily reports suggesting that filming is going over the projected length of the picture may influence the director and the producer to make deletions in the script' (1986: 72). My thanks to Daphne Paris – who sees the page/minute equation as a good *general* rule base on averages – for her discussions on this topic.

50   William C. deMille writes that 'if the writer is too exact in defining every move of the camera, every cut and every angle, he robs the director of freedom in his own proper field; he ties the director's hands to the point of cramping his cinematic style and preventing his use of the camera as an instrument for emphasising dramatic values instead of merely recording action' (1939: 157).

51   Frustrated with a perceived inability to 'convey mood' and 'to convey imagery' in such a form, Stanley Kubrick and Arthur Clarke 'proceeded to write "a 40,000 word prose piece" for *2001* before converting it into a screenplay' (Horne 1992: 52).

52   Not all approaches treat the script as a surrogate for the film, and Claudia Sternberg's work on reading screenplays is noteworthy here. Sternberg carefully explains the place and use of the script, raising wider methodological issues. She tries to distance herself from four 'fallacies', for example: i) the sequential fallacy that 'a screenplay is a by-product of a film' (2000: 153); ii) a directorial fallacy that 'the director may exercise major control over a film, but works on the basis of the screenplay. It is the writer who comes first' (2000: 154); iii) a dramatic fallacy, 'that screenplays are to film what drama is to the theatre' (ibid.); and iv) a screenplay fallacy, 'in which nothing but the script counts' (2000: 162). She is also careful to position the script not as an autonomous object, but in relation to a process of 'filmic realisation' (2000: 153).

53   Staiger sees standardisation as occurring mainly in the period from 1915 to 1931, and points to the influence of scientific management principles (see Bordwell *et al.* 1985: 134–9). My thanks to David Shepherd for this point.

54   As evidence of its awkward status, a review column in *Motion Picture Classic* was referred to as 'a review of the new screen plays' in the contents page, even though the term photoplay is used in the reviews themselves, and 'the Newest Photoplays in Review' is the title actually used (see Smith 1921b: 51).

55   Against the focus on theatre and acting, the magazine *Screen Play* or *Screen Play Secrets* which ran from the late 1920s to 1937 forms an interesting case. Combining movie and star promotion, fashion and gossip, the magazine looked at screen players at 'play', providing a glimpse of life in Hollywood.

56   In 1911, responding to the film industry's free borrowing from literary and theatrical sources as material for motion pictures – and specifically Gene Gauntier's adaptation of *Ben Hur* (see Stempel 2000: 8) – the US Supreme Court ruling KALEM CO. v. HARPER BROS. stated that a moving picture based on a literary work constituted a dramatisation of that work. This decision effectively restricted the free use of theatrical and literary source materials (see Azlant 1980: 104). On 24 August 1912, the US Copyright Act of 1909 was amended to recognise motion pictures as the product of authors, and from that date motion pictures were registered under their own category with the Copyright Office of the Library of Congress, including (albeit irregular) details of credits for direction, photography and writing. Prior to 1912 some motion pictures were registered under the categories of photographs (see

United States Copyright Office, Library of Congress 1951: v). 'Film scripts' before 1909 were also known to be copyrighted under the category of dramatic compositions (see Loughney 1990). The register is not fully reliable in that the nature of the contribution of all workers is not available for every motion picture, and the provision of this information is erratic. Only the title, name of claimant, copyright date and registration number is always given.

57 I am indebted to Rosemary C. Hanes, Reference Librarian, Moving Image Section, Library of Congress, for generously providing a description of the applications and ledgers, and research assistance in the inspection of deposit material. Thanks also to Brian Taves, Paul Spehr, Ned Comstock and Denise D. Garrett for their advice and assistance.

58 Many writers who worked for Famous Players-Lasky in the early 1920s were prominent members of the Writers' Club of the Screen Writers' Guild: June Mathis, Clara Beranger, Frances Agnew, Frank Woods and Thomson Buchanan (see Hustwick 1922). Cecil B. DeMille, William C. deMille and Thomas Ince were members. The weekly periodical of the guild, *The Script*, also tended to be produced by Lasky people.

59 Writing in 1928, Frances Taylor Patterson does not list screen play in her survey of studio vocabulary (1928: 220).

60 For an account of all of the versions of the Guild, including precursor organisations, see Wheaton (1973: 124–36).

61 My discussion of the Academy Awards is based on the nominations listed in Osborne (1989). However, I have supplemented it with an inspection of original Academy rules for each year of the Awards as many indexes to the Academy Awards streamline the wording of the category, especially the term 'screen play'.

62 As becomes evident below, this is a question with a surprisingly complex history in screenwriting. William C. deMille observes that a truce of sorts was reached between the two parties with the idea that 'Scripts are written in "master scenes" instead of detailed "cutting continuity", a method which gives the director the freedom he needs but makes it imperative that he follow the essential story as written' (1939: 160).

63 In what follows I rely on a distinction between the auteur theory as critical approach based on the personality of the director, and the *politique des auteurs* as a polemical position that has to do with expression. For an account of the process of translating and importing the *politique des auteurs* into the US, a process usually linked to Andrew Sarris (1962: 2), see Buscombe (1973: 170) and Hanet (1996). For Stephen Crofts the 'mistranslating' of *la politique des auteurs* into auteur theory was muddling and contributes to a theoretical bankruptcy (1983: 17). For a useful survey of the changing phases of auteur theory see Cook and Bernink (1999: 235–314).

64 Richard Corliss suggests the key problem arose with the uptake of auteur theory in magazines, newspapers and journals, which turned 'authorship' into 'ownership' (1974: xvii–xviii).

65　Claudia Sternberg picks up on this double-bind when she writes: 'Paradoxically, the reasons which deny the screenwriter the status of *auteur*, namely the restrictions caused by such forces as industrial production, commercialisation, censorship and collaborative structures, are seen as challenges for the director against which he or, less often, she can pit his or her *auterist* strength' (1997: 16; emphasis in original).

66　Wright for example notes that some directors work exclusively off the synopsis, which is seen as the strictly essential part (1914: 82).

67　It should be noted that it was only in 2001 that the Writers' Guild of America secured in the minimum basic agreement the principle that writers 'have the right to visit the set of the motion picture they have written'. 'NEGOTIATIONS 2001: Tentative Agreement Reached!' *NOW PLAYING* @ *wga.org* [The official e-newsletter of The Writers' Guild of America, west] IV.13, 7 May, 2001 <http://www.wga.org>.

68　Rudolf Arnheim makes a similar point: 'a director who only knows how to execute the filming of a script and who is incapable of inventing a film … is likely to be more of a routine technician than a creative artist' (1958: 12).

69　Alexandre Astruc writes that this 'implies that the scriptwriter directs his own scripts' (1968: 22). He goes on to state, 'or rather, that the scriptwriter ceases to exist, for in this kind of filmmaking the distinction between author and director loses all meaning' (ibid.).

70　Tracking the emergence of director-centred criticism would be a much larger task (see Buscombe 1973). For John Caughie, 'traditionally, the reference to the *auteur* in French film criticism had identified either the author who wrote the script, or, in the more general sense of the term, the artist who created the film. In the work of *Cahiers* the latter sense came to replace the former, and the *auteur* was the artist whose personality was "written" in the film' (1981: 9; emphasis in original).

71　Sternberg notes that 'It would be a mistake, however, to believe that the *politique des auteurs* brought an end to flourishing critical investigation of the screenplay: these investigations did not exist before the triumphs of the auteur critics. Nor are critics who oppose auteur criticism necessarily motivated by a deeper understanding of screenwriting' (1997: 16).

72　Although it should be noted that this understanding clashes with a view put by Patterson, who places interpretation in the primary position. Patterson suggests that the director gets credit for authorship because the 'secondhand authors' of the screen do not 'cast their message in screen language … they must have an interpreter. The interpreter is the director' (1928: 126).

73　William Morgan Hannon takes the opposing view: 'Broadly speaking, the writing of the scenario involves creative power; the acting, interpretive power; and the directing, creative, interpretive, and for want of a better term, executive power' (1915: 24).

74　Arnheim argues that the notion that the director is a mere executor of a work of art should not be applied to film, primarily because the distance between literary word and visual medium is much greater than in the theatre (1958: 11).

75 Astruc also used this term 'illustration': 'Direction is no longer a means of illustrating or presenting a scene, but a true act of writing' (1968: 22).

76 Another example comes from filmmaker Wong Kar-wai: 'Sometimes people think, "Well, why don't you work with a script?" I said, "The script is only a part of this process. It's only the foundations. It is only a blueprint"' (in Pomeranz 2005).

77 Beyond analogy, Patterson also describes a variation in scripting practice from the Douglas Fairbanks Company, which 'consists in the reduction of the script [from the treatment stage] to a set of blueprints drawn up exactly like an architect's plans (1928: 51–4).

78 It should be noted that different writers advance the idea of a longer, more detailed, deluxe script (see Esenwein & Leeds 1913: 145; Nichols 1942: 772; and Howard 1995: 211).

79 Sargent was a writer and journalist from a well-to-do family, formerly an influential reviewer of vaudeville, and a co-founder of Variety (see Azlant 1980: 109).

80 Ramsaye's work forms an interesting case here. His history is cast as a general history of the development of the photoplay as story-film, measuring different innovations against 'the photoplay idea' (1926: 331), and tracing the 'father of the modern photoplay' (1926: 395). Remarking on the short subjects of the late 1890s, Ramsay comments, 'it took another ten years to discover that editorial and dramatic intelligence could fuse the picture and the printed word into the hybrid screen art which today we call the photoplay' (1926: 267–8). He remarks of Edwin S. Porter's The Great Train Robbery, 'now that the motion picture had attained the photoplay it had become an independent art, seeking its own channel of service to the public' (1926: 430). For Ramsaye, then, the era of the photoplay can be tracked to at least 1905, 'when the motion picture [was] reborn with the advent of the photoplay' (1926: 440), long before the era of the multiple-reel feature.

81 Esenwein and Leeds speak of the 'huge feature photoplay' (1913: 143). Benjamin Hampton describes this length forebodingly as an 'unexplored field' (1970: 40). Frances Taylor Patterson celebrated the passing of the 'artificial' 1000 ft. limit and encouraged art patrons to 'rejoice over the emancipation of the photoplay' (1921: 114). In this usage, the photoplay is considered a feature film of usually five reels shown in one screening, the production of which was prompted by the success of European productions longer than a single reel (see Macgowan 1965: 155). Victor O. Freeburg states: 'the favourite length for serious photoplays is five reels, which requires the uninterrupted attention of the spectator for a whole hour' (1970: 234–5). The success of longer films pointed to flaws in the business assumptions surrounding the 1000 ft., one reel limit, and ultimately led to a change in distribution and exhibition practices (see Hampton 1970: 118).

82 Even if, as Richard Koszarski notes, Zukor largely abandoned the policy by 1915 in favour of screen stars (1990: 68). For Sumiko Higashi, central to Cecil B. DeMille's strategy was inserting 'the photoplay into genteel culture by exploiting parallel

discourses deemed highbrow in an era characterised by conspicuous racial, ethnic, and class distinctions' (1994: 1).

83 In his summary of the trade papers Edward Azlant notes that the magazine *Photoplay* ran with that title in 1911 (1980: 110).

84 Azlant notes the importance of this double meaning in Sargent's work (see 1980: 212), and stresses that Sargent never gets the two senses confused, but regrettably Azlant chooses to suppress this aspect of screenwriting discourse by using 'scenario' to refer to the written work. This dual meaning of the photoplay predates the ambiguity of the term 'screen play' referred to in chapter five, but nevertheless contributes to an understanding of the textuality of the screen play.

85 Sargent discusses the impact of *The Great Train Robbery* in creating a demand for stronger stories, which led to the practice of inviting outside writers to contribute (1913: 8).

86 Scenario fever is predominantly cast in terms of the interest of the general public. Wright, however, explores it as an expression of literary interest from novelists, short-story writers, journalists and poets: 'Of the two hundred thousand literary workers in our country today, it is estimated by some that at least one hundred thousand are toiling in the photoplay writing field. Writing the motion-picture story has assumed the dignity of a separate and distinct literary profession' (1914: 8). Decherney adopts a different focus, looking at efforts by Thomas Ince and Thomas Edison to approach college students for scenarios (2005: 23; see also Koszarski 1990: 106).

87 The purchasing of rights for existing plays and novels produced its own problems, however. By 1917 Eustace Hale Ball writes that the cinematograph companies have almost exhausted 'the field of novels and stage plays for picturisation' (1917: xii). Emerson and Loos declare that 'every time an original idea comes into a scenario department, everybody from the president of the company down gets on his knees and gives thanks' (1920: 3). Howard makes the same point as Ball in the 1930s which is perhaps testament to Hollywood's ability to recycle material (see 1995: 216)

88 Slevin has strong views on narrative clarity and coherence: that every scene and every bit of action in every scene must carry the story (1912: 13). For Slevin 'the great point of advantage which the picture-play has over the legitimate or stage play is that it can present almost perfect continuity of action' (1912: 54). Esenwein and Leeds insist on 'the progressive, logical development of the story in good climacteric style' (1913: 117).

89 Sargent's account of standardised script form in the third edition of his handbook is informative: 'In the beginning each studio devised its own form of script. There was no common usage. A form had to be devised and, lacking a common source of information, each pioneer Editor devised his own style of script, not differing materially from the others, but rather an individual expression of a common need. In the course of time transfer from one studio to another has brought about a combina-

tion of systems, altering the original forms, but it will be many years before there is a generally accepted standard of form and there never will be one that must be adhered to to the exclusion of all else' (1916: 99). Sargent then goes on to offer ten different styles in his appendix, varying according to indentation (or not) of description, inclusion of cast list per scene, amount of spacing per scene for director's interpolations, loose-leaf forms (one scene to a page), and a form in which the reason for the action, rather than the action itself, is the main object of description.

90   Interestingly, in 1938, Frances Marion discusses an unorthodox two-column specimen continuity (1938b: 30).

91   Against the idea that the scenario disappears with the dominance of continuity, well into the late 1920s Clara Beranger continues to refer to the scenario alongside the continuity (see 1977: 140–5). Frances Marion gives advice on 'scenario writing' in the 1930s (see 1938b). Perhaps one reason for the persistence of the notion of the scenario is that it can be seen as a plot, but also as a narrative concept. For Parsons in 1915 the scenario has a curious ambiguity. It is not restricted to the written script; it is also 'The skeleton of any play ... That part of the photoplay that unfolds the plot scene by scene' (1915: 10). The scenario seems to operate both as script form ('scenario form' (1915: 45)) and a narrative construct grounded in an older dramatic discourse. This is a construct not necessarily grounded in the written page and thus distinct from the 'manuscript of a photoplay' (1915: 12).

92   Dunne echoes this view when he writes: 'In the silent days, the director strode booted around the set, with writers trailing in his wake like courtiers trailing a king. There were "continuity writers", who wrote out the "scenario" or plot line, "title writers", who dreamed up the titles (the printed dialogue lines which the mute actors were supposed to be speaking), and "gag men", who suggested to the director the pratfalls, doubletakes, and pie-in-the-face routines which delighted audiences of the period. To this day, screen writers hate to be referred to as "script writers" or "scenario writers", both designations having originated in those bad old days of total writer subservience' (1980: 45).

93   Other writers echo Justice's call for a new arrangement around writing. For Ball, the problems of the industry have a simple solution: 'the encouragement of the independent writer, who understands technique and applies it, with variation and artistry, to every scenario' (1915: 168).

94   Anthony Slide reprints a 1916 bibliography produced by S. Gershanek of the New York State Public Library, which lists 45 works in English on photoplays and photoplay writing (1978: 112–16).

95   Censorship and public taste considerations were important (see Sargent 1912: 28). At the same time production costs and company capabilities are a concern. These primers relate mainly to the raw detail involved in the submission of acceptable photoplays. Slevin notes: 'the written picture-play, to make its proper appeal to its public, must be sent through an exceedingly complex machine, the moving picture

studio and laboratory. The methods and conditions of which are to nearly all begin-ners an attractive mystery' (1912: 10). In order to reveal this mystery, writing in this mode often describes the passage of the manuscript through the studio (see Sargent 1912: 7; Carr 1914: 21). A great amount of detail is offered, right down to the use of typewriters, the quality of the paper and size of the envelope (see Sargent 1912: 10; Palmer 1924a: 29). Sample scenarios and synopses are often presented (see Peacocke 1916: 44, 50). In some cases, advice on how to handle cut-backs (alternate editing), inserts (titles, letters, telegrams), bust pictures (close-ups) and masks is offered. This mode of handbook deals with expression in a limited way, discussing properly constructed plot and action. Too much action and the story will be 'plot ridden' (Hannon 1915: 35), not unlike 'the chase' which becomes a model to be avoided.

96 Slevin supports Sargent's understanding of the scenario when he links it to the 'brief scenario' or 'outline of scenes' used in the Italian commedia dell'arte, and the plot summaries of Shakespeare's time (Slevin 1912: 36). In the third edition of his book, Sargent capitulates to the 'errant' use of the term scenario. He refers to the '*plot of action*, which is more properly termed the scenario than the play as a whole...' (Sargent 1916: 101; emphasis in original).

97 Patterson gives special attention to one group of film workers here, 'a whole new group of directors who represent what might be called the script tradition in motion-picture directing. They have learned the camera through writing continuities' (1928: 127). Akin to modern day 'hyphenates', writer-directors, Patterson describes this group as 'the first generation of picture tellers' (ibid.).

98 As Patterson notes, the scenario is 'composed upon the typewriter, and its merit or lack of merit is judged while the idea is still clothed in words not in celluloid' (1928: 8).

99 Patterson notes: 'the term scenario is often erroneously used as a synonym for continuity, whereas, although it includes continuity, it also includes all the things listed above [cast of characters, synopsis, scene plot, plot of action or continuity]. The scenario is the completed manuscript, while the continuity is merely the action of the story' (1921: 97). In this sense, her definition goes against the one examined earlier in Sargent's work, and the shift from scenario to continuity relates more to a change in designating the plot of action.

100 Interestingly, around the same time, Frances Marion insisted that 'the original screen story had long since won its laurels' (1938a: 19).

101 Writing in 1929, thus after scenario-fever, Patterson writes: 'It must be borne in mind, however, that continuity writing is professional work. It is not the form in which to submit casual manuscript through the mails' (1929b: viii).

102 Patterson highlights how odd it is to want ideas only, synopses, and not continuities, and stresses to write the continuity 'is the only way of discovering whether an idea is really screenable' (1928: 39).

103 This is especially true in the third edition where, in the appendix, Sargent presents a range of templates from different scenario editors. He is careful in this edition to correct the impression that there is one photoplay form or an absolute law of expression (for example, in relation to the use of hyphens or punctuation in the plot of action). An earlier article by Sargent, 'The Literary Side of Pictures' (1914), profiles this network in greater depth.

104 Syd Field's concept of the 'paradigm' is a case in point. He asks: 'do all good screenplays fit the paradigm? Screenplays that work follow the paradigm' (1994: 15). The notion of what works, and the idea of following, links this paradigm to a particular set of industrial expectations, but Field uses the concept of paradigm (which has roots in linguistics and the history of science) to normalise these expectations.

105 John C. Tibbetts describes an early series of purchases of stories by successful writers by scenario staff working for D. W. Griffith (see 1977: 41); and Eileen Bowser speaks of Edison hiring and naming the famous authors of their screenplays before Goldwyn (1990: 112). Richard Fine describes efforts in this area by Universal in 1914 and Famous Players in 1916 (see 1993: 47).

106 A 1939 piece by Nichols reflects this distinction: 'It is true that it takes skill as a writer to write the dialogue, just as it takes skill as an engineer, as a constructionist to see the whole structure, the dramatic structure, to see the flow of images' (1982: 405).

107 Elmer Rice reminds us that not all writers were imported from the east as authors, but some as adapters of the eminent authors (1963: 172).

108 An example here is David Bordwell and Janet Staiger's examination of 'alternative' practice in a chapter called 'Alternative Modes of Film Practice', discussed in chapter two.

109 It could be argued that Dancyger and Rush take up some of the challenges of these different approaches in the fourth edition in their chapter on 'Digital Features', but their focus is on the feature, the aesthetics and cultural uses of film or video, and writing in a media literate way, rather than a reconceptualisation of scripting.

110 This approach is not entirely unusual, and Mack Sennett reportedly used a 'rough scenario' system in 1915, gathering together actors and crew to break down the action (a stenographer would then record instructions and the notes handed to a crew on location) (see Koszarski 1990: 220).

111 Taking the space of documentary as an example, Jakob Høgel has examined the issue of where the story takes place. He puts forward three possible responses. Firstly, that 'like other films documentaries are the realisation of the director's story ... That is why it makes sense for the director to write a script or treatment before shooting' (2001: 19). Secondly, the 'story is out there in reality and the job of the documentarist is to find a good starting point and then follow the human dramas that unfold' (ibid.). In this sense the story pre-exists the filmmaker's realisation. Thirdly, stories are the product of negotiation or collaboration. In this approach 'stories are

created in an open encounter that surpasses the intentions and knowledge of those involved' (ibid.). On the topic of structure, Høgel calls for dramaturgical openness, a situation where the documentarist's skills as a storyteller, their knowledge of structure and models, interacts with the participants 'who may have many other agendas, stories, and angles than the director does' (ibid.). Jane Young suggests that a determining aspect of structure is the events, specific times and places, that are filmed (2002: 8). While Alan Rosenthal echoes William Goldman in saying 'structure is everything' (2002: 63), clearly structure can mean many things.

112   These concerns include: the way the idea of story seems to be specific to the US; the 'universalising tendency' behind it making it a norm to which other cultures must subscribe; the way it is based on particular assumptions about the importance of conflict; the way it is privileged above the contribution of personnel (actors, directors); and the degree of executive control implicit in the system.

113   For Millard, 'The Australian film industry – like its counterpart in the United States – has adopted a series of fairly rigid conventions about how dramatic screenplays should be written and presented, sometimes even down to the use of specific fonts' (2006b).

114   While there is a tendency to associate presentational modes with pre-1910s cinema, Richard Koszarski notes how even in 1920s some exhibitors saw their work as 'closer to the work of vaudeville managers' (1990: 53). At the Eastman Theatre in Rochester, New York, the programme was tailored and presentation guided by an 'in-house "scenario editor", and staff merely to work on structure' (1990: 54).

115   For example, in 1912 Sargent is Aristotelian in insisting on simple plots and the definition of an inciting incident (1912: 17). He encourages the novice to spend time 'working out the plot' so that it is 'intelligible' to the patrons of the cheaper houses as well as 'photo-playgoers of a higher order of intelligence' (1912: 29). While Sargent articulates an early version of the central conflict theory whereby the protagonist desires an object but is opposed by the antagonist (see 1916: 26–31), he also advises that it is possible to have struggle but no interest, no suspense. He considers other forms of interest, such as 'heart interest' (1916: 56) and 'charm and distinction' (1916: 60). Using a term that has largely dropped away from contemporary writing, Sargent emphasises the importance of 'punch': 'for plot is essential to the photoplay and punch is essential to the plot' (1916: 92). 'Punch is the *idea* back of the narrative' (1916: 93; emphasis in original), and requires constantly thinking about interest and narrative.

116   Developments in digital computing mean that filmmaking has increasingly come into contact with forms and languages of scripting that in turn give rise to potentially new forms of so-called 'non-linear' writing (hypertext), or 'dynamic media'.

117   Hitchcock would allegedly keep sheets of perforated paper near the camera, and when asked what he wanted, would draw a quick sketch. Hitchcock asserts, 'I only consider that screen up there, and the whole film to me should be shot on paper

from beginning to end – shot by shot, cut by cut – and each cut should mean some-thing' (American Film Institute 1972: 8).

118   Narrative and storytelling are important issues to consider here, not solely because of the kinds of narratives being produced (interactive or storybook, for example) but the assumptions we make about narrative, and how 'telling' impacts on 'story'. Adrian Martin has discussed a similar problem in terms of the form/content distinc-tion, arguing that the notion 'form expresses content' puts form and expression in a secondary position in the hierarchy (see 2004: 86).

119   Although the erasing of the 'dividing line' between studio production and domestic or desktop work can be overstated (see McQuire 1997: 44), and O'Regan notes a 'resurgent interest in the "studio idea" in different production industries' (2000: 67).

120   As Tom O'Regan notes: 'for the core "idea" to reach audiences who live in a complex and fragmented media world, content creators increasingly have to think about producing film and television content that is creative, interactive and relevant to its audience across a variety of formats' (2000: 63).

BIBLIOGRAPHY

American Film Institute (1972) *Dialogue on Film*, 2, 1.

Anon. (1906) 'Moving Pictures Amuse and Instruct', *The Brooklyn Daily Eagle*, 6 September.

____ (1910) 'Giving Credit Where Credit is Due', *Moving Picture World*, 6, 10, 12 March, 369–70.

____ (1930) 'A Russian View of Scenarios', *New York Times*, 30 March, X3.

____ (1935) 'Writer-Producer Code Committee Disagrees', *Screen Guilds' Magazine*, 1, 2, February, 3–4, 17.

Arnheim, Rudolf (1958) 'Who is the Author of a Film?', *Film Culture*, 4, 1, January, 11–13.

Aronson, Linda (2000) *Scriptwriting Updated: New and Conventional Ways of Writing for the Screen*. North Ryde: Australian Film, Television and Radio School/St Leonards: Allen and Unwin.

Astruc, Alexandre (1968) 'The Birth of a New Avant-Garde: La Caméra-Stylo', in Peter Graham (ed.) *The New Wave*. London: Secker and Warburg, 17–24.

Australian Writers' Guild (1997) 'Submission on the Copyright Amendment Bill (Moral Rights), 8th August'. On-line. Available at http://www.awg.com.au/reports/moral_full_sub.htm (accessed 13 January 2007). The views of writers expressed in the submission are summarised separately at http://www.awg.com.au/reports/moral_quotes.htm and the Executive Summary can be found at http://www.awg.com.au/reports/moral_exec_sum.htm

Azlant, Edward (1980) 'The Theory, History, and Practice of Screenwriting, 1897–1920', unpublished PhD thesis, The University of Wisconsin, Madison.

____ (1997) 'Screenwriting for the Early Silent Film: Forgotten Pioneers, 1897–1911', *Film History*, 9, 3, 228–56.

Baines, Lawrence and Micah Dial (1995) 'Scripting Screenplays: An Idea for Integrating Writing, Reading, Thinking, and Media Literacy', *English Journal*, 84, 2, 86–91.

Baker, Fred and Ross Firestone (1972) *Movie People: At Work in the Film Industry*. London: Abelard-Schuman.

Balázs, Béla (1970) *Theory of the Film: Character and Growth of a New Art*, trans. Edith Bone. New York: Dover Publications.

Baldick, Chris (1996) *Criticism and Literary Theory, 1890 to the Present*. London: Longman.

Ball, Eustace Hale (1915) *Photoplay Scenarios: How to Write and Sell Them*. New York: Hearst's International Library.

____ (1917 [1915]) *Cinema Plays: How to Write Them, How to Sell Them*. London: Stanley Paul.

Bartlett, Lexey A. (2007) 'Who Do I Turn (in)to for Help?: Multiple Identity as Adaptation in *Adaptation*, *M/C Journal*, 10, 1. On-line. Available at http://journal.media-culture.org.au/0705/04-bartlett.php (accessed 18 July 2007).

Batchen, Geoffrey (1991) 'Enslaved Sovereign, Observed Spectator: On Jonathan Crary, *Techniques of the Observer*', *Continuum: The Australian Journal of Media and Culture*, 6, 2, 80–94. On-line. Available at http://wwwmcc.murdoch.edu.au/ReadingRoom/6.2/Batchen.html (accessed 18 April 2002).

Bazin, André (1968) '*La Politique des Auteurs*', in Peter Graham (ed.) *The New Wave*. London: Secker and Warburg, 137–56.

Beauchamp, Cari (1997) *Without Lying Down: Frances Marion and the Powerful Women of Early Hollywood*. New York: A Lisa Drew Book/Scribner.

Belton, John (1997) 'Screenwriters and Screenwriting', *Film History*, 9, 3, 226–7.

Beranger, Clara (1923) 'Good and Bad Authorship', *Motion Picture Classic*, xvii, 1, September, 11, 78.

____ (1950) *Writing for the Screen*. Dubuque, Iowa: W. M. C. Brown.

____ (1977 [1929]) 'The Story', in John C. Tibbetts (ed.) *Introduction to the Photoplay*. Shawnee Mission, Kansas: National Film Society, 133–57.

Bergman, Ingmar (1967) 'What is "Film Making"?', in Harry M. Geduld (ed.) *Film Makers on Film Making: Statements on Their Art by Thirty Directors*. Harmondsworth: Penguin, 182–94.

____ (1972) *Wild Strawberries*, trans. Lars Malmström and David Kushner. Broadway: L & S Publishing.

Bielby, Denise D. and William T. Bielby (1996) 'Women and Men in Film: Gender Inequality Among Writers in a Culture Industry', *Gender & Society*, 10, 3, June, 248–70.

Blaisdell, George (1914) 'Jesse L. Lasky in Pictures', *Moving Picture World*, 3 January, 35–6.

____ (1915) 'W. C. DeMille Talks on the Drama', *Moving Picture World*, 9 October, 258–9.

Bluestone, George (1957) *Novels into Film*. Baltimore: The Johns Hopkins Press.

Bonime, Andrew and Ken C. Pohlman (1998) *Writing for New Media: The Essential Guide to Writing for Interactive Media, CD-ROMS, and the Web*. New York: John Wiley & Sons.

Bordwell, David (1997) *On the History of Film Style*. Cambridge: Harvard University Press.

____ (2006) *As Hollywood Tells It: Story and Style in Modern Movies*. Berkeley: University of California Press.

Bordwell, David, Janet Staiger and Kristin Thompson (1985) *The Classical Hollywood Cinema: Film Style and Mode of Production to 1960*. New York: Columbia University Press.

Bowser, Eileen (1990) *The Transformation of Cinema, 1907–1915*. Berkeley: University of California Press.

Boyle, James F. (1983) 'Foreword', in Hillis R. Cole Jr and Judith H. Haag *The Complete Guide to Standard Script Formats. Part I – Screenplays*. North Hollywood: CMC Publishing, i–xi.

Bradley, Clive (1999) 'The Workings of a Dream Factory', *Worker's Liberty*, 57, September. On-line. Available at http://archive.workersliberty.org/wlmags/wl57/dreams.htm (accessed 12 July 2007).

Bradley, David (1992) *From Text to Performance In The Elizabethan Theatre: Preparing the Play for the Stage*. Cambridge: Cambridge University Press.

Brady, John (1981) *The Craft of the Screenwriter: Interviews with Six Celebrated Screenwriters*. New York: Simon and Schuster.

Braverman, Harry (1974) *Labor and Monopoly Capital: The Degradation of Work in the Twentieth Century*. New York: Monthly Review Press.

Brik, Osip (1974 [1936]) 'From the Theory and Practice of the Screenwriter', trans. Diana Matias, *Screen: The Journal of the Society for Education in Film and Television*, 15, 3, Autumn, 95–103.

Brownlow, Kevin (1968) *The Parade's Gone By...* Berkeley: University of California Press.

Brunette, Peter (2005) *Wong Kar-wai*. Urbana/Chicago: University of Illinois Press.

Brunette, Peter and David Wills (1989) *Screen/play: Derrida and Film Theory*. Princeton, New Jersey: Princeton University Press.

Buckland, Warren (2003) '"A Sad, Bad Traffic Accident": The Televisual Prehistory of David Lynch's Film *Mulholland Dr*', *New Review of Film and Television Studies*, 1, 1, November, 131–47.

Buscombe, Edward (1973) 'Ideas of Authorship', *Screen: The Journal of the Society for Education in Film and Television*, 14, 3, Autumn, 170–86.

Bush, W. Stephen (1915) 'The Dreadful Word', *Moving Picture World*, xxvi, October–December, 30 October, 760.

Cage, John (1980) *Empty Words, Writings '73–'78 by John Cage*. London: Marion Boyars.

Cameron, Sandy (2007) 'Digital Liberation: Sandy Cameron talks with *Boxing Day* director Kriv Stenders', *Realtime*, 77, Feb–March. On-line. Available at http://www.realtimearts.net/article.php?id=8363 (accessed 5 April 2008).

Carmichael, Helen (1998) 'Scriptwriting – Style and Layout', in *Scriptwriting: Style and Layout. Notes and Examples Prepared by the Writing Department*. North Ryde: Australian Film, Television and Radio School, 1.

Carr, Catherine (ed.) (1914) *The Art of Photoplay Writing*. New York: Hannis Jordan.

Carrière, Jean-Claude (1995) *The Secret Language of Film*, trans. Jeremy Leggatt. London: Faber and Faber.

Carringer, Robert (1978) 'The Scripts of "Citizen Kane"', *Critical Inquiry*, 5, 2, Winter, 369–400.

Castrique, Sue (1997) 'Add One Writer and Stir: Recipe or Feast?', *Media International Australia*, 85, 102–6.

Caughie, John (1981) 'Introduction' in John Caughie (ed.) *Theories of Authorship*. London: Routledge, 9–16.

Ceplair, Larry (1996) *A Great Lady: A Life of the Screenwriter Sonya Levien*. Lanham: Scarecrow Press.

Ceplair, Larry and Steven Englund (1980) *The Inquisition in Hollywood: Politics in the Film Community, 1930–1960*. Garden City, New York: Anchor Press/Doubleday.

Chandler, Raymond (1945) 'Writers in Hollywood', *Atlantic Monthly*, 176, 5, November, 50–4.

Cole Jr, Hillis R. and Judith H. Haag (1983) *The Complete Guide to Standard Script Formats. Part I – Screenplays*. North Hollywood: CMC Publishing.

Coleman, Todd (1995) 'The Story Structure Gurus', *Written By: The Journal of the Writers' Guild of America West*, 8, 6, June, 14–21.

Comolli, Jean-Louis (1980 [1977]) 'Le détour par le direct – Un corps en trop' [Extracts], in Christopher Williams (ed.) *Realism and the Cinema: A Reader*. London: Routledge and Kegan Paul/British Film Institute, 225–43.

____ (1985) 'Technique and Ideology: Camera, Perspective, Depth of Field', in Bill Nichols (ed.) *Movies and Methods: Volume II*. Berkeley: University of California Press, 40–57.

Conley, Tom (1991) *Film Hieroglyphs: Ruptures in Classical Cinema*. Minneapolis: University of Minnesota Press.

Cook, Pam and Mieke Bernink (eds) (1999) *The Cinema Book*, second edition. London: British Film Institute.

Corliss, Richard (ed.) (1972a) *The Hollywood Screenwriters*. New York: Avon Books.

____ (1972b) 'Introduction: The Hollywood Screenwriters', in Richard Corliss (ed.) *The Hollywood Screenwriters*. New York: Avon Books, 9–27.

____ (1974) *Talking Pictures: Screenwriters in the American Cinema, 1927–1973*. Woodstock, New York: Overlook Press.

____ (1992) 'Still Talking', *Film Comment*, 28, 6, November, 11–23.

Crimmings, Emma and Rhys Graham (2004) 'Two/Out: An Interview with Kriv Stenders', in *Short Site: Recent Australian Short Film*. Melbourne: Australian Centre for the Moving Image, 244–50.

Crofts, Stephen (1983) 'Authorship and Hollywood', *Wide Angle*, 5, 3, 16–22.

Culler, Jonathon (2000) *Literary Theory: A Very Short Introduction*. London: Oxford University Press.

Cunningham, Stuart (1987) 'Negotiating the Difference: The Chauvel School of Scenario Writing', in Tom O'Regan and Brian Shoesmith (eds) *History on/and/in Film*. Perth: History and Film Association of Australia, 81–9.

Dancyger, Ken and Jeff Rush (1990) 'Introduction', *Journal of Film and Video*, 42, 3, Fall, 3–4.

____ (1995) *Alternative Scriptwriting: Writing Beyond the Rules*, second edition. Boston: Focal Press.

Daniell, Tina (1986) 'Philip Dunne: Fine Cabinetmaker', in Pat McGilligan (ed.) *Backstory: Interviews with Screenwriters of Hollywood's Golden Age*. Berkeley: University of California Press, 151–69.

Dannenberg, Joseph (ed.) (1923) *Film Year Book 1922–1923*. New York: Wid's Films and Film Folks.

David, Ian (2000) 'I'm an Auteur, So You Can Get Fucked', *if Magazine*, 27, September, 36–7.

Davis, Gary (1984) 'Rejected Offspring: The Screenplay as a Literary Genre', *New Orleans Review*, 11, 2, Summer, 90–4.

Decherney, Peter (2005) *Hollywood and the Culture Elite: How the Movies Became American*. New York: Columbia University Press.

Deemer, Charles (2002) 'Are Screenplays Literature?', *Cyber Film School*, 5 June. On-line. Available at http://www.ibiblio.org/cdeemer/cfs0602.htm (accessed 19 August 2004).

Delofski, Maree (2006) 'Writing the "Real"/Really Writing', *Scan: Journal of Media Arts Culture*, 3, 2, October. On-line. Available at http://scan.net.au/scan/journal/display.php?journal_id=75 (accessed 12 December 2006).

de Mille, Agnes (1952) *Dance to the Piper*. Boston: Little, Brown.

deMille, William C. (1939) *Hollywood Saga*. New York: E. P. Dutton.

____ (1977 [1929]) 'The Future of the Photoplay', in John C. Tibbetts (ed.) *Introduction to the Photoplay*. Shawnee Mission, Kansas: National Film Society, 309–37

Derrida, Jacques (1976) *Of Grammatology*, trans. Gayatri Chakravorty Spivak. Baltimore: Johns Hopkins University Press.

Dimick, Howard T. (1922) *Modern Photoplay Writing: Its Craftsmanship*. Franklin, Ohio: James Knapp Reeve.

Dozoretz, David (2004) 'Pre-visualisation'. On-line. Available at http://www.aftrs.edu.au/index.cfm?objectid=9CF82098-2A54-23A3-6F8857EA50DA07DA (accessed 10 August 2007).

Dunne, Philip (1945) 'An Essay on Dignity', *The Screen Writer*, December, 1–8.

____ (1980) *Take Two: A Life in Movies and Politics*. New York: McGraw-Hill.

Dunnigan, Brian (2004) 'Scenario! A UK–France screenwriting event at Cine Lumière, Institute Français, 6–12 October 2003', *Journal of Media Practice*, 5, 1, 59–62.

Eisenstein, Sergei (1988a [1924]) 'The Montage of Film Attractions', in *Selected Works, Volume 1, Writings, 1922–34*, ed. Richard Taylor. London: British Film Institute/Bloomington: Indiana University Press, 39–58.

____ (1988b [1928]) 'Literature and Cinema: Reply to a Questionnaire', in *Selected Works, Volume 1, Writings, 1922–34*, ed. Richard Taylor. London: British Film Institute/Bloomington: Indiana University Press, 95–9.

____ (1988c [1929]) 'The Form of the Script', in *Selected Works, Volume 1, Writings, 1922–34*, ed. Richard Taylor. London: British Film Institute/Bloomington: Indiana University Press, 134–5.

Elsaesser, Thomas (ed.), with Adam Barker (1990) *Early Cinema: Space, Frame, Narrative*. London: British Film Institute.

Emerson, John and Anita Loos (1920) *How to Write Photoplays*. New York: James A. McCann.

Entman, Robert M. (1993) 'Framing: Toward Clarification of a Fractured Paradigm', *Journal of Communication*, 43, 4, 51–8.

Esenwein, J. Berg and Arthur Leeds (1913) *Writing the Photoplay*. Springfield, Mass.: The Home Correspondence School.

Fawell, John (1989) 'The Musicality of the Film Script', *Literature/Film Quarterly*, 17, 1, 44–9.

Ferster, Bill (1998) 'Idea Editing: Previsualisation for Feature Films', *Post*, April. On-line. Available at http://www.stagetools.com/previs.htm (accessed 10 August 2007).

Field, Syd (1984) *The Screenwriter's Workbook*. New York: Dell Publishing.

____ (1994) *Screenplay: The Foundations of Screenwriting*, third edition. New York: Dell Publishing.

Fine, Richard (1993) *West of Eden: Writers in Hollywood, 1928–1940*. Washington: Smithsonian Institution Press.

Foreman, Carl (1972) 'Foreword: Confessions of a Frustrated Screenwriter', in Richard Corliss (ed.) *The Hollywood Screenwriters*. New York: Avon Books, 19–35.

Foucault, Michel (1977) 'What is an Author?', in Donald F. Bouchard (ed.) *Language, Counter-Memory, Practice: Selected Essays and Interviews by Michel Foucault*. Ithaca, New York: Cornell University Press, 113–38.

Fragale, Jim (1994) 'How to Write a Hit Movie, Or Who Is Syd Field and Why Does Everybody Own His Books?', *Creative Screenwriting*, 1, 4, Winter, 119–25.

Francke, Lizzie (1994) *Script Girls: Women Screenwriters in Hollywood*. London: British Film Institute.

Freeburg, Victor O. (1970 [1918]) *The Art of Photoplay Making*. New York: Macmillan.

Froug, William (1972) *The Screenwriter Looks at the Screenwriter*. New York: Macmillan.

Fuller, Graham (1995) 'Mike Leigh's Original Features', in Mike Leigh *Naked and Other Screenplays*. London: Faber, vii–xli.

Garrett, George P., O. B. Hardison Jr and Jane R. Gelfman (eds) (1989) *Film Scripts*. New York: Irvington Publishers.

Gassner, John (1943) 'The Screenplay as Literature', in John Gassner and Dudley Nichols (eds) *Twenty Best Film Plays*. New York: Crown Publishers, vii–xxx.

_____ (1945) 'A Film Play Annual', in John Gassner and Dudley Nichols (eds) *Best Film Plays of 1943–1944*. New York: Crown Publishers, ix–xx.

_____ (1946) 'A Second Annual', in John Gassner and Dudley Nichols (eds) *Best Film Plays – 1945*. New York: Crown Publishers, ix–xxii.

_____ (1951) 'Film and Screenplay', *Theatre Arts*, xxxv, 8, August, 58, 82–3.

_____ (1959) 'Reprise for the Film Plays', in John Gassner and Dudley Nichols (eds) *Great Film Plays, Vol. 1*. New York: Crown Publishers, iii–ix.

Geuens, Jean-Pierre (2000) *Film Production Theory*. Albany, New York: State University of New York Press.

Goldman, William (1983) 'The Screenwriter', in Jason E. Squire (ed.) *The Movie Business Book*. London: Columbus Books, 51–61.

_____ (1984) *Adventures in the Screen Trade: A Personal View of Hollywood and Screenwriting*. London: Macdonald.

_____ (2000) *Which Lie Did I Tell?: More Adventures in the Screen Trade*. London: Bloomsbury.

Gray, Simon (2005) 'Beauty and the Beast: Andrew Lesnie, ASC, ACS outlines his Approach to an Ambitious Remake of *King Kong*', *American Cinematographer*, December. On-line. Available at http://www.theasc.com/magazine/dec05/kingkong/page1.html (accessed 4 May 2007).

Gross, Roger (1974) *Understanding Playscripts: Theory and Method*. Bowling Green, Ohio: Bowling Green University Press.

Gunning, Tom (1991) *D. W. Griffith and the Origins of American Narrative Film: The Early Years and Biograph*. Urbana: University of Illinois Press.

Hamilton, Ian (1990) *Writers in Hollywood, 1915–1951*. New York: Harper and Row.

Hampe, Barry (1995) 'Scripting a Documentary', *Creative Screenwriting*, 2, 2, 67–75.

Hampton, Benjamin B. (1970 [1931]) *History of the American Film Industry: From Its Beginnings to 1931*. New York: Dover Publications.

Hanet, Kari (1996) 'The Auteur Theory: Myths and Magic', *Newsletter of the Australian Screen Directors Association*, April, 4–6.

Hannon, William Morgan (1915) *The Photodrama: Its Place Among the Fine Arts*. New Orleans: The Ruskin Press.

Hansen, Miriam (1985) 'Universal Language and Democratic Culture: Myths of Origin in Early American Cinema', in Dieter Meindl and Friedrich W. Horlacher with Martin Christadler (eds) *Myth and Enlightenment in American Literature*. Erlangen: Universitätsbund Erlangen-Nürnberg, 321–51.

Harrington, John (ed.) (1977) *Film and/as Literature*. Englewood Cliffs, New Jersey: Prentice-Hall.

Harris, Erich Leon (1996) *African-American Screen-writers Now: Conversations With Hollywood's Black Pack*. Los Angeles: Silman-James Press.

Herman, Lewis (1952) *A Practical Manual of Screen Playwriting: For Theater and Television Films*. Cleveland: World Publishing.

Higashi, Sumiko (1990) 'Cecil B. DeMille and the Lasky Company: Legitimating Feature Film as Art', *Film History*, 4, 3, 181–98.

____ (1994) *Cecil B. DeMille and American Culture: The Silent Era*. Berkeley: University of California Press.

Higgins, Scott (1995) 'Moviemaker's Workspace Article'. On-line. Available at http://alumni.media.mit.edu/~scott/MWarticle.html (accessed 4 June 2007).

Hillier, Jim (1993) *The New Hollywood*. London: Studio Vista.

Hiltunen, Ari (2002) *Aristotle in Hollywood: The Anatomy of Successful Storytelling*. London: Intellect Books.

Høgel, Jakob (2001) 'Where's the Story: Dramaturgy in the Documentary', *Film*, 19, November. On-line. Available at http://www.dfi.dk/english/filmmagazine/filmmagazine.htm (accessed 4 June 2007).

Horne, William (1992) '"See Shooting Script": Reflections on the Ontology of the Screenplay', *Literature/Film Quarterly*, 20, 1, 48–54.

Horton, Andrew (1992) 'The "How to Write the Best Ever Screenplay" Book Biz', *Cineaste*, XIX, 2–3, 12–14.

Howard, Sidney (1937) 'The Story Gets a Treatment', in Nancy Naumburg (ed.) We Make the Movies. New York: W. W. Norton, 32–52.

____ (1995 [1937]) 'The Story Gets a Treatment', in John Boorman, Tom Luddy, David Thomson and Walter Donohue (eds) *Projections 4: Film-Makers on Film-Making*. London: Faber and Faber, 205–17.

Hustwick, Alfred (1922) 'The Screen Writers' Guild and Its Club, "The Writers"', in *Opportunities in the Motion Picture Industry — and how to qualify for positions in its many branches, Volume II*. Los Angeles: Photoplay Research Society, 65–9.

Ingarden, Roman (1973) *The Literary Work of Art: An Investigation on the Borderlines of Ontology, Logic, and Theory of Literature*, third edition, trans. George G. Grabowicz. Evanston: Northwestern University Press.

Iser, Wolfgang (1978) *The Act of Reading: A Theory of Aesthetic Response*. Baltimore: Johns Hopkins University Press.

Jacobs, Lewis (1939) *The Rise of the American Film: A Critical History*. New York: Harcourt, Brace.

____ (1970) *The Movies as Medium*. New York: Farrar, Straus and Giroux.

Jensen, Paul (1970) 'The Career of Dudley Nichols', *Film Comment*, 6, 4, 1970/71, 56–64.

Johnstone, Calder (1914) 'Why So Many Photoplays Fail to "Land"', in Catherine Carr (ed.) *The Art of Photoplay Writing*. New York: Hannis Jordan, 108–9.

Jones, Henry Arthur (1977 [1921]) 'The Dramatist and the Photoplay', in John Harrington (ed.) *Film and/as Literature*. Englewood Cliffs, New Jersey: Prentice-Hall, 53–4.

Justice, Maibelle Heikes (1917) 'The Photodrama', in Louella O. Parsons *How to Write for the 'Movies'*, revised edition. Chicago: A. C. McClurg, 237–55.

Kahan, J. H. (1950) 'Scripting', *Sight & Sound*, 19, 2, 80.

Keisling, Barrett C. (1937) *Talking Pictures: How They Are Made, How to Appreciate Them*. Richmond: Johnson Publishing.

Kelly, Kevin and Paula Parisi (1997) 'Beyond *Star Wars*: What's Next for George Lucas', *Wired*, 5, 2, February, 160–66, 210–12, 216–17. On-line. Available at http://www.wired.com/wired/archive/5.02/fflucas.html (accessed 9 September 2007).

Kemm, James O. (1997) *Rupert Hughes: A Hollywood Legend*. Beverly Hills, California: Pomegranate Press.

Knudsen, Erik (2004) 'The Eyes of the Beholder: Does Responsibility for the Lack of Quality Screenplays Really Lie at the Door of Inadequately Trained Screenwriters?', *Journal of Media Practice*, 5, 3, 181–3.

Kohn, Nathaniel (2000) 'The Screenplay as Postmodern Literary Exemplar: Authorial Distraction, Disappearance, Dissolution', *Qualitative Inquiry*, 6, 4, 489–510.

Korte, Barbara and Ralf Schneider (2000) 'The Published Screenplay – A New Literary Genre?', *AAA–Arbeiten aus Anglistik und Amerikanistik*, 25, 1, 89–105.

Koszarski, Richard (1990) *An Evening's Entertainment: The Age of the Silent Picture, 1915–1928*. Berkeley: University of California Press.

Kouvaros, George (1998) 'Where Does It Happen? The Place of Performance in the Work of John Cassavetes', *Screen*, 39, 3, 244–58.

Kuleshov, Lev (1987 [1920]) 'The Banner of Cinematography', in *Selected Works: Fifty Years in Films*, ed. Ekaterina Khokhlova, trans. Dmitri Agrachev and Nina Belenkaya. Moscow: Raduga, 37–55.

_____ (1987 [1929]) 'The Art of the Cinema: My Experience', in *Selected Works: Fifty Years in Films*, ed. Ekaterina Khokhlova, trans. Dmitri Agrachev and Nina Belenkaya. Moscow: Raduga, 130–85.

Kurman, George (1990) '*Scarlet Street*: A "Remake" with a Key', *Literature Film Quarterly*, 18, 2, 111–16.

Lane, Tamar (1936) *The New Technique of Screen Writing: A Practical Guide to the Writing and Marketing of Photoplays*. New York: Whittlesey House.

Lasky, Jesse L. (1914) 'Accomplishments of the Feature', *Moving Picture World*, 11 July, 214.

_____ (1937) 'The Producer Makes a Plan', in Nancy Naumburg (ed.) *We Make the Movies*. New York: W. W. Norton, 3–20.

Lawson, John Howard (1949) *Theory and Technique of Playwrighting and Screenwriting*. New York: G. P. Putnam's Sons.

Le Dœuff, Michèle (1989) *The Philosophical Imaginary*, trans. Colin Gordon. Stanford, California: Stanford University Press.

_____ (1991) *Hipparchia's Choice: An Essay Concerning Women, Philosophy, Etc.*, trans. Trista Selous. Oxford: Basil Blackwell.

Leff, Leonard J. (1981) 'I Hear America Typing: A Survey of Scriptwriting Manuals', *Quarterly Review of Film Studies*, 6, 3, Summer, 279–94.

Leigh, Mike (1995) *Naked and Other Screenplays*. London: Faber.

Lent, Michael (1998) 'Beyond Syd Field: A New Spec Format', *Creative Screenwriting*, 5, 2, 4–5.

Lindsay, Vachel (2000) *The Art of the Moving Picture*. New York: Modern Library.

Lonergan, Lloyd (1997 [1917]) 'How I Came To Write Continuity', *Film History*, 9, 3, 275–6.

Loughney, Patrick G. (1990) 'In the Beginning Was the Word: Six Pre-Griffith Motion Picture Scenarios', in Thomas Elsaesser with Adam Barker (eds) *Early Cinema: Space, Frame, Narrative*. London: British Film Institute, 211–19.

____ (1997a) 'From Rip Van Winkle to Jesus of Nazareth: Thoughts on the Origins of the American Screenplay', *Film History*, 9, 3, 277–90.

____ (1997b) 'Appendix: Selected Examples of Early Scenario/Screenplays in the Library of Congress', *Film History*, 9, 3, 291–9.

Lumme, Helena and Mika Manninen (1999) *Screenwriters: America's Storytellers in Portrait*. Santa Monica: Angel City Press.

Macdonald, Ian W. (2003) 'Finding the Needle: How Readers See Screen Ideas', *Journal of Media Practice*, 4, 1, 27–39.

____ (2004a) 'Disentangling the Screen Idea', *Journal of Media Practice*, 5, 2, 89–99.

____ (2004b) 'Manuals are not Enough: Relating Screenwriting Practice to Theories', *Journal of British Cinema and Television*, 1, 2, 260–74.

____ (2007) 'The Struggle for the Silents: The British Screenwriter from 1910 to 1930', *Journal of Media Practice*, 8, 2, 115–27.

MacDonald, Scott (ed.) (1995a) *Screen Writings: Scripts and Texts by Independent Filmmakers*. Berkeley: University of California Press.

____ (1995b) 'Introduction', in Scott MacDonald (ed.) *Screen Writings: Scripts and Texts by Independent Filmmakers*. Berkeley: University of California Press, 1–14.

Macgowan, Kenneth (1965) *Behind the Screen: The History and Techniques of the Motion Picture*. New York: Dell Publishing.

Macpherson, Jeanie (1922) 'Functions of the Continuity Writer', in *Opportunities in the Motion Picture Industry – and how to qualify for positions in its many branches, Volume II*. Los Angeles: Photoplay Research Society, 25–35.

Madsen, Axel (1975) *The New Hollywood: American Movies in the '70s*. New York: Thomas Y. Crowell.

Maras, Steven (2005) 'The Problem of Theory and Practice: Towards a Constitutive Analysis', *Journal of Media Practice*, 6, 2, 93–103.

Marion, Frances (1938a) *How to Write and Sell Film Stories*. London: John Miles.

____ (1938b) 'Scenario Writing', in Stephen Watts (ed.) *Behind The Screen: How Films are Made*. London: A. Barker, 29–39.

____ (1972) *Off With Their Heads: A Serio-Comic Tale of Hollywood*. New York: Macmillan.

Martin, Adrian (1992) 'Mise-en-Scène is Dead, or The Expressive, The Excessive, The Technical, and The Stylish', *Continuum: The Australian Journal of Media and Culture*, 5, 2, 87–140.

____ (1999) 'Making a Bad Script Worse: The Curse of the Scriptwriting Manual', *Australian Book Review*, 209, April. On-line. Available at http://home.vicnet.net.au/~abr/April99/mar.html (accessed 17 February 2006).

____ (2000) 'Auteur Auteur', *Sydney Morning Herald*, 25 November, 94.

____ (2004) 'There's a Million Stories, and a Million Ways to Get There from Here', *Metro Magazine*, 142, 82–90.

Mathews, Jack (1990) 'Rules of the Game', *American Film*, XV, 6, March, 32–5, 58–9.

McCreadie, Marsha (1994) *The Women Who Write the Movies: From Frances Marion to Nora Ephron*. New York: Birch Lane Press.

McFarlane, Brian (1996) *Novel to Film: An Introduction to the Theory of Adaptation*. Oxford: Clarendon Press.

McGilligan, Pat (1986) *Backstory: Interviews with Screenwriters of Hollywood's Golden Age*. Berkeley: University of California Press.

____ (1989) 'Review of *Framework: A History of Screenwriting in the American Film*', *Film Quarterly*, 42, 4, 49–50. Berkeley: University of California Press.

____ (ed.) (1997) *Backstory 3: Interviews with Screenwriters of the 60s*. Berkeley: University of California Press.

____ (ed.) (2006) *Backstory 4: Interviews with Screenwriters of the 1970s and 1980s*. Berkeley: University of California Press.

McKee, Robert (1997) *Story: Substance, Structure, Style and the Principles of Screenwriting*. London: Regan Books.

McMackin, Archer (1909) 'How Moving Picture Plays Are Written', *The Nickelodeon*, II, 6, December, 171–3.

McMerrin, Michelle (2007) 'Agency in *Adaptation*', *M/C Journal*, 10, 2. On-line. Available at http://journal.media-culture.org.au/0705/03-mcmerrin.php (accessed 15 July 2007).

McQuire, Scott (1997) *Crossing the Digital Threshold*. Brisbane, Griffith University: Australian Key Centre for Cultural and Media Policy.

Mehring, Margaret (1990) *The Screenplay: A Blend of Film Form and Content*. Boston: Focal Press.

Mercurio, James P. (1998) 'When to Go to a Movie Guru ... and When to Go to a Movie: A Review of Six Major Screenwriting Seminars', *Creative Screenwriting*, 5, 5, 32–9. On-line. Available at http://www.jamespmercurio.com/storygurus.pdf (accessed 19 February 2004).

Merwin, Bannister (1912) 'The Future of the Photoplay', *Moving Picture World*, 1 June, 805–6.

Metz, Christian (1974) *Film Language: A Semiotics of the Cinema*, trans. Michael Taylor. New York: Oxford University Press.

Millard, Kathryn (2006a) 'Cinematic Scriptwriting', *Scan: Journal of Media Arts Culture*, 3, 2, October. On-line. Available at http://scan.net.au/scan/journal/display_synopsis.php?j_id=8 (accessed 12 December 2006).

_____ (2006b) 'Writing for the Screen: Beyond the Gospel of Story', *Scan: Journal of Media Arts Culture*, 3, 2, October. On-line. Available at http://scan.net.au/scan/journal/display.php?journal_id=77 (accessed 12 December 2006).

Miller, Pat P. (1986) *Script Supervising and Film Continuity*. Boston: Focal Press.

Morey, Anne (1997) '"Have You the Power?": The Palmer Photoplay Corporation and the Film Viewer/Author in the 1920s', *Film History*, 9, 3, 300–19.

Morris, Gouverneur (1934) 'Scripts', *The Screen Writers' Magazine*, 1, 1, July, 4.

Morsberger, Robert E. and Katharine M. Morsberger (1975) 'Screenplays as Literature: Bibliography and Criticism', *Literature/Film Quarterly*, 3, 1, Winter, 45–59.

Münsterberg, Hugo (1970 [1916]) *The Film: A Psychological Study: The Silent Photoplay in 1916*. New York: Dover Publications.

Munt, Alex (2006) 'Digital Kiarostami & The Open Screenplay', *Scan: Journal of Media Arts Culture*, 3, 2, October. On-line. Available at http://scan.net.au/scan/journal/display.php?journal_id=74 (accessed 12 December 2006).

_____ (2008) '"Am I Crazy To Make a Film for only $100,000 or am I Crazy Not To?": Kriv Stenders goes Micro-Budget Digital for Boxing Day', *Senses of Cinema*, 46. On-line. Available at http://www.sensesofcinema.com/contents/08/46/kriv-stenders-boxing-day.html (accessed 5 April 2008)

Murnau, F. W. (1928) 'The Ideal Picture Needs No Titles', *Theatre Magazine*, XLVII, 322, 41, 72.

Musser, Charles (1990) *The Emergence of Cinema: The American Screen to 1907*. Berkeley: University of California Press.

_____ (1991) *Before the Nickelodeon: Edwin S. Porter and the Edison Manufacturing Company*. Berkeley: University of California Press.

Naumburg, Nancy (ed.) (1937) *We Make the Movies*. New York: W. W. Norton.

Nelmes, Jill (2007) 'Some Thoughts on Analysing the Screenplay, the Process of Screenplay Writing, and the Balance Between Craft and Creativity', *Journal of Media Practice*, 8, 2, 107–13.

Nelson, John Arthur (1913) *The Photoplay: How to Write, How to Sell*, second edition, revised and enlarged. Los Angeles: Photoplay Publishing.

Nichols, Dudley (1942) 'Film Writing', *Theatre Arts*, 26, 7, December, 770–4.

_____ (1943) 'The Writer and the Film', in John Gassner and Dudley Nichols (eds) *Twenty Best Film Plays*. New York: Crown Publishers, xxxi–xl.

_____ (1945) 'Writer, Director and Film', in John Gassner and Dudley Nichols (eds) *Best Film Plays of 1943–1944*. New York: Crown Publishers, xxi–xxx.

_____ (1982 [1939]) 'The Making of a Scenario', in Stanley Hochman (ed.) *From Quasimodo to Scarlett O'Hara: A National Board of Review Anthology, 1920–1940*. New York: Frederick Ungar, 405–11.

Norman, Marc (2007) *What Happens Next: A History of American Screenwriting*. New York: Harmony Books.

O'Regan, Tom (2000) 'New Stories for a Digital Age', in Bronwen Levy and Ffion Murphy (eds) *Story/telling*. St Lucia: University of Queensland Press, 61–78.

Osborne, Robert (1989) *70 Years of the Oscars: The Official History of the Academy Awards*. New York: Abbeville Press.

Palmer, Frederick (1924a) *Authors Photoplay Manual*. Hollywood, California: Palmer Institute of Authorship.

____ (1924b) *Technique of the Photoplay*. Hollywood, California: Palmer Institute of Authorship.

Panofsky, Erwin (1947) 'Style and Medium in the Motion Picture', *Critique*, 1, 3, January/ February, 5–28.

Parsons, Louella O. (1915) *How to Write for the 'Movies'*. Chicago: A. C. McClurg.

____ (1917) *How to Write for the 'Movies'*, new revised edition. Chicago: A. C. McClurg.

Pascal, Ernest (1935) 'The Author of the Piece', *The Screen Guilds' Magazine*, 2, 6, August, 8.

Pasolini, Pier Paolo (2005) *Heretical Empiricism*, second edition, ed. Louise K. Barnett, trans. Ben Lawton and Louise K. Barnett. Washington, D. C: New Academic Publishing LLC.

Patterson, Frances Taylor (1921) *Cinema Craftsmanship: A Book for Photoplaywrights*. New York: Harcourt, Brace.

____ (1923) 'Signs and Portents', *Exceptional Photoplays*, 3, 6, April, 4.

____ (1928) *Scenario and Screen*. New York: Harcourt, Brace.

____ (ed.) (1929a) *Motion Picture Continuities*. New York: Columbia University Press.

____ (1929b) 'Preface' in Frances Taylor Patterson (ed.) *Motion Picture Continuities*. New York: Columbia University Press, v–ix.

____ (1937) 'The Author and Hollywood', *North American Review*, 244, 1, 77–89.

Paul, William (1997) 'The Uncanny Theater: The Twin Inheritances of the Movies', *Paradoxa*, 3, 3–4, 321–47.

Paxton, John (1947) 'Collected Blueprints, Volume III', *Hollywood Quarterly*, 2, 3, April, 308–9.

Peacocke, Captain Leslie T. (1916) *Hints on Photoplay Writing*. Chicago: Photoplay Publishing.

Perry, Louis and Richard Perry (1963) *A History of the Los Angeles Labor Movement, 1911–1941*. Berkeley: University of California Press.

Phelan, Peggy (1997) *Mourning Sex: Performing Public Memories*. London: Routledge.

Phillips, Henry A. (1914) *The Photodrama*. Brooklyn, NY: The William G. Hewitt Press.

Phillips, Richard (2007) '"I'm Interested in a Documentary and Fiction Hybrid": Filmmaker Kriv Stenders speaks with WSWS', *World Socialist Web Site*, 24 July. On-line. Available at http://www.wsws.org/articles/2007/jul2007/sff6-j24.shtml (accessed 5 April 2008).

Pipolo, Tony and Grahame Weinbren (1991) 'Editors' Introduction: The Script Issue', *Millennium Film Journal*, 5–7.

Polan, Dana (2001) 'Auteur Desire', Screening the Past: An International, Refereed, *Electronic Journal of Screen History*, 12. On-line. Available at http://www.latrobe.edu.au/screeningthepast/firstrelease/fr0301/dpfr12a.htm (accessed 17 April 2008)

____ (2007) *Scenes of Instruction: The Beginnings of the U.S. Study of Film*. Berkeley: University of California Press.

Pomeranz, Margaret (2005) 'Interview with Wong Kar-wai', *At the Movies*. On-line. Available at http://www.abc.net.au/atthemovies/txt/s1397057.htm (accessed 22 July 2007).

Popple, Simon and Joe Kember (2004) *Early Cinema: From Factory Gate to Dream Factory*. London: Wallflower Press.

Potamkin, Harry (1977) *The Compound Cinema: The Film Writings of Harry Alan Potamkin*. New York: Teachers College Press.

Powdermaker, Hortense (1950) *Hollywood: The Dream Factory. An Anthropologist Looks at the Movie-Makers*. Boston: Little, Brown.

Pratt, George C. (1973) *Spellbound in Darkness: A History of the Silent Film*, revised edition. Greenwich, Connecticut: New York Graphic Society.

Pudovkin, Vsevolod I. (1958 [1929]) *Film Technique and Film Acting*, ed. and trans. Ivor Montagu. Memorial Edition. London: Vision Press/Mayflower.

Pye, Michael and Lynda Myles (1979) *The Movie Brats: How the Film Generation Took Over Hollywood*. London: Faber and Faber.

Ramsaye, Terry (1926) *A Million and One Nights: A History of the Motion Picture*. New York: Simon and Schuster.

Raynauld, Isabelle (1997) 'Written Scenarios of Early French Cinema: Screenwriting Practices in the First Twenty Years', *Film History*, 9, 3, 257–68.

Rice, Elmer (1963) *Minority Report: An Autobiography*. London: Heinemann.

Rinehart, Mary Roberts (1931) *My Story*. New York: Farrar & Rinehart.

Rizzo, Sergio (undated) 'Adaptation and the Art of Survival', *M/C Journal*, 10, 2. On-line. Available at http://journal.media-culture.org.au/0705/02-rizzo.php (accessed 16 July 2007).

Robinson, Casey (1978) 'Casey Robinson on Dark Victory', *The Australian Journal of Screen Theory*, 4, 5–10.

Ropars, Marie Claire (1981) 'The Graphic in Filmic Writing: /À bout de souffle,/or the Erratic Alphabet', *Enclitic*, 5, 2 and 6, 1, 147–61.

Ropars-Wuilleumier, Marie-Claire (1985) 'Film Reader of the Text', *Diacritics*, 15, 1, 18–30.

Rosenthal, Alan (2002) *Writing, Directing and Producing Documentary Films and Videos*. Carbondale: Southern Illinois University Press.

Ross, Murray (1941) *Stars and Strikes: Unionization of Hollywood*. New York: Columbia University Press.

Routt, William D. (1997) 'Textual Criticism in the Study of Film', *Screening the Past*, 1. On-line. Available at http://www.latrobe.edu.au/www/screeningthepast/firstrelease/firjul/wdr.html (accessed 16 March 1998).

Ruiz, Raúl (1995) *Poetics of Cinema*. Paris: Dis Voir.

Rush, Jeff and Cynthia Baughman (1997) 'Language as Narrative Voice: The Poetics of the Highly Inflected Screenplay', *Journal of Film and Video*, 49, 3, Fall, 28–37.

Russell, David (2003) 'Narrative Structure: Can Media Studies Deliver?', *ScriptWriter*, 11, July, 36–40.

Sainsbury, Peter (2003) 'Visions, Illusions and Delusions: Part II', *Realtime*, 54. On-line. Available at http://www.realtimearts.net/ (accessed 10 April 2003).

Sands, Pierre Norman (1973) *A Historical Study of the Academy of Motion Picture Arts and Sciences (1927–1947)*. New York: Arno Press.

Sargent, Epes Winthrop (1912) *Technique of the Photoplay*. New York City: Moving Picture World.

_____ (1913) *Technique of the Photoplay*, second edition. New York City: Moving Picture World.

_____ (1914) 'The Literary Side of Pictures', *Moving Picture World*, 21, 2, 11 July, 199–202.

_____ (1916) *Technique of the Photoplay*, third edition. New York City: Moving Picture World.

Sarris, Andrew (1962) 'Notes on the Auteur Theory in 1962', *Film Culture*, 27, Winter 1962–63, 1–8.

_____ (1974) 'Preface', in Richard Corliss *Talking Pictures: Screenwriters in the American Cinema, 1927–1973*. Woodstock, New York: Overlook Press, xi–xvi.

Schaefer, Dennis and Larry Salvato (eds) (1984) *Masters of Light: Conversations with Contemporary Cinematographers*. Berkeley: University of California Press.

Schatz, Thomas (1997) 'The Return of the Hollywood Studio System', in Patricia Aufderheide (ed.) *Conglomerates and the Media*. New York: The New Press, 73–106.

Schudson, Michael (2001) 'The Objectivity Norm in American Journalism', *Journalism: Theory, Practice, Criticism*, 2, 2, August, 149–70.

Schwartz, Nancy Lynn (1982) *The Hollywood Writers' Wars*. New York: Alfred A. Knopf.

Seger, Linda (1994) *Making a Good Script Great*, second edition. Hollywood: Samuel French.

Seger, Linda and Edward Jay Whetmore (1994) *From Script to Screen: The Collaborative Art of Filmmaking*. New York: Henry Holt.

Shand, John and Tony Wellington (1988) *Don't Shoot the Best Boy: The Film Crew at Work*. Sydney: Currency Press.

Sheldon, Sidney (1951) 'The Hollywood Writer', *Theatre Arts*, xxxv, 8, August, 31.

Singer, Ben (2001) *Melodrama and Modernity: Early Sensational Cinema and Its Contexts*. New York: Columbia University Press.

Slevin, James (1912) *On Picture-Play Writing: A Handbook of Workmanship*. Cedar Grove, New Jersey: Farmer Smith.

Slide, Anthony (1978) *Aspects of American Film History Prior to 1920*. Metuchen, NJ: The Scarecrow Press.

____ (1994) *Early American Cinema*, revised edition. Metuchen, NJ: The Scarecrow Press.

Smith, Frederick James (1921a) 'Truth on the Screen', *Motion Picture Classic*, xii, 2, April, 36, 75.

____ (1921b) 'The Celluloid Critic', *Motion Picture Classic*, xii, 6, August, 50–1, 78.

Spigelgass, Leonard (ed.) (1970) *Who Wrote the Movie: And What Else Did He Write? An Index of Screen Writers and their Film Works, 1939–1969*. Los Angeles: Academy of Motion Picture Arts and Sciences and the Writers' Guild of America–West.

Staiger, Janet (1979) 'Dividing Labor for Production Control: Thomas Ince and the Rise of the Studio System', *Cinema Journal*, 18, Spring, 16–25.

____ (1980) 'Mass Produced Photoplays: Economic and Signifying Practices in the First Years of Hollywood', *Wide Angle*, 4, 3, 12–27.

____ (1983) '"Tame" Authors and the Corporate Laboratory: Stories, Writers and Scenarios in Hollywood', *Quarterly Review of Film Studies*, 8, 4, Fall, 33–45.

____ (1985) 'Blueprints for Feature Films: Hollywood's Continuity Scripts', in Tino Balio (ed.) *The American Film Industry*, revised edition. Madison, Wisconsin: University of Wisconsin Press, 173–92.

____ (ed.) (1995) *The Studio System*. New Brunswick: Rutgers University Press.

Stanislavski, Constantin (1987) *Creating A Role*. London: Methuen.

Stempel, Tom (1982) *Screenwriting*. San Diego: A. S. Barnes/London: Tantivity Press.

____ (2000 [1988]) *FrameWork: A History of Screenwriting in the American Film*, third edition. New York: Syracuse University Press.

Sternberg, Claudia (1997) *Written for the Screen: The American Motion-Picture Screenplay as Text*. Tübingen: Stauffenburg-Verlag.

____ (2000) '"Return, I Will, to Old Brazil" – Reading Screenplay Literature', in Eckart Voigts-Virchow (ed.) *Mediatized Drama/Drama Mediatized*. Trier, Germany: Wissenschaftlicher, 153–66.

Styan, John Louis (1984) *The State of Drama Study*. Sydney: Sydney University Press.

Tasker, Yvonne (1996) 'Approaches to New Hollywood', in James Curran, David Morley and Valerie Walkerdine (eds) *Cultural Studies and Communications*. London: Arnold, 205–17.

Taylor, John Russell (1964) *Cinema Eye, Cinema Ear: Some Key Film-Makers of the Sixties*. London: Methuen.

Taylor, Thom and Melinda Hsu (2003) *Digital Cinema: The Hollywood Insider's Guide to the Evolution of Storytelling*. Studio City: Michael Wiese Productions.

Thomas, Bob (ed.) (1973) *Directors in Action: Selections from Action, the Official Magazine of the Directors' Guild of America*. Indianapolis: Bobbs Merrill.

Thomas, Sam (1986a) 'Introduction', in *Best American Screenplays*. New York: Crown Publishers, 1–11.

____ (ed.) (1986b) *Best American Screenplays*. New York: Crown Publishers.

____ (ed.) (1990) *Best American Screenplays 2: Complete Screenplays*. New York: Crown Publishers.

Thompson, Kristin (1999) *Storytelling in the New Hollywood: Understanding Classical Narrative Technique*. Cambridge: Harvard University Press.

Tibbetts, John C. (ed.) (1977) *Introduction to the Photoplay*. Shawnee Mission, Kansas: National Film Society.

Tretler, Lawrence J. (1981) 'Literature and Playscript: A Primer for English Teachers who Teach Drama', *The English Journal*, 70, 2, February, 45–7.

Trottier, David (1997) 'Ask Dr Format', *Scr(i)pt: the Screen-Writer's Magazine*, 3, 2, March/April, 14.

Truby, John (1994) 'Why the Producers Are Winning and What Writers Can do About It', *Creative Screenwriting*, 1, 2, 83–9.

Truffaut, François (1976) 'A Certain Tendency in the French Cinema', in Bill Nichols (ed.) *Movies and Methods: Volume I*. Berkeley: University of California Press, 224–37.

Trumbo, Dalton (1933) 'Hollywood Pays: Providing You Can't Fool All of the People All of the Time', *The Forum*, February, 113–19.

Ulmer, Shirley and C. R. Sevilla (1986) *The Role of Script Supervision in Film and Television: A Career Guide*. Hastings House.

United States Copyright Office, Library of Congress (1951) *Motion Pictures, 1912–1939. Catalog of Copyright Entries: Cumulative Series*. On-line. Available at http://www.archive.org/details/motionpict19121939librrich (accessed 26 August 2007).

Vale, Eugene (1982) *The Technique of Screen and Television Writing*. Englewood Cliffs, New Jersey: Prentice-Hall.

Various (1991) 'The Script Issue', *Millennium Film Journal*, 25, Summer.

Vertov, Dziga (1967) '"Kinoks-Revolution", Selections', in Harry M. Geduld (ed.) *Film Makers on Film Making: Statements on Their Art by Thirty Directors*. Harmondsworth: Penguin, 89–114.

____ (1984) *Kino-Eye: The Writings of Dziga Vertov*, ed. Annette Michelson, trans. Kevin O'Brien. Berkeley: University of California Press.

Waugh, Patricia (1992) 'Canon', in David Cooper (ed.) *A Companion to Aesthetics*. Oxford: Blackwell, 59–61.

Weinbren, Grahame (1979) 'Six Filmmakers and an Ideal of Composition', *Millennium Film Journal*, 3, Winter/Spring, 39–54.

Wheaton, Christopher D. (1973) 'A History of the Screen Writers' Guild (1920–1942): The Writer's Quest For A Freely Negotiated Basic Agreement', unpublished PhD thesis. University of Southern California (Communications-Cinema), Los Angeles.

Wingate, David and Tine Fischer (2001) 'There is No Such Thing as a Documentary Script', *Dox*, 35, June, 18–20.

Winston, Douglas Garrett (1973) *The Screenplay as Literature*. London: Tantivity Press.

Woods, Frank (1977 [1929]) 'Growth and Development', in John C. Tibbetts (ed.) *Introduction to the Photoplay*. Shawnee Mission, Kansas: National Film Society, 42–61.

Wright, William Lord (1914) *The Motion Picture Story: A Textbook of Photoplay Writing*. Chicago: Cloud.

____ (1922) *Photoplay Writing*. New York: Falk Publishing.

Wyatt, Justin (1994) *High Concept: Movies and Marketing in Hollywood*. Austin: University of Texas Press.

Young, Jane (2002) 'Structure and Script', in Searle Kochberg (ed.) *Introduction to Documentary Production: A Guide for Media Students*. London: Wallflower Press, 5–27.

INDEX